# Conversion of Chinese Students in Korea to Evangelical Christianity

# Evangelical Missiological Society Monograph Series

Anthony Casey, Allen Yeh, Mark Kreitzer, and Edward L. Smither

<small>SERIES EDITORS</small>

---

A Project of the Evangelical Missiological Society

www.emsweb.org

# Conversion of Chinese Students in Korea to Evangelical Christianity

## Factors, Process, and Types

Chang Seop Kang

PICKWICK *Publications* · Eugene, Oregon

CONVERSION OF CHINESE STUDENTS IN KOREA TO EVANGELICAL
CHRISTIANITY
Factors, Process, and Types

Evangelical Missiological Society Monograph Series 13

Pickwick Publications
An Imprint of Wipf and Stock Publishers
199 W. 8th Ave., Suite 3
Eugene, OR 97401

www.wipfandstock.com

PAPERBACK ISBN: 978-1-6667-0352-8
HARDCOVER ISBN: 978-1-6667-0353-5
EBOOK ISBN: 978-1-6667-0354-2

*Cataloguing-in-Publication data:*

Names: Kang, Chang Seop, author.

Title: Conversion of Chinese students in Korea to Evangelical Christianity : factors, process, and types / by Chang Seop Kang.

Description: Eugene, OR: Pickwick Publications, 2022 | Evangelical Missiological
Society Monograph Series 13 | Includes bibliographical references.

Identifiers: ISBN 978-1-6667-0352-8 (paperback) | ISBN 978-1-6667-0353-5 (hard-
cover) | ISBN 978-1-6667-0354-2 (ebook)

Subjects: LCSH: Evangelicalism—Korea | Chinese students—Korea (South)

Classification: BV3460 K364 2022 (print) | BV3460 (ebook)

01/03/22

For my loving family.

# Abstract

IN SOUTH KOREA, THERE are about 54,000 Chinese university students, and approximately 3,000 Chinese students are attending churches and Christian activities in more than 150 churches. Ministries for Chinese international students is strategically significant because students who convert to Christianity may become future leaders of Chinese churches. The purpose of this study is to explore and identify the factors, process, and types of conversion among Chinese international students in South Korea and to formulate a theory on their conversion.

This study utilized grounded theory methodology, conducting interviews ($n$=30) and generating the following conversion theory grounded in the data. Chinese students studying in Korea were inclined to convert to Christianity upon experiencing God. Experiencing God was the turning point in which they overcame their obstacles to conversion, they overcame their problems, and they no longer viewed their lives as problematic.

Based on this theory and key findings, this study presents three approaches to potential Chinese converts: the overcoming problems approach, the coming home approach, and the role model approach. Finally, this study recommends phenomenology as a method for studying conversion in future research.

# Contents

# Preface

ALTHOUGH CHRISTIANITY'S CENTER OF gravity has long since shifted beyond the West, theology, including missiology, still relies heavily on Western Christianity. While it is true that both mission and missiology are indebted to Western scholarship, there is a need for a different research methodology and for missiology to be appropriate for specific mission field contexts. Top-down, deductive research, which typically begins with theological themes to study contexts, can be methodologically limited in understanding how God is working in specific field contexts. This may subsequently limit how research can propose principles and strategies appropriate for such contexts. Currently, deductive methodologies depend on existing theories and the dualism of separating the Word of God from human experiences. To establish a field-centric missiology, we require a research methodology that not only generates new theories, but also opens the way for more holistic perspectives.

To this end, grounded theory may be considered one of the most ideal research methodologies. Grounded theory was developed for the purpose of generating new knowledge (or theories) concerning areas of study that are relatively unknown. I have seen many missionaries struggling to do research using deductive methodologies, because these methodologies seek to verify hypotheses generated from existing theories or theoretical frameworks that are often inapplicable to rapidly changing mission fields. Since grounded theory uses data to develop concepts and generate new theories, it is particularly useful for missionaries who are experts in the language and culture of their mission fields and want to conduct research on little-researched areas. Such research would contribute greatly to mission through the development of new theories relevant to mission fields.

Furthermore, since grounded theory does not seek to prove a hypothesis, it allows for unexpected discoveries. For instance, I was holding an assumption in approaching my primary research question, "What are the factors, processes, and types of conversion of Chinese students in Korea?" Since atheism and evolutionism are solidified into Chinese education, I had assumed that the Chinese international students would have undergone a cognitive-heavy process of conversion in which discussions and explanations transformed their beliefs. However, my preconceptions were shattered when data analysis revealed that most students had undergone conversion by personally experiencing God, instead of any intellectual approach. As such, the data analysis of grounded theory methodology can allow the researcher to discover unexpected concepts or theories grounded in the data.

Overall, it is an honor to hope that, through this publication, ministries can witness how God brings about conversion through the commitment of God's workers and researchers, while appreciating how grounded theory guides the construction of a theory through intensive data analysis.

# Acknowledgments

I THANK GOD FOR allowing me to study at Torch Trinity Graduate University, which trains students to carry out the Great Commission, to spread the gospel to all the nations of the world. After serving over two decades as a missionary, studying missiology at this school with such supportive and academically excellent professors was an immense blessing to me. During this academic journey, the Lord allowed me to get help from many faithful servants of God. This research project would never have been finished if the Lord had not provided the necessary health, intellect, spiritual insight, and financial support. I would like to specially recognize the following people.

Dr. Eiko Takamizawa, my supervisor, provided substantial insight and invaluable support throughout the project. Dr. Hyung Jin Park opened up a new world for me with respect to studying creatively using primary sources, which contrasts the traditional way of studying in Korea. He also opened my eyes to see world Christianity and the translatability of the gospel. Dr. Ah Young Kim helped me gain new insights on postmodernism and Muslim studies with her exceptional academic abilities. Dr. Hyun Joo Oh kindly taught me qualitative research methodology and how to use NVivo. I give special thanks to Dr. Lewis R. Rambo, who kindly gave me a great deal of advice and reading materials on conversion studies. Dr. Priscilla Choi helped me in proofreading the introduction of the dissertation, Kathy McKay was instrumental for proofreading this dissertation.

I give my deep appreciation to each of the participants in this study. I also extend my very grateful acknowledgement to those church pastors who willingly recommended their church members to have interviews with me. Special thanks also go to the members of Incheon Chinese Christian Church, who granted me the time to study and prayed for me. Special thanks are also due to Elder Young Su Seo, who financially supported me and my family.

I am also grateful to the Evangelical Missiological Society of North America, the series editors, and especially Dr. Anthony Casey, for accepting this dissertation in the EMS Monograph Series. In addition, I must thank Pickwick Publications, including my editor, Dr. Chris Spinks, Matthew Wimer, and George Callihan, for encouragingly guiding me through the publishing process. I want to give special thanks to my professors at Torch Trinity, including president Dr. Yoon Hee Kim and Dr. Enoch Wan of Western Seminary, for endorsing my book.

Finally, I extend a special note of my appreciation and love to my wife, Sukwha. She has endured many hardships while I was studying, all the while faithfully serving the church in my place. I also thank my lovely daughter Grace and son-in-law William Scott for proofreading, and my son David for editing and polishing the manuscript for publication.

# Abbreviations

| | |
|---|---|
| CBMC | Connecting Business and Marketplace to Christ |
| CCC | Campus Crusade for Christ |
| CCCOWE | Chinese Coordination Centre of World Evangelism |
| CCP | Chinese Communist Party |
| CHISTA | Chinese Students All Nations |
| KOSTA | Korean Students All Nations |
| KOWSMA | Korean World Student Missions Association |
| NIV | The Holy Bible, New International Version |

# 1

## Introduction

### Statement of Research Problem

ACCORDING TO MIIKKA RUOKANEN, Protestant Christianity has become one of the fastest growing religions in the People's Republic of China (hereafter China).[1] The total number of Christians in China is about 130 million, which is second only to the United States.[2] The Chinese church has experienced phenomenal growth since the Chinese government implemented its Open Door Policy in 1979. Because the Chinese government and enterprises have been able to provide job opportunities, many Chinese people who studied overseas have been returning to their home country. Among the returnees, called *hai-gui*, there are many Christians who converted to Christianity while studying overseas. These Christian returnees are forming a new type of Chinese church, the urban intellectual house church, which is distinct from both the house church and the registered church (Three-Self Patriotic Movement Church).[3] This new category of the Christian church makes Christianity no longer a religion only for the marginalized—the old, the sick, the illiterate, and women—as people used to characterize the house church movement.[4]

In 2012, I attended a forum, hosted by the Association of Chinese Mission Organizations, for those working to evangelize Chinese students. Many attendees asked for more information that could help them work more effectively. Since Korea began receiving Chinese students in 1994, the number of Chinese students in Korea has been gradually increasing. In 2011, there were 47,725 students in degree programs in Korea. In 2015, the Korean Ministry of Education estimated that approximately 54,000

1. Ruokanen, *Christianity and Chinese Culture*, viii.

2. Sisci, *China*, 17.

3. Zhou, *Chinese vs. Western Perspectives*, 152.

4. Wielander, *Christian Values*, 90.

1

Chinese students were currently studying in Korea, on almost every university campus.[5] Although the significance of the ministry to Chinese students is apparent, little research has been conducted regarding their conversion to Christianity. Many pastors and missionaries in Korea who work with Chinese students mention the need for more research in order to help them understand the conversion of Chinese students.

## Statement of Purpose

Conversion happens due to certain factors in the process of decision-making, and it may be of a particular type. The purpose of this study is to discover the primary factors, process, and types of conversion of Chinese students in Korea to Evangelical Christianity. Understanding why some factors are more positive in the process of conversion, whereas others may negatively affect the process can be beneficial to pastors who are reaching out to Chinese students.

Conversion does not happen in an instant but takes place through a process in which several factors work together in each stage, from the initial encounter to the decision to convert. Exploring the dynamism of the steps of the conversion process will give a big picture of conversion. My research was designed to identify specific types of conversions along with the factors that might distinctively affect particular types of conversion. For example, Chinese students, because they were brought up in strong, atheistic environments, might struggle to accept the concept of a deity. How do they come to accept this idea? What are the factors that contribute to such change? What does the process look like? What are the types of conversion? These are the questions that I address in this study.

## Research and Interview Questions

The research question for this study is as follows: What are the primary factors, process, and types of conversion to Christianity among Chinese students studying in various programs in universities in South Korea? The question has three aspects: the primary factors, the process, and the types

5. Korean Ministry of Education, "Statistics of Education."

of conversion. In order to establish a religious conversion theory, I utilize the methodology of grounded theory.[6]

As grounded theory emphasizes, interview questions are simple and open-ended at the initial stage. One of the specific features of grounded theory methodology is that it is generative in terms of creating interview questions according to the principle of theoretical sampling. The researcher develops interview questions by way of theoretical sampling rather than preparing the questions beforehand. I developed four initial interview questions for this project:

1. What was your life like before you became a Christian?

2. What made you decide to become a Christian?

3. What were the difficulties for you in becoming a Christian?

4. How did you overcome these difficulties?

## Definition of Terms

For the purposes of this study, certain terms are defined as follows.

- *Chinese student*: One who was born in China, came to Korea after graduating high school in China, is studying in or has graduated from a Korean university, and is currently residing in Korea.

- *Conversion*: An experience in which a person comes to believe in Jesus Christ with the accompanying acts of repenting, turning from sin, and deciding to follow the teachings of the gospel with the ritual of baptism (Acts 2:38). In the Chinese church, Christian conversion is called *chongshengdejiu* ("being saved and born again").

- *Conversion factor*: Something that affects a person in their conversion to Christianity. For instance, doctrinal factors are associated with the existence of God, creation, sin, and salvation; affective factors with feelings of security, love, and affirmation; communal factors with friendship and relationship; and religious experiential factors with dreams, miracles, visions, and answered prayers.

---

6. Strauss and Corbin, *Qualitative Research*; Corbin and Strauss, *Qualitative Research 3e*; Charmaz, *Constructing Grounded Theory*.

- *Conversion process*: Religious converts go through a process that moves from the initial encounter to the commitment stage.

- *Conversion type*: The defining characteristics of a particular conversion that reveals the distinctiveness of the conversion experience. In analyzing the factors and the process, the conversion can be categorized as one of several typical types of conversion.

- *Evangelical Christianity*: The movement of Christian faith affiliated with Protestant Christianity that holds to the following beliefs: (1) the authority, inerrancy, sufficiency, and inspiration of the entire Bible, (2) salvation by grace through faith alone, (3) the total corruption of human beings and their need to be converted, and (4) the effectiveness of the atoning work of Christ on the cross to save human beings. According to Berkhof, the total corruption (depravity) of humans means that: (1) the inherent corruption extends to every part of man's nature, to all the faculties and powers of both soul and body, and (2) there is no spiritual good, that is, good in relation to God, in the sinner at all, but only perversion.[7]

- *Korea*: Republic of Korea (also known as South Korea). The southern part of the Demilitarization Zone of the Korean peninsula, with Seoul as its capital city. Christianity is one of the major religions in Korea. There are 77,000 Protestant churches in the country,[8] and 13,731,000, or 28 percent of the population is Christian (Protestant or Catholic).[9] People who live in Korea have many opportunities to encounter Christians and Christian churches.

## Assumptions

This study is based on the following assumptions:

1. The Word of God (the Bible) is inerrant and sufficient to convert a person through the work of the Holy Spirit.

---

7. Berkhof, *Systematic Theology*, 246–47.
8. Lee, "Why So Many Churches?"
9. Park, *Religions of Korea*, 17–19.

2. Chinese people in Korea have the freedom to interact with Christians. Once they arrive in Korea, they are free to go to church and to meet Christians, without restrictions.

3. The participants who were interviewed in this study provided honest answers to the questions they were asked.

## Significance of the Research

This study is significant in the following areas:

First, this research will help Korean churches plan and prepare evangelism and discipleship. Knowing how conversion takes place can help Christian workers prepare in ways that are appropriate for Chinese students. Currently, the Korean Church has an unprecedented opportunity to do mission work among Chinese students. According to the Korean Ministry of Education, 54,214 future leaders of China are studying on the campuses of Korean universities.[10] Most were not Christians before coming to Korea, but now they have the chance to hear the gospel from Christian workers and churches that are passionate about converting these Chinese students.

Second, this study will help Korean churches approach Chinese students with the sensitivity of cross-cultural understanding, for this study approaches conversion among Chinese students as a cross-cultural ministry. Today, the interactions between Chinese students and many gospel sharers take place in cross-cultural surroundings. Mission-minded Korean churches and missionaries are the most important driving force of evangelism among Chinese students in Korea. For instance, some Korean churches not only employ Chinese missionaries and pastors from mainland China, but they also mobilize all possible resources to reach out to Chinese students. One such example is Kon-kuk Chinese Church, which is primarily operated by a couple of Chinese professors with the cooperation of Korean lay-professional Christians. In this regard, the ministry to Chinese students in Korea is a cross-cultural mission of sorts. Therefore, anyone willing to serve the conversion of international students in Korea should employ the perspective of cross-cultural ministry.

Third, this research offers both theoretical and practical explanations of conversion among Chinese students that will be helpful to those serving

10. Korean Ministry of Education, "Statistics of Education."

Chinese students in other parts of the world, although the different contexts require different theories and approaches.

For instance, several studies have been done on the conversion experience of Chinese intellectuals in North America.[11] The conversion process of Chinese intellectuals in North America may be significantly different, however, from that of Chinese students in Korea. First of all, most of the Chinese intellectuals in the studies in North America were immigrants, whereas the subjects of this study are students who mostly do not intend to live permanently in South Korea. Moreover, the conversion of Chinese intellectuals in America is related to identity reconstruction,[12] assimilative transformation,[13] Chinese churches, and institutions.[14] According to the Chinese Coordination Centre of World Evangelism (CCCOWE), there are around 1,444 Chinese churches in North America.[15] However, only a handful of Chinese immigrant churches exist in South Korea: there are only seven Chinese immigrant churches in Korea. These are called *hwakyo* churches, and each has less than one hundred members. I have been serving one such church in Incheon.

Fourth, this study on conversion discloses the holistic and sequential nature of conversion. The approach of this study is holistic in the sense that it explores significant factors reported by the participants, rather than focusing on any predetermined hypothesis or theoretical framework. It is also sequential in the sense that it explores the entire process of how people experience conversion.

Lastly, unlike research done by secular social scientists on conversion, this study places a high value on the work of the Holy Spirit. Studies of religious conversion have been mostly conducted by social scientists, and their theories are developed based on their disciplines. However, the most crucial factors in Christian conversion are the gospel and the work of the Holy Spirit. Keeping this in mind, I explore the factors that affect conversion and the process and types of conversion.

---

11. Wong, "From Atheists to Evangelicals"; Temple, "Perspective Transformation"; Wang, "Conversion to Christianity"; Zhang, "Chinese Conversion."

12. Wong, "From Atheists to Evangelicals," 179–86.

13. Temple, "Perspective Transformation," 62–67.

14. Zhang, "Chinese Conversion," 149–59.

15. CCCOWE, "List of Chinese Churches."

## Delimitations

The participants in this study are Chinese students from mainland China who converted to Christianity within an evangelical Protestant context since their arrival in South Korea. The scope of this research includes the factors, process, and types of conversion of Chinese students to Evangelical Christianity in Korea. Factors such as personal traits or characteristics, ethnic origins, regional differences (rural/urban), educational background, and financial background are not considered in this study.

The philosophical framework used throughout this study is not positivism, which holds to the belief in "a unitary method of systematic observation, replicable experiments, operational definitions of concepts, logically deduced hypotheses, and confirmed evidence."[16] Rather, the philosophical framework of this study is social constructivism (often called interpretivism).[17] Individuals seek and develop subjective meanings of their experiences in the world.[18] Researchers need to look for the complexity of meaning rather than categorize it into a narrow framework or the participants' views of the situation.[19] Social constructivism sees subjective meanings as negotiated socially and historically. That is, "they are not imprinted on individuals but are formed through interactions with others."[20] According to John W. Creswell, with social constructivism, rather than starting with a theory, inquirers generate or inductively develop a theory or pattern of meaning and address processes of interaction among individuals in a specific context.[21]

Thus, social constructivism is appropriate for this study, because I aim to identify the factors of conversion of people in a specific context and the process and types of conversion experience in the dynamic interactions among the people involved, such as Christian workers, other Christians (friends, professors, and others), non-Christians, and the participants. In addition, I want to interpret their conversion experiences by relying as much as possible on the participants' views.

16. Charmaz, *Constructing Grounded Theory*, 4.

17. Denzin, "Interpretation," 500–15.

18. Creswell, *Qualitative Inquiry*, 24.

19. Creswell, *Qualitative Inquiry*, 24–25.

20. Creswell, *Qualitative Inquiry*, 25.

21. Creswell, *Qualitative Inquiry*, 25.

## Limitations

Even though most of the participants in this study have similar ideological and educational backgrounds, they come from a variety of cultural and social backgrounds. There are fifty-six different ethnic groups in China, and a vast gap exists between the rich and the poor, between urban areas and rural areas. Since this study is descriptive in nature, its findings are not to be taken as conclusive. The goal is to extend our understanding about the factors affecting conversion in cross-cultural contexts, as well as to show the process and typical types of conversion of Chinese students in Korea. This study illustrates how conversion in this context proceeds.

## Methodology

I have chosen to use qualitative methodology. I also utilize the methodology of grounded theory to develop a theory of conversion. The following three books were utilized in developing the methodology of this research: Strauss and Corbin, *Basics of Qualitative Research*; Corbin and Strauss, *Basics of Qualitative Research 3e*; and Charmaz, *Constructing Grounded Theory*. This study focuses on a sample of thirty Chinese student converts. The data gathered from in-depth interviews, observations, and written materials were analyzed by the methodology of grounded theory utilizing NVivo 11 software.

This introductory chapter has presented statement of research problem, statement of purpose, research and interview questions, definition of terms, assumptions, significance of the research, delimitations, limitations, and methodology. The next chapter presents precedent and related literature.

# 2

# Precedents and Related Literature

THIS CHAPTER ADDRESSES ESSENTIAL subjects related to the theme of the study, including the religious background of China. The chapter is comprised of six sections that establish the background knowledge and rationale for this study of the conversion experience of Chinese students in Korea. First, the biblical understanding of conversion and Christian conversion from a theological perspective are explored. Then, religious conversion from social science perspectives and models of the conversion process are presented. The second section reviews diasporas and international students, focusing on the topic of diasporas. The third section discusses ministry to Chinese students in Korea, including the state of international students in Korea and ministries for Chinese students in Korea. The fourth section presents an overview of the Chinese Church since 1949, addressing reformation in China after 1979 and church growth after 1979. The fifth section treats Chinese traditional religions and culture from the perspective of Christianity. The sixth section presents literature on research methodology, including qualitative research methodology, phenomenology and conversion study, and grounded theory.

## Understanding Conversion

There exist as many conversion experiences as there are Christians. The authenticity of one's conversion should be critically evaluated by the Bible, though the conversion experience of any single person cannot be exactly compared to those of Bible characters. This section addresses the biblical understanding of conversion, Christian conversion from a theological perspective, the social sciences perspective on religious conversion, and particular models of the conversion process.

## Biblical Understanding of Conversion

In the Old Testament, the Hebrew verb *šwb* ("to turn or return") has the closest meaning to the English word conversion, and it refers to one's return from waywardness to a God-centered life. The word is mainly used to refer to the spiritual relationship of the Israelites with God in the covenantal context.[1] Therefore, *šwb* is not used to indicate a change of religion or a sudden transformation of life. Instead, *šwb* emphasizes maintaining an existing covenant relationship through continual turning away from evil and turning to God.[2]

In the New Testament, the Greek word *epistrephō* is used for conversion in reference to the Jews (Acts 3:19) and the Gentiles (Acts 11:21). The conversion passages of outsiders in the New Testament include two distinct elements: return *from* the old sinful way of life *to* a "new and opposite allegiance."[3] These two elements are shown in *metanoeō* ("to repent") and *pisteuō* ("to believe"), which together denote the full process of the conversion process. Paul often uses *pistis* ("faith") in order to express the act of conversion (1 Thess 1:9). The Apostle John also uses *pisteuō* to describe the conversion of the Samaritans (John 4:39). Thus, the three words— *epistrephō*, *metanoeō*, and *pisteuō*—convey the meaning of conversion in the New Testament. Those within the Old Testament context (the Jews) need to maintain a covenantal relationship with God. Those outside the covenant (the Gentiles) need to turn to God, who wants to save sinners by the grace shown on the cross, through faith. Only then can they enter into a new covenantal relationship with God.

As Frederick J. Gaiser states, it is important to understand what the Bible says about "the nature and work of both God and humanity," in order to comprehend conversion.[4] There has been a controversy over the matter of conversion, whether it is solely God's work (divine sovereignty) or solely human work (human response). Gaiser argues that we do not need to divide the two, because "the Bible's incarnational perspective insists that God's work in the world need not be neatly distinguished from the work of his creatures."[5] Indeed, in the Old Testament, conversion has

---

1. Wells, *Turning to God*, 32.
2. Wells, *Turning to God*, 33.
3. Wells, *Turning to God*, 35.
4. Gaiser, "Theology of Conversion," 93–107.
5. Gaiser, "Theology of Conversion," 95.

a twofold aspect: the covenantal God turns his covenantal people who broke the covenant, the Israelites, back to God. God calls out to the fallen Israelites, "Return, Israel, to the Lord your God" (Hos 14:1). At the same time, Israel calls upon God for restoration: "Restore me, and I will return" (Jer 31:18). For the authors of Scripture, Yahweh's demand ("Return, faithless children," Jer 3:14) is in no way incompatible with Israel's cry ("Restore us, O God," Ps 80:3).

In the New Testament, conversion is inseparably related to the work of the Holy Spirit. Gaiser points out that the conversions effected by the message of the apostles were manifestations of the Spirit's presence and the fulfillment of God's word prophesied by Joel: "I will pour out my Spirit on all people" (Joel 2:28).[6] Conversion includes repentance, baptism, and the gift of the Holy Spirit. Yet, this may not be the normative pattern of conversion in Acts of the Apostles, for the conversion stories in the book vary and do not reveal a systematic, typical, and ideal pattern of conversion. In Acts, conversion is not an end but only a beginning. Conversion is a more complex process than a simple and instantaneous event, except in a very few cases like Paul's.[7] David F. Wells also views conversion as the threshold, "the way into Christian faith," rather than "the entirety of Christian faith."

> Conversion does not stand alone; it is the beginning of a lifelong journey of growing in Christ and being conformed to his image. Discipleship must follow on conversion as living and breathing follow on birth. . . . Just as there is no discipleship without conversion, so there also can be no conversion without discipleship. The two belong together. That, at least, should be our insistence. And if we fail here, our testimonies to God's grace in our conversion become empty, discordant, and unbelievable.[8]

There is both continuity and discontinuity between the converted, new person and the old person prior to conversion.[9] Though the old is passed away, its character continues to affect the new. Therefore, the newly converted must be edified by continuing discipleship training. Wells points out that rather than emphasizing the moment of conversion to test one's spiritual life, we need to emphasize "the renewing works of the Spirit, the

---

6. Gaiser, "Theology of Conversion," 99.

7. Wells, Turning to God, 69.

8. Wells, Turning to God, 23.

9. Gaiser, "Theology of Conversion," 105.

fruitful life, and obedience."[10] Authentic conversion should be accompanied by much effort and discipleship training.

The biblical writers did not focus on the convert's feelings or emotions, but on the content of the gospel. Thus, the New Testament records several dramatic conversion experiences without showing interest in the psychology of conversion. New Testament writers interpret conversion theologically with words such as faith, repentance, grace, forgiveness, and regeneration. Though the process of conversion may be different in individual cases, both the content of the gospel and the principle of conversion are unchanged. A conversion story should include the description of both the transforming action of the converter and the work of the gospel in the process. Thus, a conversion story can be shown to be authentic if it reflects a turning away from sinful living and receiving Christ as Savior through the gospel.

## Christian Conversion in Theological Perspective

As Christianity has shifted from the Northern hemisphere to the Southern, non-Christian faiths have gained influence even in countries that were formerly predominantly Christian. Moreover, postmodernism has influenced people's mindsets, especially in terms of the denial of any principles or truths as universal criteria. The development of information technology like the Internet has also facilitated access to a variety of spiritual traditions. Other cultures' spiritualities and religions are similar to the Christian faith and practice, even having their own versions of conversion. For non-Christians, these phenomena considerably weaken the Christian claim of Christian doctrine as the absolute norm.

Wells summarizes and interprets the eight papers presented at the Lausanne Consultations on Conversion and World Evangelization held in Hong Kong, in 1988. He concludes that two central principles regarding Christian conversion, that Christian conversion is both supernatural and unique, are non-negotiable.

Wells points to three reasons for the supernatural character of Christian conversion.[11] First, conversion is impossible without God's saving action. Second, "the convincing work of the Holy Spirit" makes conversion desirable.[12] Third, only the inspired Scriptures can give a framework for

10. Wells, *Turning to God*, 69.

11. Wells, *Turning to God*, 18.

12. Wells, *Turning to God*, 18.

truth in thinking about authentic Christian conversion. Wells claims that Christian conversion is supernatural because God's grace alone, manifested in Jesus' cross, can redeem sinners, who need to repent and believe.

Christian conversion is unique because it is centered on Christ alone. It is "rested upon Christ, is grounded in him, looks to him, is supernaturally caused, and has eternal results."[13] Christ has delivered those who believe in him from sin, death, the devil, and God's judgment. Without Christ, there can be no authentic faith and conversion in any biblical sense.

George E. Morris views Christian conversion as "a dynamic, complex, ongoing process which is greatly impacted by particular times and places and considerably shaped by contexts."[14] Conversion always takes place within a particular historical culture. Furthermore, Christian conversion cannot be understood apart from the convert's cultural context, nor does it deny one's life before conversion. Therefore, Christian conversion cannot be viewed as a transcultural, non-contextual event. In *The Mystery and Meaning of Christian Conversion*, Morris states, "This non-contextual view opens up the possibility of a more devastating error—that of assuming that Christian conversion happens to all believers, everywhere, at the same point in life, and in the same way."[15] Conversion happens in a specific context of personal and cultural influences at the intersection between God's way and human ways.

Christian conversion has a profound and mysterious aspect so that any analysis of the conversion experience has severe limitations. Morris puts it this way:

> No one can hope to encompass in word and thought the mystery and meaning of Christian conversion in all its concrete actuality. For in this experience one is confronted with the ultimate mystery in which the love of God lays hold upon the mind, heart, and conscience of a human being. . . . We deceive ourselves when we think we can dissect Christian conversion and describe it in detail.[16]

The experience itself should be judged by its authority and content rather than by prior standards of genuine Christian faith. Christian conversion is an experience that affects the human mind, heart, and spirit in significant ways.

13. Wells, *Turning to God*, 21.
14. Morris, *Christian Conversion*, 4–5.
15. Morris, *Christian Conversion*, 4.
16. Morris, *Christian Conversion*, 9.

No religious experience can be the criterion of authentic Christian conversion. In fact, it is actually dangerous to structure an understanding of Christian conversion around human experience. Morris argues that we must relate the gospel to our understanding of Christian conversion, saying that "[bringing] the gospel to bear on the nature of Christian conversion means involving ourselves and a critical assessment, allowing the light of the gospel to illumine, assess, and where necessary, correct our experiences."[17] In sum, the only legitimate criterion for Christian conversion is the gospel.

## Social Science Perspectives on Religious Conversion

Conversion is a comprehensive phenomenon. It is so complicated and diverse that many questions have been raised about conversion, including the question of how it is initiated (by God or humans) and when it takes place (instantaneous or gradual).[18] Due to the significant effects of religious conversion on people's lives, scholars in various fields of the social sciences have studied conversion. Different academic disciplines have contributed to the understanding of conversion, such as anthropology, sociology, psychology, history, and religious studies. As Christopher Lamb and M. Darrol Bryant claim, diverse meanings and understandings of conversion pose difficulties for theorists of conversion.[19] Lewis Rambo argues, "Ideally, multidisciplinary studies of conversion will access the full richness of models and understandings that already exist in each of these disciplines but at the same time will recognize the limitations of each discipline."

According to Rambo, the significant contribution of anthropologists to the study of religious conversion is their deep analysis of the context of conversion, that is, of the contextual matrix of conversion. Anthropologists also provide analysis and insight into the long-term consequences of religion, providing rich data, whereas psychologists and sociologists study conversion synchronically, of one particular time in time.[20] The psychological analysis of religious phenomena may be reductionist in nature because it relates the emotional or psychological experience of a person to their religious conversion, omitting the spiritual realm of religious experience. Sociologists have studied the sources and nature of religious conversion,

17. Morris, *Mystery of Conversion*, 10–11, 13.

18. Lamb and Bryant, *Religious Conversion*, 1.

19. Rambo, "Anthropology and Conversion," 217.

20. Rambo, "Anthropology and Conversion," 213.

though sociology has limitations in researching the supernatural. In his book *A Theology of Religious Change: What the Social Science of Conversion Means for the Gospel*, David J. Zehnder argues that "though a conversion theology may use science to explain how the gospel speaks to people amid life's changes, the starting point must be a theological account of conversion that preserves its independent authority."[21] The gospel is the criterion of religious change. The gospel's presence is crucial for people to have the opportunity to convert to Christianity.

Zehnder studies the causes of religious change and their implications for communicating theology, utilizing the psychology and sociology of religious change to explain the factors and process of conversion. He states that the social sciences can explain some of the factors that cause people to change, explaining that social networks and parents have decisive influences on faith development.[22] He starts to resolve a doctrinal problem, the tension between the role of God and of people in conversion, but discovers that the social sciences are very helpful in explaining how theology communicates the various changes that people experience by helping us understand how people process concepts. Regarding the psychological study of conversion, he states, "Though the psychological account cannot ground conversion's theological validity, it expands our knowledge of human nature and explains the material through which salvation appears."[23]

Meredith McGuire sees conversion as consisting of a change in the individual's meaning system and self.[24] She holds that conversion has social, psychological, and ideational components.[25] The social component consists of the interaction between the recruit and his or her circles of associates. The psychological component refers to emotional and affective aspects of conversion, as well as changes in values and attitudes. The ideational component includes the actual ideas the convert embraces or rejects during the process. These three components appear to encompass different theories of conversion.

In a psychological study of religious conversion, Ullman finds that conversion, in contrast to her initial assumption of "ideology change," hinges on a sudden attachment, "an infatuation with a real or imagined

21. Zehnder, *Religious Change*, 2.

22. Zehnder, *Religious Change*, xiv–xv.

23. Zehnder, *Religious Change*, 36.

24. McGuire, *Religion*, 74.

25. McGuire, *Religion*, 74.

figure which occurs on a background of great emotional turmoil."[26] The conversion, through intense and omnipresent attachment, could lead the convert to anticipate everlasting guidance and love, for the object of the convert's infatuation was perceived as infallible. Thus, Ullman's study reveals the importance of emotional attachment in the process of religious conversion. She argues that the context of the individual's emotional life is the most important factor in understanding conversion, saying, "It occurs on a background of emotional upheaval and promises relief by a new attachment."[27] To the converts in her study, conversion appears to be an answer to their search for psychological salvation and offers the haven discovered in a new relationship.[28] She found that most of the conversion stories in her study were based on an infatuation with a powerful authority figure, such as a leader or a mentor.

Religious conversion by nature results in the convert's attachment to a new group of peers who lavish acceptance and love on the convert, who turns away from previous affiliations to become a member of a new community.[29] Since the new group offers an emotional haven, the convert may find new hope, happiness, and emotional rapture there. Thus, Ullman's study presents the importance of attachment in the process of religious conversion in which the convert can have new relationships, new emotional and psychological experiences, and new hope.

Ullman also finds that cognitive questions—beliefs, ideology, the universal question of meaning, and questions about theological correctness—were not germane to the religious conversions in her study. The significant factors were preoccupation with the self, emotional turmoil in the person's life, and urgent need in the particular circumstances of the convert's life.[30] Ullman explains the experience of religious conversion as "a change in the self."[31] Religious conversion may affect the major components of people's self-definition, including their ideological affiliations and beliefs, their social ties, and their lifestyle.

According to control theory, individuals tend to act in a conventional way so long as they possess a strong bond to the conventional social

26. Ullman, *Transformed Self*, xvi.
27. Ullman, *Transformed Self*, xvii.
28. Ullman, *Transformed Self*, xvii.
29. Ullman, *Transformed Self*, xviii.
30. Ullman, *Transformed Self*, 4.
31. Ullman, *Transformed Self*, vii.

order. This bond includes attachments to other individuals, "the standard societal institutions, constant involvement in conventional activities, and belief in the correctness of social order."[32] Individuals who lack these bonds to conformity will be free to experiment with new alternatives. From this perspective, those most likely to convert to a new religious affiliation are those who have lost a sense of connection. Thus, students studying abroad have less of a burden based on their former social bonds when converting to a new religion.

Subculture theory emphasizes the role of a group of like-minded people in establishing a distinctive way of thinking and acting. In a group of close friends, the majority can easily control the others in terms of decision-making. Group members strengthen their bond through repeated social interactions by sharing information, emotions, and material rewards. Strong friendships between members can draw people in, and the friendless, whose social bonds are weak, may be attracted to the group as well. This can also give some important insights to those who work for international students in relation to the lack of strong bonds. Thus, social influence theory stresses the importance of the church's social life; the church can utilize social influences not only as a medium for the translation of faith, but also as a strong power in sustaining faith.[33]

Cognitive belief theory stresses ideational components of the process, specifically, that people readily commit themselves to a particular religion because of what they believe.[34] This theory is quite different from those regarding conversion and commitment as the result of external compelling factors.[35] For instance, Brian Taylor criticizes sociologists who view conversion exclusively through the lens of pre-dispositional sociocultural perspectives, background circumstances, or situational contingencies.[36] He suggests that conversion theory must include cognitive components in addition to "ecological factors."[37]

Cognitive belief theory argues that a person's adjustment to life's stresses and developmental crises centers on a search for meaning through which one gains mastery and control over one's life. Snow et al. conducted

32. Bainbridge, "Sociology of Conversion," 182.

33. Bainbridge, "Sociology of Conversion," 184.

34. Kilbourne and Richardson, "Paradigm Conflict," 1–21.

35. Lane, "Conversion in Evangelical Context," 186.

36. Taylor, "Conversion and Cognition," 16.

37. Taylor, "Conversion and Cognition," 16.

an empirical study that validated the notion that converts want to join religious groups with which they can align their conceptual worldviews.[38] It seems that Christian workers need to understand the cognitive patterns or ways of thinking of the people they are serving, in order to effectively render the truth. Nevertheless, we also need to acknowledge that ideas alone do not necessarily persuade a person to convert. Without the work of the Holy Spirit, no one can believe in Jesus as their savior (1 Cor 12:3).

Ullman, in *The Transformed Self: The Psychology of Religious Conversion*, reports on the findings of her conversion study of American college students, some of which can be viewed as motifs of conversion. For example, she writes about the haven of last resort (conversion and the search for relief), the relationship with authority (conversion and the quest for the perfect father), infatuation with the group (conversion and social influence), adolescent conversion and the search for identity, the merger with the perfect object (conversion and the narcissistic condition), conversion and the quest for meaning, and "the transformed self."[39] Personal motifs of conversion within the above psychological factors of conversion may be categorized as *affectional motifs* (the search for relief, the perfect father, the infatuation with the group, and merger with the perfect object), *intellectual motifs* (the quest for meaning and the search for identity), and the *consequences of conversion* (the transformed self).

John Lofland and Norman Skonovd explore the defining experiences that enable each type of conversion to be distinctive.[40] In their study, Lofland and Skonovd isolate key, critical, orienting, defining, or motif experiences in the process of conversion.[41] The notion of a motif experience aims to account for the conversion perceived by the convert. They suggest that holistic, subjective conversions vary because the convert's motif experiences are different. Lofland and Skonovd describe the characteristics of motif experiences as follows: "Motif experiences, then, are those aspects of a conversion which are most memorable and orienting to the person *doing* or *undergoing* personal transformation—aspects that provide a tone to the event, its pointedness in time, its positive or negative affective content, and the like."[42]

38. Snow et al., "Frame Alignment Process," 464.
39. Ullman, *Transformed Self*.
40. Lofland and Skonovd, "Conversion Motifs," 373–85.
41. Lofland and Skonovd, "Conversion Motifs," 374.
42. Lofland and Skonovd, "Conversion Motifs," 374.

In order to describe conversion motifs objectively, Lofland and Skonovd combine salient thematic elements and key experiences with objective situations. They identify six motifs of conversion that are delineated by the five major variations (or dimensions). The six motifs are intellectual, mystical, experimental, affectional, revivalist, and coercive. The five dimensions are the degree of social pressure, temporal duration, level of affective arousal, affective content, and belief participation sequence. The five dimensions comprise the traditional trinity of the intellectual, physical, and emotional. The authors identify significant aspects of some conversion motifs, namely, that the converts often participate actively in their new role before they intellectually assent to its theological implications.

In intellectual conversion, the active role in the conversion is practiced by the person who is seeking alternative knowledge about religion, spiritual issues, and ways of life—new grounds of being, personal fulfillment, theodicies, etc.—via books, media, lectures, and other impersonal ways without interacting with religious advocates.[43] This pattern is also referred to as the activist model of conversion.[44] In intellectual or self-conversion motifs, conversion occurs prior to active participation in religious activities of the organizations. As the result of the rapid development of information technologies, people have an increasing array of opportunities for obtaining religious knowledge.

Experimental conversion denotes the active involvement of a prospective convert who has an experimental attitude and a pragmatic *show me* mentality in relation to pursuing religious faith prior to conversion.[45] Through intensive interaction, the prospective convert becomes committed. Thematic words such as socialization process and situational adjustment are appropriate for describing this conversion motif.[46]

Affectional conversion was first identified by Lofland and Stark in 1965, and this type emphasizes the importance of positive and affective interpersonal bonds in the conversion process. Central to the conversion process in this motif are the personal attachments or strong liking for

---

43. Lofland and Skonovd, "Conversion Motifs," 376.

44. See Lofland, "Becoming a World-Saver," 805–18; Straus, "Changing Oneself," 252–72.

45. Lofland and Skonovd, "Conversion Motifs," 378.

46. Lofland and Skonovd, "Conversion Motifs," 379.

practicing believers generated by the "experience of being loved, nurtured, and affirmed by a group and its leaders."[47]

Revivalism has tended to decrease in the contemporary globalizing techno-information society. Revival gatherings or conferences do still occur throughout the world, however. The central feature of conversions in such gatherings is generally emotional due to the powerful music, evangelistic preaching, and group experience.[48]

The coercive motif is relatively rare, because it requires special conditions in which the religious advocate pressures the prospective convert to participate, conform, and confess. Such a process is also labeled as brainwashing, programming, mind control, coercive persuasion, and thought reform.

Lofland and Skonovd have contributed to our understanding of the phenomena of conversion as follows. First, the study of conversion motifs delineates the schema of conversion types, identifying conversion motifs and themes. Second, they refer to the historical and social dimension of conversion motifs. Trends of conversion are related to social conditions.

Mystical conversion is typically represented by the case of Paul's dramatic incident on the road to Damascus. Mystical conversion generally occurs suddenly in a way that is beyond logical description, such as through visions, voices, or other paranormal experiences.

## Models of the Conversion Process

In order to more precisely analyze the complexity of conversion, some scholars study the process of conversion and present models of the conversion process which show the integrative nature of conversion and its patterns and structures. This section reviews Eiko Takamizawa's model of religious commitment, Alan R. Tippet's model of the conversion process, and Rambo's seven-stage model.

Takamizawa developed a new theoretical framework for studying the religious commitment of Japanese Christians, one that is not monolithic but integrative and holistic. Her model is based on doctrinal, communal, religious experiential, and ritual factors, and she analyzes these factors according to five stages of commitment: context, conversion, incorporation, crisis, and recommitment. To be baptized has crucial meaning in the

47. Rambo, *Understanding Religious Conversion*, 15.
48. Lofland and Skonovd, "Conversion Motifs," 380.

20

communal society of Japan, which has a very strong religious bond. Her model seems to be relevant to studies of people in communal societies such as Japan's, where living in the "co-web of Japanism" often results in great challenges when it comes to committing to Christianity.[49]

Kwon Shik Han studied the conversion factors of Iranian and Indonesian Muslims who became Christian in South Korea, focusing on three factors, sociocultural, doctrinal, and experiential, which is based on Takamizawa's conversion theory.[50] In this study, Han finds that "these Muslims who were embedded in Muslim culture evaluated the Christian culture through the lenses of their own cultures and traditions and decided to convert to Christianity."[51] Han found that in the process of conversion, Iranians converted to Christianity through traditional truth seeking and supernatural experiences, whereas Indonesian Muslims became Christians due to an intuitive inner feeling and the practical help they received in daily life.

Alan R. Tippett, in an article entitled "Conversion as a Dynamic Process in Christian Mission," studied the dominant pattern of conversion among the people of Oceania. He found that the structure of the conversion pattern was fairly regular, and he provides a schematization of the conversion process.[52] Tippett defines the schematization as "more of a frame of reference, within which to arrange, classify and discuss data, than a complete theory of conversion."[53] He was concerned with the process of conversion: How are people separated from the old context, and incorporated into the new? Tippett originally had conceptualized the conversion process in units of time (before he witnessed an abrupt end of the incorporation of groups of converts in the mission field), such as the period of awareness, the moment of decision, and incorporation. There are a number of points of realization and points of encounter in this process. Therefore, the model has three specific characteristics: it is processual, measures periods, and is marked by points.

Tippett confirms four different possible decisions a communal group may make in the period of decision. The group may decide against conversion or totally accept Christianity. In order for the acceptance to be stable, the process of acculturation should be exceedingly rapid and should satisfy the

49. Takamizawa, "Religious Commitment Theory," 171.

50. Han, "Conversion of Iranian," 54.

51. Han, "Conversion of Iranian," iv.

52. Tippett, "Anthropology of Conversion," 203–5.

53. Tippett, "Anthropology of Conversion," 210.

acceptors. People may accept the conversion but with an act of modification. One form of this is syncretism, in which people modify Christianity with their own traditional or cultural content, which is not what the advocates envisioned. The other pattern of adjustment is that the acceptors maintain the basic content of the beliefs modeled by their own cultural structures, procedures, authority patterns, and way of life.

After the decision to convert has been made, the new convert needs to be instructed and trained in how to acquire new norms and a new group identity. This is a kind of transition that can be "ritually effected and finally completed by means of an act of incorporation," as in the case of baptism.[54] Tippett points out the importance of drawing on a conceptual field with which the new converts are familiar, saying, "for any religious conversion to be permanent its new structure should both meet the needs of the converts and operate in meaningful forms."[55] The above-mentioned three units of time in the process of conversion are separated into the point of realization and the point of encounter. According to Tippett, the point of realization ends the period of awareness and begins the period of decision. There comes a moment when a person or a group suddenly but clearly realizes the reality of the passage of the old context and the possibility of the new context.

Tippett emphasizes the importance of a clear-cut termination of the old way, saying, "there is clearly a relationship between the manifest form of encounter and the subsequent stability of the new religion, or to state the principle the other way—avoid the encounter and increase the reversions."[56] Tippett has witnessed large numbers of converts in the mission field presumed to have been well incorporated into church for a long time suddenly turn away as a body to "a highly institutionalized and enthusiastic social pattern of their own."[57] Actually, his original idea is that following the period of incorporation should be the move into *glory*. Because the period of incorporation can come to an abrupt end, which goes against his original model, he finds that his model does not account for all the phenomena related to the conversion process. Therefore, he expands his model by adding the point of *consummation* (or confirmation), which leads to the period of maturity "where people, having learned to

54. Tippett, "Anthropology of Conversion," 211.
55. Tippett, "Anthropology of Conversion," 211.
56. Tippett, "Anthropology of Conversion," 213.
57. Tippett, "Anthropology of Conversion," 219.

use the means of grace and to study Scripture, and so forth, now pass on into a deepening experience of faith, growing in grace, or *sanctification*."[58] This model sheds light on the importance of continuing the education of converts to the point of qualitative commitment.

As Tippett admits, this perspective accords with the traditional Wesleyan understanding on the order of salvation (*ordo salutis*), which emphasizes personal experience with an emphasis on sanctification. There seems to be some difficulty separating the work of the Spirit solely for the point of consummation in confirming the trueness of a conversion. The Spirit works in the whole process of conversion, whether or not the phenomena of the experience of the Spirit manifests. In addition, not all converts abruptly terminate the period of incorporation by leaving their newly acquired Christian faith.

Rambo regards surrender as "the inner process of commitment that continues over a lifetime" and also as "the turning point away from the old life and the beginning of a new life."[59] Surrender is a process, just as sanctification is not a one-time experience for Christians. In the life-long process of surrender the convert disconnects from "old ways and patterns and gradually is able to consolidate the new life into firmer, growing commitment."[60] Total submission to God is the goal of every convert, just as Paul states: "I have been crucified with Christ and I no longer live, but Christ lives in me. The life I now live in the body, I live by faith in the Son of God, who loved me and gave himself for me" (Gal 2:20).

Rambo views religious conversion as a complex process, interweaving personal, social, cultural, and religious forces.[61] He also stresses the spiritual dimension of conversion while utilizing concepts from the social sciences, saying, "However scholars may choose to delineate its causes, nature, and consequences, conversion is essentially theological and spiritual. Other forces are operative, but the meaning, the significance, and the goal are religious and/or spiritual to the convert."[62] Therefore, as mentioned above, although we need to study the phenomena of conversion with the help of the methodologies of social science, we must also recognize that the work

---

58. Tippett, "Anthropology of Conversion," 219.

59. Rambo, *Understanding Religious Conversion*, 136.

60. Rambo, *Understanding Religious Conversion*, 136.

61. Rambo, "Psychology of Conversion," 159.

62. Rambo, *Understanding Religious Conversion*, 10.

of the triune God is the major force of conversion: "and no one can say, 'Jesus is Lord,' except by the Holy Spirit" (1 Cor 12:3b).

Rambo proposes a stage model of conversion using an interdisciplinary approach (integrating psychology, sociology, anthropology, and religious studies) to understand this complicated multilayered phenomenon. His stage model consists of seven stages: context, crisis, quest, encounter, interaction, commitment, and consequences.

*Context* is the total environment of conversion process. In the stage of *crisis*, some motifs are included in the catalysts for conversion, which includes mystical experiences, near-death experiences, illness and healing, the question, "Is this all there is?," the desire for transcendence, altered states of consciousness, and externally stimulated crises.[63] The term *catalysts of conversion* can be interpreted as the factors affecting conversion, which also affect motifs of conversion.

In the stage of the *quest*, Rambo primarily addresses motivational structures, which include experiencing pleasure and avoiding pain, the convert's conceptual system, enhanced self-esteem, establishing and maintaining relationships, power, and transcendence.[64] The fourth stage, *encounter*, includes benefits of conversion, such as system of meaning, emotional gratification, techniques for living, leadership, and power.[65] The *commitment* stage includes motivational reformation. In the last stage, *consequences* treat the nature of consequences that may be the result of motifs such as affective, intellectual, ethical, religious, social, and political.[66]

Rambo's model is holistic and process-oriented, though not sequential. It may be appropriate in analyzing conversion experiences in cross-cultural contexts. Due to the complex nature of religious conversion, a one-dimensional theory of conversion cannot fully encompass the conversion experience of people in diverse contexts. After examining whether Rambo's stage model would be appropriate for describing and assessing the conversion experiences of Chinese intellectuals in the United States, Wong concludes that it offers a systematic framework that includes different aspects of their conversion experiences.[67]

---

63. Rambo, *Understanding Religious Conversion*, 44–65.

64. Rambo, *Understanding Religious Conversion*, 56–65.

65. Lamb and Bryant, *Religious Conversion*, 29.

66. Rambo, *Understanding Religious Conversion*, 144–48.

67. Wong, "From Atheists to Evangelicals," 214.

This section has treated a biblical understanding of conversion, Christian conversion in theological perspective, social science perspectives on conversion, and models of the conversion process. The next section addresses diasporas and international students.

## Diasporas and International Students

The phenomenon of diaspora has significantly affected the mode of mission as it gives unprecedented opportunities for mission. Here, diaspora refers to the scattered people who have settled for a long period in a foreign country, outside of their native country. According to Enoch Wan, one of the pioneers of diaspora missiology, "the size and significance of diaspora have increased in the twenty-first century. Approximately 3 percent of the global population resides in countries other than their places of birth."[68] While emigration may be related to particular economic, social, political, cultural, religious, and natural situations, in this age of migration, many people are moving across borders to pursue a better life.[69]

Wan, in *Diaspora Missiology: Theory, Methodology, and Practice,* stresses that a new paradigm in missiology, one that is different from traditional missiology, is needed "to cope with the new demographic reality of large scale and intensified diaspora movement of people in the twenty first century."[70] Based on my own experience, some of the people living in foreign countries are more receptive to the gospel and have a greater understanding of foreign culture than the people in their home country. Therefore, Christian missionaries should pay special attention to people on the move and know that God has a sovereign purpose and leads the world and people to fulfill his own will. We can find evidence of this in the narratives of the Bible. International students studying in foreign countries are a strategically important group of people, for once the students return to their home country, they will likely be leaders and influential members of their society.

The following section discusses diasporas and international students, including diasporas with respect to missions and ministry with international students.

68. Wan, "Phenomenon of Diaspora," 12.

69. Castles and Miller, *Age of Migration,* 6–20.

70. Wan, "Phenomenon of Diaspora," 13.

## Diasporas and Missions

The Greek word *diaspora* is translated in the Bible as "scattered" (see John 7:35; Jas 1:1; 1 Pet 1:1). God planned to have people scattered in the world, even before they sinned, to cultivate them as agents of his blessings (Gen 1:26–28). This blessed commandment was repeated with the covenant of preserving the world after the judgment of the flood (Gen 9:1–7). God did not want people to rebel against this commandment of scattering throughout the world (Gen 11:1–9). God's first words to Abraham were a commandment to leave for a new and unknown land. In the Old Testament, the narratives of Abraham's descendants show the theme of the deliverance of God among his people scattered, in Palestine, Egypt, Babylon, Persia, Greece, and Rome. Jesus himself experienced migration with his family. Narry F. Santos offers insights about the dispersion of the Jewish diaspora in the Old Testament era: (1) God's orchestration and control of the spread of Jews, (2) the hope and reality of the people's regathering after the scattering, (3) Israel's role as witness to the nations, and (4) sovereign preparation for the advent of Christ and the spread of Christianity.[71] Thus, God had a special purpose in scattering his people abroad. That is, by scattering his chosen people, he wanted to save not only the Israelites, his chosen people, but also the heathens.

Jesus commanded his disciples and churches to scatter to the end of the world, in order to save people from their sins. The first church in Jerusalem led by his disciples was scattered to places such as Cyprus and Antioch, where they won people to Christ and established churches. God wants his people to globally disperse to show others how much he loves to save people. This is the Great Commission, which can be accomplished only by scattering (Matt 28:18–20; Mark 16:15–17; Luke 24:46–49; John 17:18; Acts 1:8). As Wan and Tira state, "all historical events happen along a divinely-set trajectory, and diaspora would seem to be one of God's ways of working among the nations."[72] They also note that "the scattering of Christians could be God's provision of outreach and church planting."[73]

A paper prepared for the Lausanne Movement uses the word *diaspora* to describe the "large scale movement of people from their homeland to

---

71. Santos, "Exploring the Dispersion," 22–23.
72. Wan and Tira, "Diaspora Missiology," 39.
73. Wan and Tira, "Diaspora Missiology," 41.

settle permanently or temporarily in other countries."[74] The host Christian communities have the opportunity to: (1) "provide loving hospitality to care for the immediate needs of the 'stranger,'" (2) "shape leaders from around the world," (3) "create new relevant forms in expressing Christianity," and (4) "provide training for Christian leaderships."[75]

On the other hand, the diaspora Christian communities have opportunities to: (1) "contribute to the society of their new country," (2) "reach out to others in their own diaspora through hospitality" (Acts 8:4), reach out to other diaspora communities (Acts 11:19–20), (3) reach out to the marginalized people in their own country who may not be receptive to those from the host country and "be bridges of the gospel to the people in their countries of origin and in other countries," and (4) "revitalize the Christian community in their host country."[76]

Wan and Tira classify the factors creating diaspora as either voluntary or involuntary: "urbanization, rapid globalization in the labor industry, geopolitical shifts, catastrophic natural disasters (such as hurricane, flood, earthquake, or tsunami), national and ethnic conflicts, socio-economic advancement, cultural exchanges, and pandemics resulting in crippling of the work force (e.g., HIV/AIDS)."[77] They also use the terms *push* and *pull* to categorize the factors of migration. Push factors are the undesirable and negative situations, such as war, natural disaster, and poverty that push people to move from their origin of place to other countries. Pull factors, such as political freedom, a better quality of life, and economic opportunity, pull immigrants to host countries to improve their lives. As Tira notes, "most immigration is a result of a combination of several push and pull factors."[78]

As mentioned above, the migration experience can increase the possibilities for searching for a new religion. This can be attributed not only to "the alienation inherent in the immigration experience," but also to the freedom in the newly adopted country.[79] Sam George states, "The changing demographics of Christianity call for fresh reflection on the missionary task and our theological understanding of Christian Mission as from everywhere

---

74. Houston et al., "New People Next Door," 9.

75. Houston et al., "New People Next Door," 30–31.

76. Houston et al., "New People Next Door," 31–32.

77. Wan and Tira, "Diaspora Missiology," 28–29.

78. Tira, "Landscape of Diaspora," 3.

79. George, "Diaspora," 48.

to everywhere. The roles that scattered communities play in the advancement of the Kingdom also need fresh missiological consideration."[80] Jehu Hanciles also emphasizes that the contemporary global transformations are significantly affecting the geographic and demographic features of the world religions and offer a great opportunity for missionary expansion.[81]

Comparing traditional missiology and diaspora missiology in terms of how they conduct ministry, Wan and Tira point to several specific aspects of ministry patterns in diaspora missiology as a new way of realizing Christian missions: "mission at our doorstep," "ministry without border," "networking and partnership" for the Kingdom, "the borderless church," "the liquid church," and "the church on the ocean."[82] They clearly categorize the distinct characteristics of diaspora mission with a table titled, "the yes and no of mission at our doorstep."[83] Within the *yes* categories include: yes, door opened; yes, people accessible; yes, missions at our doorstep; yes, ample opportunities; yes, holistic ministries; and yes, powerful partnership. The *no* categories are items such as: no visa required, no closed door, no international travel required, no political/legal restrictions, no dichotomized approach, and no sense of self-sufficiency and unhealthy competition.

More than two decades ago, before I served Chinese contract workers in Saipan, the Korean diaspora church in Saipan invited me to evangelize the Chinese workers there. At that time, there was no diplomatic relationship between Korea and China. The door was wide open, however, for Korean Christians to reach out to the Chinese people in Saipan. The Chinese people had more opportunity to pursue religious searches (*people accessible*) with the help of Korean Christians who wanted to make the best use of the *ample opportunity* to do *missions at their doorstep*. The Korean Christians served the Chinese not only with the gospel, but also with care for their physical needs with the love of Christ (*holistic ministries*). Later on, overseas Chinese Christians who were very moved to know that Korean Christians had served their fellow brethren cooperated with Korean Christians to serve Chinese contract workers from mainland China (*powerful partnership*).

Wan and Tira assert that "in the present technological age and in our increasingly 'borderless' world, missions strategies must be multi-directional,

80. George, "Diaspora," 46.

81. Haniles, "Migration and Mission," 146–53.

82. Wan and Tira, "Diaspora Missiology," 5.

83. Wan and Tira, "Diaspora Missiology," 56.

riding on the 'wave' of mass movements of people and having a 'high touch' relational approach."[84] We need to be aware of new mission opportunities in the movements of people around the world. Craig Ott views the diaspora and relocation as a divine impetus for mission in the early church in terms of the cross-cultural spread of the gospel to the nations.[85] God's sovereignty is active in the movement of people in the globalizing world today; that is, God is using diaspora for his missional purposes, spreading his glory among people and preparing people to receive that message. In this vein, Ott's suggestion seems to be insightful. He says, "We act in alignment with the missional trajectory of the New Testament in identifying open doors for the gospel in migration and diaspora today."[86]

Ott investigates four aspects of diaspora and relocation in relation to mission in the book of Acts.[87] First, persecution scattered Christians, bringing bearers of the gospel to new locales. These Christians brought the gospel beyond the bounds of Judea, Samaria, Phoenicia, Cypress, and Antioch (Acts 8:5; 11:19). Second, non-Christians who relocated came into proximity to the gospel, such as Cornelius, the Roman centurion who became a "God fearer" and led his family to be baptized by Peter. Another example is Apollos, a native of Alexandria who later joined Paul's missionary band (Acts 18:24–28). Third, diaspora communities provided an entry point for the gospel. Jews scattered throughout the Roman Empire established diaspora communities and synagogues that facilitated the spread of the gospel. This is evident in Paul's ministry, as he always began his witness in a synagogue. Fourth, the diaspora was a preparation for gospel messengers.[88] Paul is a special example of a diaspora Jew who was competent in the language and culture of the Greek world, which enabled him to work for the gospel in the Roman Empire.

Living in a globalizing world today, we have great opportunities to act as witnesses for Christ. Scattered Christians have been establishing churches for both themselves and other ethnicities wherever they have settled down, from early Christianity to the present. Today, we can see many Asian diaspora Christians engaged in sharing the gospel with other ethnic groups in many cities around the world. According to Ott,

84. Wan and Tira, "Diaspora Missiology," 57.
85. Ott, "Diaspora and Relocation," 73.
86. Ott, "Diaspora and Relocation," 88.
87. Ott, "Diaspora and Relocation," 88.
88. Ott, "Diaspora and Relocation," 75.

many Christians among the ten million Filipinos working in 193 differ-ent countries are sharing the gospel, even in the Arab world.[89] Christians living in this globalized world have unprecedented opportunities to reach out to foreigners in their homeland with the gospel and Christian love and hospitality. For instance, many witnesses speak about how students experience conversion while studying abroad.

The most common type of immigrants in Korea work 3D (difficult, dirty, and dangerous) jobs. Others are those in international marriages, in-ternational students, and businesspeople. These immigrants may experience a lot of problems while working and living in Korea, including labor exploi-tation of illegal immigrant workers, sexual violence in the workplace, and international marriage problems (mostly caused by Korean husbands). Gwi-sam Cho suggests mission strategies for immigrants in Korea that involve a change of attitude, such as "the acceptance of the gospel through a change in worldview" and a "mutual understanding of inclusive multi-culture."[90] He also suggests "family evangelization through social welfare," saying that after we open immigrants' hearts with inclusive attitudes, we can share the gospel through social welfare. He stresses a holistic approach for holistic salvation; that is, the salvation of souls and bodies.[91]

According to Chan Shik Park, in 2010, about five hundred Korean churches were involved in serving migrants and one hundred independent churches of immigrants, and in 2014, a reported 208,778 of the 1,797,618 foreigners living in Korea were of illegal status.[92] Guen Seok Yang analyzes how the changed situation under globalization presents a challenge to Ko-rean churches' understanding and practice of mission. He points out two different responses of Korean churches. They have either used the changed situation as an opportunity for the expansion of mission or they have tackled various social problems caused by the impact of globalization.[93] Further-more, according to Dong Hun Seol, the Korea International Labor Foun-dation identified 121 Christian organizations among the 159 organizations actively working on behalf of migrant workers in Korea.[94] Korean churches help the migrants with their difficulties, such as work-related human rights

89. Ott, "Diaspora and Relocation," 93.

90. Cho, "Missiological Answer," 81–84.

91. Cho, "Missiological Answer," 85.

92. Park and Jung, *Diaspora Mission*, 25–26.

93. Yang, "Globalization," 43.

94. Seol, *Migrant Workers*, 24.

violations, dangerous working conditions, legal disputes, immigration issues, disputes caused by racial and cultural prejudice, conflicts in families with international marriages (in Korea, the term *multi-cultural family* is used), and issues regarding medical services. Korean churches perform such mercy ministries—serving the afflicted immigrants in alienated circumstances with Christian love—while serving these people's spiritual needs by inviting them to church and planting churches for them.

Tira suggests the following three forms of diaspora mission: ministry of hospitality, ministry to the displaced, and mobilization of the Church for global ministry.[95] Since the Bible instructs the people of God to be hospitable to those who are afflicted as refugees and aliens, we need to be hospitable to diaspora groups. Many immigrants who have relocated due to push factors are uprooted, therefore having no safety net. Christians should be like the good Samaritan, acting as friends in suffering, sorrowful, and displacement situations. As Tira states, churches in the twenty-first century should accelerate holistic missions to the scattered and the distressed.[96] The churches should utilize their resources to bless these people and plant churches for the scattered. He also points out the importance of training and mobilizing leaders and members of the churches to serve those who are scattered and afflicted.[97] Networking among Christian diaspora groups not only fosters cooperation, but also will lead to the sharing of resources around the world. For example, the Filipino International Network, the Chinese Coordination Centre of World Evangelization, and the North American Council for South Asian Christians facilitate cooperation around the world.

## Diasporas and Ministry to International Students

*Panta ta ethnē* (Greek for "all nations"; Matt 28:19) is traditionally rendered inclusively, including both Jews and Gentiles as the object of the missionary activity of the Church. Contemporary readings of *panta ta ethnē* are influenced by the sociological understanding offered by Donald McGavran and Peter Wagner. It is understood as people groups or all peoples, meaning all the tribes, castes, lineages, and people of the earth. *Panta ta ethnē* is also sociologically rendered as the dispersed nations, which includes the immigrants or peoples from various lands scattered

95. Tira, "Landscape of Diaspora," 12.
96. Tira, "Landscape of Diaspora," 12.
97. Tira, "Landscape of Diaspora," 12.

all over the world.[98] Dispersed people can be mobilized as the missional power who will work for their homeland, as is seen today when the overseas Chinese help churches in China.

Therefore, *panta ta ethnē* should be the mission goal of every Christian and local church. Sang In Lee asserts that "the final pericope of Matthew (Matt 28:18–19) is acknowledged as the most important one in the entire Gospel and is regarded as the key to grasping the whole work."[99] There are no geographical or ethnic boundaries that exclude certain people from hearing the gospel. Mission has long been understood as crossing the border to take the gospel to those living far away. However, since we live in a globalizing world, this traditional concept of mission has to be transformed. We are living in all nations, and people from all nations are our neighbors.

The Lord initiated the spread of the gospel to the non-Israelites by calling his disciples to save them. Receiving a special vision and hearing the voice of the Lord, Peter was called to go to Cornelius, a Roman centurion who was living among the Jews. This was a transforming experience for both of them. God also called the non-Israelites to see and hear his great works and believe in him. The Queen of Sheba was amazed to see and hear the wisdom and glory that God had given to Solomon, and she praised God in Jerusalem. An Ethiopian eunuch became a Christian through Philip, who was guided by the Holy Spirit; the eunuch then spread the gospel in his home country. God's sovereign hand guides people's movements, as well as his church and the people who bear witness to him.

Jesus instructs the disciples to treat people with hospitality, especially those who are from other places, by identifying with them: "I was a stranger and you invited me in . . . whatever you did for one of the least of these brothers of mine, you did it for me" (Matt 25:35, 40). There are many testimonies of international students becoming Christians as a result of receiving hospitality in Christian homes. God has used foreigners to fulfill his purposes in the history of the world. In the Old Testament, Moses, Joseph, and Daniel are good examples of this; they were educated in a foreign land and became influential leaders. To serve international students is to serve God in fulfilling his eternal purpose of gathering people from "every nation, tribe, people and language" (Rev 7:9).

98. Casino, "Diaspora Missions," 132.
99. Lee, "*panta ta ethne*," 50.

International migration creates great opportunities for mission. As Korea has become rapidly globalized, churches and mission organizations have been expending great effort to reach out to foreigners in word and deed. International students have great potential to become influential leaders in their home countries after they become Christians while studying in Korea. God has moved the students and scholars to other countries where they can be more receptive to the gospel. God has given this strategic opportunity to local churches so that they may impact the world for Christ. The international student ministry is strategic because it is beneficial to the students, local churches, and the gospel. The students can receive Christian love in the forms of kindness, friendship, caring, and help during a time when they are feeling lonely in a foreign land. Additionally, students from restrictive societies can freely access and explore the gospel. Some of the international students may be "more curious, open, and responsive to the gospel than they would be at home."[100]

Lausanne's International Student Ministry Group reports that local churches can be beneficial as they serve international students in the following ways: (1) members can communicate the gospel with international students by building friendships; (2) in particular, those who want to serve abroad can learn cross-cultural skills; (3) the churches can join the mission with "cost-effective ways of reaching the world for Christ" through prayer and giving; and (4) Christian international students can also contribute to the Christian community in the host country.[101]

International students returning to their home countries can help advance the kingdom of God. They have no difficulty reaching out to people in their own country in terms of language, culture, and relationship, whereas missionaries have to devote their lives to acquiring these skills. John Sung is an extraordinary case of a returned student who dedicated himself to evangelizing the people of his own country. After receiving his PhD in chemistry in the United States, he returned to China in the 1920s and became an evangelist for China and the Chinese diaspora in Southeast Asia.[102]

This section has presented diasporas and international students, diasporas and missions, and ministry to international students, focusing on the significance of the ministry to the diasporas in the globalizing world and the ministry to the international students who will be leaders after

100. Houston et al., "New People Next Door," 48.

101. Houston et al., "New People Next Door," 48.

102. Tow, *John Sung*, 277.

returning home. The next section will present the ministry for Chinese students in Korea.

## The Ministry for Chinese Students in Korea

Korean churches and mission organizations have shown great zeal in serving international students studying in Korea, in order to win them to Christ. In almost every university, Christian workers lead a Christian fellowship or church among international students. This section surveys the overview of international students in Korea and the types of Christian workers and ministries, and the state of the ministry.

### International Students in Korea

According to a report by the Korean Ministry of Education, the number of international students in Korea has gradually been increasing. In 2015, there were 91,332 international students, which is 7.6 percent (6,441) more than the previous year (see Figure 1).[103] The number of international students in degree programs is 55,739, and 35,593 are in non-degree programs.[104]

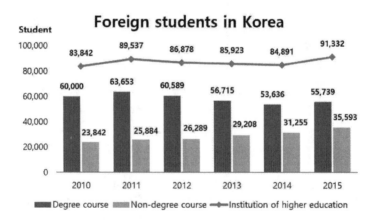

Figure 1. The Number of International Students in Korea

*Source:* Korean Ministry of Education, "Summary of the Basic Statistics of Education for 2015"

103. Korean Ministry of Education, "Statistics of Education."
104. Korean Ministry of Education, "Statistics of Education."

The number of Chinese students studying degree programs in Korea decreased from 2011 (47,725 students) to 2014 (34,482). In 2015, the total number of Chinese students was 54,214, with 19,327 (54.3 percent of the Chinese students) in non-degree programs (see Figure 2). This represents an increase of 21.9 percent (3,473) from the previous year, and 62.6 percent (34,887) of the Chinese students were in degree programs.[105]

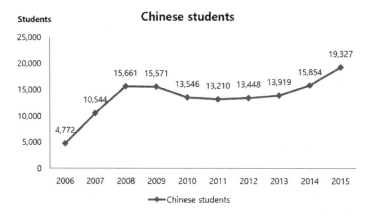

Figure 2. The Number of Chinese Students in Non-degree Programs in Korea

*Source*: Korean Ministry of Education, "Summary of the Basic Statistics of Education for 2015"

There seem to be two major factors in the increase of international students coming to study in Korea. First, there are some pull factors. That is, as Korea becomes more industrialized and technologically advanced, more students want to study in Korea. Also, Korean culture, such as drama (K-drama) and music (K-pop), attracts international students to Korea. Second, universities in Korea face a growing need for more students. Due to the declining birth rate in Korea, the number of higher education students has also been declining in recent years. Universities recruit international students to improve their finances and reputations. The Korean government keenly supports the recruitment of international students through various policies and financial aid for universities. For instance, in 2013, the prime minister created the Study Korea 2020 Project, a long-term plan for recruiting additional international students to Korean universities. This project aims to develop a global network that is aware of and friendly towards Korea and seeks to

105. Korean Ministry of Education, "Statistics of Education."

welcome 200,000 international students into Korea by 2020. To implement the project, the government will raise its annual budget for higher education to ten billion won by 2015, and further increase it to twenty billion won by 2020.[106] The Ministry of Education plans to continuously support the recruitment of international students in order to attract the world's future leaders to study and be successful in Korea.

## Overview of Ministries for Chinese Students in Korea

Korean church leaders consider themselves indebted to the work of past foreign missionaries, who established some of the first educational institutions in Korea. With this in mind, the Korean Church seeks to serve international students in hopes that they will return to their home countries as leaders. Some mission organizations are adopting a class in "Mission for the Foreign Students in Korea" as part of their missionary training course. For instance, the Global Mission Society has offered training on this topic since 2014, because it recognizes the importance of practical training in this time of a shifting mission paradigm.[107] Global Mission Society is a mission organization of the General Assembly of Presbyterian Church in Korea, which has about 2,400 missionaries in 105 countries.

Professor Yoo Jun Kim of Yonsei University outlines the history of the founding of the university with the help of missionaries as follows: Missionary Horace N. Allen (1885–1932) and Oliver R. Avison (1860–1956), who was a doctor and professor at the University of Toronto Medical School, established *Jae Jung Won* in 1885, a hospital that later became Severance Hospital of Yonsei University. When Horace G. Underwood (1859–1916) and Henry G. Appenzeller (1858–1902) arrived at Incheon on April 5, 1885, Yonsei University came into existence in Korea.[108]

### Types of Christian Workers for Chinese Students

In order to evangelize to international students, Christians from various walks of life make use of their talents and opportunities. Christian professors who can freely contact students have the greatest authority and opportunity

106. "Government Attracting Foreign Students."
107. Kang, "Foreign Students."
108. Kim, "Foreign Student Ministry," 25.

36

to guide them to Christ. Many dedicated professors are involved in various activities for missions, such as establishing a church, preaching and leading Bible study groups, and cooperating with pastors or missionaries, to name just a few. Some professors who have established Chinese churches on or off campus have even become pastors of those churches. For instance, Dr. Lee is a professor at K University and senior pastor of a church for Chinese students on his campus. Dr. Park is the dean of the Korean language department of I University and pastors Chinese students at his church next to the campus. At P University, four Christian professors are pastoring a Chinese students' church on their own, without a pastor.

Some Korean pastors work to serve these students after they discover the significance of evangelizing to international students. Churches near campuses often become a center for evangelizing to students under the leadership of dedicated pastors, who also mobilize church members to become involved. Chaplains of Christian universities have a crucial role in reaching out to international students on campus. They organize various activities, inviting them to the gospel in ways other than leading them to a chapel. Recently, retired missionaries and missionaries who have unwillingly left their mission fields due to visa problems have joined campus ministries. With their rich experience and linguistic and cultural competence, most of them are working as pastors in the Chinese services in Korean churches or in their own Chinese churches that they planted on their own.

Most of the pastors working with Chinese students in Korea are Korean-Chinese from China who graduated from Korean seminaries. Some Han Chinese pastors are also serving Chinese ministries in Korean churches, but the linguistic and cultural limitations of some Chinese pastors have caused difficulties in their communications with the leaders of Korean churches who supervise these ministries. This is the most difficult aspect of the work of Chinese pastors within Korean churches. Different styles and methods of ministry between Chinese pastors and Korean pastors often lead to great tension and result in separation. Some Chinese missionaries from Hong Kong who have worked in Korean churches had to leave because of this problem in Daegu.

Campus mission organizations such as Campus Crusade for Christ (CCC), Inter-Varsity Christian Fellowship, International Student Fellowship, Worldwide Evangelization for Christ, International Corporation (Inter-Corp), and University Bible Fellowship are working with Chinese students. CCC, for example, has six missionaries who had served in China but had to leave due to visa problems. They are cooperating with local churches to serve the Chinese students. Many of the Christian Korean language teachers in language schools or centers also serve the students with Christian love, to win them for Christ.

Most of the local churches near the campuses have great zeal for evangelizing Chinese students. Some church members do their best to serve the Chinese students in various ways. For instance, they invite students to their homes or to restaurants, offer scholarships, and provide counseling.

## Types of Ministry to Chinese Students

The types of Chinese ministry to Chinese students in Korea vary. Most of the Chinese ministries are not independent, as Korean churches run mission programs for the Chinese students through Chinese-speaking pastors (i.e., Chinese, Korean-Chinese, or Korean missionaries or lay leaders). In this structure, Chinese pastors face difficulties caused by communication challenges and cultural misunderstandings. Only a few Chinese churches are independent from Korean churches, and these are run by Chinese pastors, Chinese professors, Korean professors, Korean-Chinese pastors, or Korean missionaries, whereas others have services that provide Chinese translation.

## The Korean World Student Missions Association (KOWSMA)

The Korean World Student Missions Association (KOWSMA), established in 2013 by Rev. Seong Ju Moon, is actively coordinating and working for the mission of international students in Korea. Rev. Moon started the organization with the vision of evangelizing to international students. He states, "This is a shortcut to the world mission; by sowing the seed of the gospel among them we can harvest fruits in 230 countries."[109] In order to realize this vision, KOWSMA wants to cooperate with Christian workers serving international students, the leaders of church and mission organizations, professors, and even the government and private companies to develop programs.

KOWSMA has organized an annual Forum for Mission for Foreign Students, inviting missionaries, church leaders, and professors. At the

109. KOWSMA, "KOWSMA Bulletin."

forums, I have learned that many Christian professors, mission-minded professors, and non-ordained Christians are working actively to share the gospel with international students through Christian love. KOWSMA also annually organizes a three-day retreat for international students, the Global Student Mission Conference, during which pastors and overseas missionaries are invited as speakers and lecturers to emphasize this mission.[110] During the first retreat, held in 2013, at the Songdo International Campus of Yonsei University, about forty international students committed their lives to world mission. KOWSMA also conducts worship and fellowship in renowned and popular locations near Hongik University, inviting talented Christian musicians. A Chinese student who attended the worship shared what he experienced: "I was profoundly moved and spiritually touched at the meeting."[111] For the holidays, KOWSMA organizes festivals for international students with diverse programs and food. In 2014, 130 international students from thirty-three countries attended the Full Moon Festival.[112]

## Chinese Students All Nations (CHISTA)

Chinese Students All Nations (CHISTA) is an organization that was established in 2010, with the purpose of serving Chinese students in Korea with the gospel. The leaders of CHISTA are Chinese pastors serving Chinese students in Korea, most of whom are Korean seminary graduates. From the beginning, they have cooperated with the leaders of Korean Students All Nations (KOSTA), who have served Korean students studying overseas since 1986. KOSTA was founded by several Korean pastors, including Rev. Jung Kil Hong and Rev. Dong Won Lee, who were concerned about the spiritual needs of Korean students. Their primary vision was to equip students, so that they could transform Korea with the gospel and also become future leaders who integrate academics and faith. In 1988, KOSTA started its ministry in France, Italy, and Germany. Today, its ministry expanded to twenty-six countries, with annual retreats in thirty cities of these countries and a total attendance of about twenty thousand students.[113]

CHISTA annually organizes a four-day retreat for Chinese students during the Full Moon Festival in Korea, which has been attended by about

110. Kang, "Foreign Students."
111. Kim, "Foreign Students as Leaders."
112. Kang, "Foreign Students."
113. KOSTA, "Vision."

1,000 students in recent years. The leaders of CHISTA organized CHISTA Singapore and CHISTA Mongolia in 2013, and they have also held retreats for Chinese students in Mongolia and Thailand. Under the umbrella of CHISTA International, there are regional branches, such as CHISTA Korea and CHISTA Singapore. The organization is now preparing to set up regional CHISTAs in the United States, France, Italy, Australia, and Japan.

The goals of CHISTA can be summarized as follows: (1) to save souls—to seek the conversion and spiritual transformation of Chinese students so that they can transform China in the future; (2) discipleship training—to make disciples who can change Chinese society when they return to China; and (3) to mobilize students for world mission.[114] CHISTA has three major ministries: (1) organizing the annual four-day retreat during the Full Moon Festival, mainly targeting converted students, with the purpose of renewing their spiritual life and mobilizing them for world mission; (2) evangelizing twice a year to non-Christians; (3) running a leadership school, offering three different sets of courses for lay leaders, seminarians, and holders of doctoral degrees in theology.[115]

The future plans of CHISTA can be summarized as follows: (1) to plant Chinese-speaking churches in countries that have CHISTA; (2) to set up Chinese services through cooperation with Korean churches; (3) to mobilize Chinese students for world mission by selecting missionary candidates to train and to dispatch and manage the missionaries; 4) to establish a seminary to create a team of those who have earned doctorates in theology; (5) to network with mainland Chinese churches, overseas Korean churches, Korean diaspora churches, and Korean missionaries; and (6) to create a pastoral academy to introduce the pastoral experience of Korean churches to the world.[116]

CHISTA establishes churches in China for international students who will return to their home country.[117] In order to follow up with returned Christian students, CHISTA dispatches pastors who graduated from seminary in Korea and requires them to plant churches in China. It also organizes retreats in China twice a year for those who have returned. It asks the churches in the hosting countries of the Chinese students to join in the ministries for them.

114. Chul Soo Kim, email to the author, June 20, 2015.
115. Kim, email to the author.
116. Kim, email to the author.
117. Kim, email to the author.

## Ministry to Chinese Students in Seoul

There are forty-five universities in Seoul, most of which have Chinese students. In 2013, the total number of Chinese students in Seoul was 18,235, which represented 62 percent of the total number of international students (29,071).[118] According to Jun Min Zhang, a Chinese pastor serving Chinese students in S Church in Seoul, twenty churches hold services in Chinese.[119] Of these, only four are independent Chinese churches, and the others hold Chinese services in Korean churches. I conducted a survey in September 2015 and found that fifty-five churches in Seoul hold Chinese services.

Most of the Chinese churches in Seoul have been cooperating together to organize CHISTA and its programs, such as the retreat during the Full Moon Festival and the one-day retreat every year. Because many seminaries in Seoul have Chinese students (including Korean-Chinese), the churches have no difficulty in recruiting workers for the Chinese student ministry.

Some Protestant Christian universities have chapel services through which international students may have a chance to hear the gospel. Chapel is mandatory for some universities, including Yonsei University, Ewha Woman's University, Myongji University, and Soongsil University. The International Church of Seoul National University holds a Chinese Sunday service on campus. Yonsei University has 3,653 international students, of whom almost 40 percent are Chinese.[120] As a Christian university established by missionaries, the school's chaplains, Christian professors, the Christian Student Union, and the university's church all work together in organizing joint worship services, Bible study for professors and students, and various activities for evangelizing the students.[121]

Most of the pastors of the Chinese churches in Seoul are Korean-Chinese who graduated from seminaries in Korea. Only three pastors are Han Chinese. According to Zhang's study of the five Chinese services within five mega-churches in Seoul, although Korean-Chinese students comprise only 3 percent of the international students in Korea, they account for 21 percent of the attendants of those five churches.[122] This is because most of the pastors are Korean-Chinese, an ethnic group with a relatively high

118. Seoul Metropolitan Government, "Inconveniences."

119. Zhang, "Ministry for Chinese Students," 14.

120. Yim, "Yonsei University."

121. Kim, "Foreign Student Ministry," 23–24.

122. Zhang, "Ministry for Chinese Students," 31.

percentage of Christians compared to other ethnicities in China. They are more easily influenced by Korean Christianity because the language and culture are more familiar to them than for the Han Chinese who are now living in Korea. In Zhang's own Chinese church, only 8 percent of the members are Korean-Chinese students, while the rest are Han Chinese, as is their pastor. Zhang suggests that churches need to expand their ministry more towards the Han Chinese students since these students have more contacts in a wider range of the society than Korean-Chinese students and can more strongly affect their society when they return to China.[123]

Zhang's survey of the motives that led the Chinese students to come to church shows the importance of recommendations by Christians. In his study, 40 percent of the students came to church through the recommendation of Christians on campus: Chinese students (28 percent), Korean students (6 percent), and professors (6 percent). The survey also shows that many Chinese students (37 percent) are primarily motivated to go to church for religious reasons. Religious curiosity (8 percent) is also a significant factor in leading Chinese students to go to church, which is another reminder to Christians that some Chinese students are interested in religion. Some students (5 percent) go to church due to their loneliness of living in a foreign country. Christians can approach international students with their kindness and friendship. Table 1 summarizes the results of Zhang's survey on the motives of Chinese students for going to church in Korea.

Table 1. Motives for Going to Church

| Motive | Students (n=103) |
|---|---|
| Studying Korean | 3 |
| Recommendation of a professor | 6 |
| Recommendation of a Chinese friend | 28 |
| Recommendation of a Korean friend | 6 |
| Curiosity | 8 |
| Financial support | 1 |

123. Zhang, "Ministry for Chinese Students," 31.

| Motive | Students ($n=103$) |
|---|---|
| Loneliness | 5 |
| Religious motive | 37 |
| Other | 9 |

*Source:* Data adapted from Zhang, "A Study of the Ministry for Chinese Students in Korea," 34.

## Ministries in the Yeong-nam Area

There are about eighty churches that have services for approximately 10,000 Chinese students in the southeast part of Korea (called Yeong-nam), including the cities of Daegu, Busan, Ulsan, and the provinces of North and South Gyeongsang. Almost half of the churches have ministers who can conduct services in Chinese, whereas the other churches have services that are translated by Korean-Chinese, Korean-speaking Chinese students, and Chinese-speaking Koreans. The leaders serving each church are composed of people from diverse backgrounds: Korean missionaries who once served in China (ten churches), Chinese pastors who studied in Korean seminaries (twenty churches), Korean-Chinese pastors who studied in Korean seminaries (ten churches), Korean pastors (ten churches), and Korean professors (ten churches).[124] The number of Chinese students attending these churches varies from twenty to more than one hundred students.

The strength of the ministry for Chinese students in the Yeong-nam area lies in the strong cooperation among Christian professors, pastors of the churches, and mission organizations. The Christian professors and the Chinese University Mission play a leading role in arranging Easter service and a retreat during the Full Moon holidays. There are two fellowships of Christian professors for missions, targeting mainly international students: the Fellowship of Christian Professors in Daegu and Gyeong-buk for Missions and the Fellowship of Christian Professors in Busan, Ulsan, and Gyeong-nam for Missions. The Christian leaders serving the Chinese

124. Young Chu Lee, interview with author, July 7, 2015.

43

students in the area of Yeong-nam holds a monthly prayer meeting for ministry growth, information, and strategy sharing.

The Christian professors in Daegu and Gyeong-buk Province and mission organizations like the Christian University Mission have organized the CHISTA retreat for Chinese students in the Yeong-nam area since 2011. Professor Sang Shick Lee, vice president of the department of international students of the Fellowship of Christian Professors in Daegu and Gyeong-buk Province for Missions, recalls that "the retreat, in a word, was a grace-filled one, with the strong work of the Holy Spirit, and about 400 Chinese students attended, whom 100 Korean Christians served. About half of the students decided to live their lives for evangelizing the gospel."[125] Since 2013, the two Fellowships of Christian Professors for Missions and the Network of Christian Workers for Chinese Students have organized the annual retreat for Chinese students in the Yeong-nam area.

The retreat is composed of worships, lectures, and workshops. The speakers deal with the problems and difficult situations that the students may face when they return to China. On the usefulness of the workshop for Christian workers serving the Chinese students during the retreat, Professor Sang Shick Lee states that the great worry of the Christian workers serving Chinese students is how to help those returning students to pursue their careers and continue their faith once they return home. It is said that only 12.5 percent of returned Chinese students attend church.[126]

In 2015, the Chinese University Mission and Christian professors in the Yeong-nam area held a two-day retreat for the Chinese students at Sooyoungro Church in Busan. The purpose of the retreat was to mainly help converted students in the areas of vision finding, spiritual growth, and dedication for the kingdom of God. Five hundred Chinese students attended, along with one hundred Christian workers and retreat staff members. The program was composed of worship services, lectures on career development and spiritual growth after returning to China, counseling, and workshops for Christian workers serving Chinese students.

The role of Christian professors at Busan National University, an academically rigorous university in the Yeong-nam area with 1,300 Chinese students, was impressive. The Christian professors began their Chinese worship service in 2010, after the Night for the Chinese Students, an event

125. Lee, "Cooperating Mission," 156.
126. Lee, "Cooperating Mission."

which 150 Chinese students attended.[127] Since then, they have organized this event every year at the beginning of the academic year, with the cooperation of nearby Korean churches. Now, between three hundred and four hundred students attend. The event has been quite effective in establishing contact with new Chinese students and inviting them to church. Since this event first started, about three hundred Chinese students have registered with the Chinese church annually over the past three years.

The Christian professors leading the church call this group A Mission for the Chinese Students in Busan National University, which excludes the word *church* from the name. In Gee Choi, one of the leaders of the church, explained during an interview that the omission was intentional, as they wanted to serve by themselves rather than under the supervision of a pastor in the traditional form of church. The Christian professors alternate preaching with the help of a translator and also conduct a small group Bible study in Korean without a translator. The average number of attendants of the worship service is thirty students.[128] Recently, they have found the need to have a Chinese-speaking pastor due to the low ratio of consistent church attendants and the weakness of their follow-up programs. Therefore, they have decided to invite a Chinese seminary graduate and seven Korean students who belong to CCC to take care of the Chinese students. In an interview, In Gee Choi said, "Now, we should change the mindset and format of the ministry in order to break through the current stagnant situation; the professors need to be helpers rather than to hold the initiative in the ministry."[129]

## Chinese Student Ministries in Incheon and Gyeong-gi Province

As of 2015, there are about two thousand Chinese students attending three universities in Incheon: Inha University, the National University of Incheon, and the Songdo International Campus of Yonsei University. In Gyeong-gi Province, there are approximately six thousand Chinese students in sixty-five universities. About twenty-five churches are serving these Chinese students. Many diverse Christians, such as professors, missionaries, and Korean-Chinese pastors, also serve them.

---

127. Choi, "Chinese Students Ministry," 36–38.

128. In Gee Choi, interview with author, July 11, 2015.

129. In Gee Choi, interview with author, July 11, 2015.

In particular, the ministry for the Chinese students of Inha University is active compared to those at the other universities. Three independent Chinese churches and Korean churches served the 728 Chinese students of Inha University in 2015. A Chinese church for older-generation Chinese immigrants, which I am serving, is cooperating with a Chinese missionary who was converted while studying in Korea and who also graduated from seminary in Korea. Recently, we started a church near the university for Chinese students. Also, a Korean language professor has established another church for international students.

Though most of the Christian professors are humbly cooperating with missionaries and pastors of the church, some of the Christian professors prefer to take the initiative in ministry. They cannot speak Chinese, but this does not hinder them in their ministries. For instance, the professor directing the Korean language department of an urban university has been leading a church for international students. Nearly all of the thirty to forty students are Chinese students, most of whom are majoring in Korean. He and his wife lead the church in Korean, along with the worship services, Bible study, and fellowship. The director of a Chinese mission organization in Hong Kong and I visited this church with the purpose of helping them in their mission but found that the professor did not want to engage in cooperative efforts. Although Chinese students majoring in the Korean language can understand more than 70 percent of the communications in church, I have found that students want to sing hymns and listen to sermons in their native language, Chinese.[130]

## Chinese Student Ministries in Other Areas

In Jeonbuk Province, there are about 4,000 Chinese students, and several Korean missionaries, a Chinese pastor, and a number of Korean-Chinese pastors are serving these Chinese students in six churches. One Korean pastor's ministry is actively serving the three universities of Woosuk, Jeonju, and Jeonbuk. He is also a professor at one of these universities, cooperating with other dedicated Christian professors who serve three churches for these universities. According to this pastor, proper caring for the students requires the help of Chinese-speaking coworkers. One Chinese pastor is working for the Chinese students at a Korean church in this area, leading worship services and visiting universities. He says there is some conflict

130. In Gee Choi, interview with author, July 11, 2015.

regarding the ministry between the Korean leaders and himself due to cultural differences.[131] This is a common problem that Chinese and Korean-Chinese pastors face when working in Korean churches.

In the city of Daejeon and in Chung-nam Province, six churches serve about seven thousand Chinese students. A Chinese church at Mokwon University has about one hundred students, and a Chinese pastor studying the Old Testament in a doctoral program there is working for the church. This Chinese pastor has also studied in Korea for ten years, doing undergraduate, seminary, and doctoral studies.

In Chungbuk Province, there are about six churches serving about two thousand Chinese students. Three churches are actively involved in the ministry for these Chinese students: Jungbu Meongseong Church, Joeun Methodist Church, and Sachang Full Gospel Church.[132] As in other churches, deacons and deaconesses who cannot speak Chinese fervently work for these Chinese students to win them over to Christ. In Gangwon Province, there are about 1,200 Chinese students. In Jeju-do, there are about 1,000 Chinese students served by three churches.

## Summary

In summary, this section has treated the overviews of international students in Korea, the types of ministries to Chinese students, and the states of ministries to Chinese students in Korea. The leaders of Korean churches have been exerting their best to serve the Chinese students. As a result, there are about 150 to 200 Chinese churches serving Chinese students in Korea. Almost all of the university campuses have Chinese churches serving Chinese students in Korea. The next section will present overview of the Chinese church in Communist China since 1949.

# Overview of the Chinese Church in Communist China since 1949

It is generally thought that by 1949, there were an estimated 625,000 Chinese Protestants who were served by ten thousand pastors and evangelists in

---

131. Yong Suk Yang, interview with author, May 6, 2015.
132. In Su Kim, interview with author, May 10, 2015.

twenty thousand churches throughout China.[133] Since then, the Communist government has strictly controlled all churches and their members, with the restrictions peaking during the Cultural Revolution (1966–1977). A campaign was launched to attack traditional ideas, cultures, customs, and habits, including those related to Confucianism.[134] Although Chinese Christians underwent severe hardship under this ideological campaign, they did not give up their faith and witness. When Deng Xiaoping effectively initiated a reformation policy in 1978, Protestant Christianity markedly progressed, and churches were reopened. The reformation policy resulted in free-market economic activities and considerable political liberation for the Chinese, even for those in the countryside. Most people started to enjoy the fruits of the free-market economy and greater freedom to participate in religious activities. By 1988, around 6,500 churches were reopened, and 15,000 meeting places were registered. At that time, Christians in China numbered approximately five million.[135] In this section, I discuss Chinese Christianity and the new China from 1949 to 1979, reformation after 1979, church growth since 1979, and the gospel and culture in Chinese history.

## Chinese Christianity and the New China: 1949–1979

After the Chinese Communist Party (CCP) took over the Kuomintang ("the National Party") in 1949, they launched a series of political movements aimed mainly at brainwashing, with an emphasis on the class struggle theory of Marxism and Leninism. The intellectuals were among those targeted to be attacked. The government tried to eliminate all religions, philosophies, and cultures, both Chinese and foreign, except for their Communist ideologies. Based on Marx's materialism, the Communists regarded the reality of the universe as changing matter, including the spiritual realm. They insisted that the spiritual realm is an advanced state of matter. Within this atheistic materialism, religion had no place at all and was targeted to be eliminated. Christianity was attacked as the opium of the people and as a tool of imperialism and cultural infiltration.[136] Regarding this kind of propaganda, Kun Shi, former researcher at the National Science Academy in Beijing, remarks, "In this way the Communists are in reality worshipping Marxism, Leninism

133. Hunter and Chan, *Protestantism in China*, 118.
134. Hunter and Chan, *Protestantism in China*, 2.
135. Hunter and Chan, *Protestantism in China*, 72.
136. Chuang, *Ripening Harvest*, 83.

and Maoism as religion."[137] The Cultural Revolution instigated by Mao in 1966 tried to destroy all remnants of the old society. In particular, intellectuals were targeted and severely persecuted; as a result, outside observers thought that Chinese Christianity was completely extinguished during the Cultural Revolution.[138] Until 1979, Chinese churches experienced severe trauma under the new Chinese Communist Party.

The CCP believed that religion was a product of feudalism and would die out in the new social order, but believers had to be controlled in the meantime.[139] In addition, the CCP related Christianity to U.S. imperialism and bureaucratic capitalism, thus producing the *Christian Manifesto* with the purpose of purging such influences from churches. In 1950, the CCP forced Christians to sign the manifesto approved by Premier Zhou Enlai, and around 400,000, half of the Protestants in China, signed it. The manifesto required that Christians recognize the damage that imperialism had caused China and pledge to eliminate its influence.[140] This signature campaign was combined with the creation of the Three-Self Reform Movement, which promoted the CCP's control over the churches. The CCP successfully campaigned with denunciation meetings, political study, and thought reform. Significant content of the manifesto is as follows:

> Recognize clearly the evils that have been wrought in China by imperialism; recognize the fact that in the past imperialism has made use of Christianity; purge imperialistic influences from within Christianity itself; and be vigilant against imperialism, especially American imperialism, in its plot to use religion in fostering the growth of reactionary forces.[141]

The movement to urge Christians to sign the manifesto proceeded together with a campaign against counter-revolutionaries and leaders of the churches. Both missionaries and Chinese Christians were subjected to denunciation meetings.

As a result of these movements, a new organization designed to control religion in China, the Three-Self Patriotic Movement, was launched in May of 1954. Under this new organization, Chinese churches nationwide were forced to support the ideological concerns of the government and the

137. Shi, "Knowing Chinese Students," 83.

138. Lambert, *Resurrection of Chinese Church*, 9.

139. Hunter and Chan, *Protestantism in China*, 23.

140. Bays, *Christianity in China*, 162.

141. Bays, *Christianity in China*, 158.

building of socialist China. Alan Hunter and Kim Kwong Chan describe the situation as follows: "There was a strong insistence on this-worldly rather than other-worldly concerns, and a tendency to proclaim a justification by works rather than by faith alone."[142] The pulpit became a forum for political propaganda throughout the 1950s and 1960s. All churches were closed from 1966, the year the Cultural Revolution began, until 1979, and during this period pastors were unable to function at all. When the churches were under the strict control of the government, the Christian movement went underground, and this lasted for about twenty years in China.[143] In those years, the Christian faith did not diminish. Instead, it gradually spread through personal evangelism. Hunter and Chan point out that "Protestantism in Contemporary China with the Party and widespread insecurity made people receptive to the Christian message."[144] When Deng started the reform policy in 1979, former Three-Self Patriotic Movement officials were recalled to manage the reopening of churches—this was the start of a remarkable Christian revival.[145]

## Reform in China after 1979

After the Cultural Revolution ended in failure in 1976, the newly emerged leaders encouraged intellectuals to freely express their criticism of Mao's methods of mass mobilization and ideological movements that had ruined the country's economy. The intellectuals' criticism of the leaders and the system of the Communist government led the government to recognize the "crisis of three faiths" (sanxin weiji, a term created by the government); this referred to the loss of faith in Marxism, Maoism, and Communism. In addition, the "crisis of trust" (xinren weiji) referred to the loss of trust in party-state officialdom and in the future of the socialist system and the official modernization program. Intellectuals in open forums confessed their disillusionment, "saying that all their cherished ideals and values were smashed and that they simply did not know what they could rely on and where they should head."[146] The intellectuals stressed technological-economical change rather than class struggle as the motivating force of

142. Hunter and Chan, *Protestantism in China*, 24.
143. Hunter and Chan, *Protestantism in China*, 26.
144. Hunter and Chan, *Protestantism in China*, 28.
145. Hunter and Chan, *Protestantism in China*, 27.
146. Chuang, *Ripening Harvest*, 45.

history, which is also the government's present emphasis. Chinese traditional Confucianism, which had previously been attacked by the government, was revived again in the post-Mao era.

Chinese scholar Cai Xuanging, who left for America in 1986 to pursue a PhD degree, said the following on what he learned in China, "The whole philosophical system in Mainland China is built solely on Marxist materialism; that is, material comes first, spirit second, metaphysics, idealism, and religions are taught as premature epistemology, and only Marxist dialectical materialism is the perfect one."[147] Chinese students were taught in this type of educational system, one that denies religious beliefs, especially Christianity. Once the Chinese government started its Open Door Policy in relation to the economy, people were allowed to join religious activities under the principles of the Three-Self Patriotic Movement. Chinese students who grew up in the 1990s have not been taught as much Marxism, Leninism, and Maoism as earlier students but are still influenced by the ideological Communist educational system, which is atheistic and materialistic.

By the late 1980s, there were hot debates known as *culture fever* about the nature of Chinese and Western culture. There were two extremes. Some radical reformers desired to completely replace Chinese culture, which they thought hindered progress, with Western ideas. Extreme conservatives, on the other hand, feared Western influence and wanted Chinese people to preserve their own *spiritual civilization*. There were also some moderates who wanted to retain what was worthwhile in their own culture while accepting useful aspects of Western culture.

*River Elegy (he shang)*, a mini-series televised by Peking Central Television in the spring of 1988, ignited much debate among Chinese people. The program raised a historical rationale for the Open Door Policy and condemned the feudalistic culture of Chinese agriculture. The episodes were initially highly favored by Chinese leaders for their pro-reform stance. Later on, the government put restrictions on the earlier ideological challenges raised by intellectuals and restricted democratic movements such as Tiananmen Square. Though the student movement was not successful, some Chinese came to understand how the basic tenets of Christianity are different from those of Confucius, who held that men are born good and become even better through education. Contrary to Confucius' teaching, Christians believe in the fallen nature of human

---

147. Ging, "Unexpected Harvest," 31.

beings, although humans were originally created good. Only through faith in Jesus Christ can people become unselfish.

As Chinese students, especially those who are studying abroad, have ever-increasing opportunities to access foreign religions and various perspectives due to the development of information technologies, they have more options for dealing with their problems or pursuing their intellectual or spiritual quests. Until recently, some Chinese people have regarded religion as a *spiritual shelter*, especially for those who are vulnerable, and also as a superstitious belief system.[148] However, some negative views of religion have significantly changed in the past decade. Chinese students are now more open than the older generations were towards religion and religious practices. In a study published in 2010, Y. Hua shows that 58.5 percent of non-Christian university students see the nature of Christianity as *spiritual belonging*, whereas only 12.2 percent see it as superstition or the *opium of the people*.[149]

According to Hua, more than half of Chinese Christian students converted to Christianity during their school years in university.[150] Protestant Christianity is not only the fastest growing, but also the largest religion among university students. As Fengjiang recognizes in her discussion of the importance of Chinese university students, these students may have a strong influence on the religious landscape of China.[151]

The overall reform program under Deng's leadership significantly affected religious life in China, especially for Christians. The free-market economic system was evaluated as successful in raising living standards and stimulating production, although it caused some environmental problems and social polarization. The new open-market system created new social forces, a spirit of competition, mobility, diversification, and independence among people in rural areas. At the same time, the re-emergence of materialism and commercialism led to new and unwelcome results, such as drugs, prostitution, crime, and corruption.[152] The Communist Party tried to strike a balance between the market economy system and Marxist-Leninist ideologies, eventually deciding to maintain its ideology while implementing economic reformation in the 1980s. The whole process of "bringing order

---

148. Rambo et al., "Psychology of Converting," 901.

149. Hua, "Chinese Student Conversion," 75–80.

150. Hua, "Chinese Student Conversion," 75–80.

151. Hua, "Christian Beliefs," 27–34.

152. Hunter and Chan, *Protestantism in China*, 47.

out of the chaos" (*ba luan fang zheng*) focused on social and economic development, with the well-known catch phrase of "seeking truth from facts" (*shi shi qiu shi*), rather than ideological propaganda.[153] The strategic objectives were those of the Four Modernizations regarding agriculture, industry, science, and technology. The Chinese government did not want friction or factionalism or the sudden influx of Western ideology and sought to maintain a coherent national state under one dominant ideology.[154]

## Church Growth Since 1979

The three decades since the early 1950s proved to be the darkest time for all Christians in China. Churches went through a seemingly endless valley of shadows. Christian faith was suppressed, and Christians were denounced and persecuted until the reformer Deng Xiaoping initiated his reformation policy in 1978. The government made the restoration of a judicial process. In November 1978, the government announced rehabilitation for those who had been wrongly labeled and denounced over the past twenty years. Churches reopened during the Christmas season in 1978, but the return of church property often took a considerable time, even into the 1990s. As Philip L. Wickeri states, "the restoration of religious policy after 1978 created the conditions for an unprecedented revival of religious life all over China."[155]

In March 1982, the government issued a significant directive on the restoration of religious freedom, entitled "The Basic Viewpoint and Policy on the Religious Question during Our Country's Socialist Period." This directive, which is also known as Document 19, explained the details of the government's religious policy and gave guidelines for policymakers appropriate for China during the reform period.[156] Though it maintained the Marxist-Leninist interpretation of religion, it did not describe religion adversely, as had the previous label *opium of the people.* The directive rejected the coercive oppression of religion and positively stated that religion would continue to exist under socialism for a long time. Document 19 supported the security of Christians in China more than any other government policy,

153. Wickeri, *Christianity in China*, 202.
154. Hunter and Chan, *Protestantism in China*, 47.
155. Wickeri, *Christianity in China*, 206.
156. Bays, *Christianity in China*, 190.

so long as they were engaging in normal religious activities.[157] The artificial distinction between normal and abnormal religious activities has always caused tension between the Party's policy and house churches that did not want to register. If the officers of the Party regarded the activities of those attending a house church as abnormal, the house church leaders might be sanctioned. In line with the government's concerns for maintaining social order, house churches were profiled as potential adversaries to the Party.[158] In the 1980s, Protestant churches gained stability through the framework of Document 19 and the revised state constitution. According to Wickeri, religious life was revived in many major cities, especially along the east coast, while in rural areas, house churches that had disappeared entirely became more public.[159] Church buildings were restored, pastors were rehabilitated, and seminaries were reopened.

Though Bible schools and seminaries were allowed to open, and several new ones were created, but they did not meet the need of the explosively growing churches. Due to the considerable shortage of well-trained pastors and leaders, churches faced problems of syncretic sectarianism and heterodox ideas and rituals, especially in rural areas lacking educated leaders and afflicted with a high illiteracy rate.[160] The five major cults are as follows: the Established King (*beili wang*), the Lord God (*zhu shen jiao*), the Narrow Gate in the Wilderness (*kuang ye zhai men*), the Three Grades of Servants (*san ban pu ren*), and the Lightening out of the East (*dong fang shan dian*). The churches were not prepared to face challenges such as rapidly growing numbers of converts and ever-powerful heresies, because few pastors or Bible teachers had been trained during the past three decades—no official services had been allowed and all of the seminaries had closed during the dark era of the Cultural Revolution.

In 1984, Bishop Ting K. H., then head of the Three-Self Patriotic Movement, stated that Protestant Christians had multiplied more than fourfold since 1949, from 700,000 to three million.[161] The number of Chinese Christians had mysteriously grown faster than it had during any other era in Chinese history. Tony Lambert, in his book *The Resurrection of the Chinese Church*, explained this phenomenon as follows:

157. Wickeri, *Christianity in China*, 211–12.
158. Wickeri, *Christianity in China*, 210.
159. Wickeri, *Christianity in China*, 208.
160. Bays, *Christianity in China*, 191.
161. Lambert, *Resurrection of Chinese Church*, 10.

The Cultural Revolution was a severe trial to the Chinese Christians, but also, as they often themselves relate, used by God to create a church refined by fire and uniquely adapted to reach out to millions disillusioned with Maoism. It destroyed the last vestiges of the institutional churches in China but, paradoxically, created conditions in Chinese society from which the church was to re-emerge invigorated in new, largely de-institutionalized forms when the fury of the storm had passed.[162]

During the two decades since the reopening policy, many churches recovered, and others were newly founded; more than 20,000 churches registered with the Three-Self Patriotic Movement.[163] Many scholars tried to understand the factors affecting the growth of the Chinese church under the control of the atheistic Communist Party. Hunter and Chan analyze the growth of Chinese churches from 1979 to the early 1990s and find three significant factors that affected conversion: social and political factors, the continuing influence of religious traditions, and the perceived advantages of conversion. Their analysis presents a comprehensive understanding of contemporary history and culture in China.[164]

According to Hunter and Chan, social and political unrest caused by imperialistic Western powers and the Japanese invasion (1937–1944) contributed to the process of unlocking the Chinese people from their traditional beliefs. The living conditions of the ordinary people were desperate due to China's semi-colonial status before 1949. In addition, the ideological campaign of the new Communist government, with its many coercive reforms, caused a spiritual crisis for many people, especially those who valued traditional thinking or philosophy and religion. Also, the failure of the Cultural Revolution created a spiritual and ideological vacuum for former zealots of Maoism, such as intellectuals and students. Hunter and Chan state, "After the Cultural Revolution, observers recognized a kind of spiritual vacuum in China. Traditional values had long been in crisis, and most people were deeply disillusioned with Marxism."[165] In the same vein, Lambert, in his book *The Resurrection of the Chinese Church*, states that "the traumatic event of the Cultural Revolution, and subsequent

162. Lambert, *Resurrection of Chinese Church*, 10.
163. Bays, *Christianity in China*, 190.
164. Hunter and Chan, *Protestantism in China*, 168–71.
165. Hunter and Chan, *Protestantism in China*, 168.

disillusionment, have created a climate conducive to the revival of religion, and of Christianity in particular."[166]

As the entire social atmosphere changed, religion became a serious option for many people. The deeply ingrained humanism of the Chinese people had been totally shaken by the events of the last four decades, and in particular, the Confucian teachings of the basic goodness of human nature, self-control, and moderation were severely undermined.[167] The Christian teaching of original sin was more easily understood than ever before by those who had lost faith in the essential goodness of human nature. Accordingly, the message of salvation from sin became attractive to many people.[168]

Hunter and Chan study the growth of the churches in the twentieth century in China from a sociological perspective. To analyze the phenomena of the growth, they divide the social and political factors of conversion and ongoing adherence to religion into four items with specific examples. Under social conditions, they examine factors such as rural isolation, poverty, boredom, the breakdown of kinship networks, greater social mobility, and low levels of education. Political factors include China's semi-colonial status pre-1949, disillusionment with the Kuomintang and the CCP, people's low opinions of government officials, and the dangers of political activism. Psychological stress was caused by the devaluation of traditional culture and a personal search for meaning, as well as the need for comfort during wars and other disasters. The underprivileged status applied to women, minority groups, and retired workers.

The second group of factors is the continuing influence of religious traditions such as traditional religions and Buddhism and also Christians. Traditional religions influenced the local culture, especially in the form of gods and ghosts. Hunter and Chan argue that Christianity can be easily accepted because it has some congruencies and commonalities with traditional religions in China, such as prayer, healings, fellowship, a powerful system of morality and a philosophical message, a rationale for suffering, and the promise of salvation. Regarding this argument, Lambert raises a critical question: "If Christianity is only a variant form of syncretistic folk religion, as the argument seems to imply, why do so many rural people not stick with the various Buddhist and Daoist sects they are familiar

---

166. Lambert, *Resurrection of Chinese Church*, 103.

167. Lambert, *China's Christian Millions*, 202.

168. Lambert, *China's Christian Millions*, 202.

with?"[169] Though syncretism exists on the fringes of Christianity, Christians have made a radical break from idolatry and their former religious practices. Therefore, Hunter and Chan's argument on this seems to be incomplete. It is necessary to consider the uniqueness of the Christian faith, the providential works of God in saving people, and also the fact that unlike other religions in China, Chinese Christians have had both fervor and skill when it comes to evangelism.

Hunter and Chan point out the perceived advantages of conversion. In the twentieth century, there were no external inducements or significant material advantages that could be derived from converting to Christianity, except during the republican era (1911–1949). Regarding spiritual benefits, the following factors were significant: magical powers, an all-powerful God, healing and exorcism, the actualization of personal potential, and fellowship/love/support. The social benefits included an ecclesiastical community as surrogate family/pseudo-kinship network and a channel to Westernization or modernization. Christianity can provide self-respect and an enhanced personal identity to those who feel weak in the world, whereas Buddhism emphasizes the doctrine of non-self. Christianity was able to grow because it had the ability to meet the needs of different kinds of people, including different social classes or personalities, and the many varieties of subcultures in a huge continent.[170]

Hunter and Chan stress that flexible and successful organizational form is helpful in maintaining worship in a religiously sanctioned society. In relation to this idea, Lambert stresses the flexible structure of religions such as Buddhism and Daoism. However, it seems that Hunter and Chan are referring to the simple characteristics of house churches, which allows people to easily access nearby homes used for religious activities. A small number of believers were able to hold religious meetings secretly in house churches, even during the strongly repressive period of the Cultural Revolution.

A study on modern religion in China conducted by the Shanghai Academy of Social Sciences in 1987 pointed out the reasons for the growth of Christianity in China as follows: (1) The attraction of novelty, (2) the decline in prestige of the Party and of Socialism because of the Cultural Revolution, (3) the creation of an ideological vacuum, which allowed for the revival of religion, (4) the role of healing in attracting new converts, (5) the lack of education and of scientific knowledge, and (6) the provision

169. Lambert, *China's Christian Millions*, 206.
170. Hunter and Chan, *Protestantism in China*, 173.

of strong bonds, comfort, encouragement in this life and hope of happiness in the next.[171] Only one item, number five, is different from the factors discussed by Hunter and Chan. This is because the Chinese sociologists perceived religion as superstition.

It is difficult to identify the overall pattern of church growth in China. The fastest growing churches are in coastal areas, such as Fujian, Zhejiang, and Jiangsu, and northern Anhui in the Central Plain, and among certain minorities in Yunnan and Guizhou, as well as elsewhere.[172] The evangelistic endeavors of independent, indigenous churches, such as the Little Flock founded by Watchman Nee and the Jesus Family, are also significant factors in church growth.[173] The Little Flock strongly believes the direct headship of Christ over each local assembly, and they survived the persecutions of the 1950s and the Cultural Revolution. They focus on Scripture and close fellowship in small group meetings. Jesus Family was founded by Jing Dianying in the 1920s in Shandong, and its distinctive characteristics are Christian Communism, Pentecostalism, and the ascetic pursuit of end-time salvation.[174]

The church in China has multiplied over the past thirty years due to the spontaneous evangelism of humble Christians. Itinerant evangelists have travelled from village to village with the spirit of *faith mission*, relying only upon God for supplies. Lambert also points to the initiative role of God in the growth of the church in China, claiming that "it is my conviction after over 20 years firsthand contact with the house churches that the heart of the movement is thoroughly biblical, evangelical and led by the Spirit of God."[175]

Lambert identifies the role of suffering as the most important reason for the growth of the church in China. Suffering has purified and strengthened the faith of the people. Those who suffered have witnessed the gospel for the people and also have proved the power of the gospel and its supernatural origin. The spirit of suffering for the cause of the gospel seems to have gradually become lost in places where Christianity is well established. Many churches have been closed, not because of persecution but because of abuse of the freedom.

171. Lambert, *Resurrection of Chinese Church*, 114.

172. Lambert, *Resurrection of Chinese Church*, 114.

173. Lambert, *China's Christian Millions*, 64–65.

174. Xi, *Conversion Missionaries*, 863.

175. Lambert, *China's Christian Millions*, 180.

The Christians in China have proved their genuine faith throughout the three decades of hardships they had to endure and also through their extraordinary zeal and sacrifices for evangelism that resulted in the phenomenal growth of the church in China. Lambert points out some of the strengths of the church in China, one of which is that the church has become indigenous.[176] Without foreign aid for almost three decades and suffering many hardships, Chinese churches have not only survived but have also grown extraordinarily. The church in China has proven the ability to develop Christianity distinctively to fit the Chinese situation. It also has developed its own theology, spirituality, and practices under the control of an atheistic government. Lambert argues that the house churches throughout China have developed as "an indigenous movement which has shown a remarkable gift for acculturation."[177] Chinese Christians have lived up to the teachings of the Bible under harsh conditions with unyielding faith, fervent prayer, and sacrificial evangelism. We can learn from the Chinese churches, especially their emphasis on the authority of Scripture, prayer, repentance, and the endurance of hardship.

The Chinese church has also walked the way of the cross, not fearing the fiery trial that lasted for almost three decades since 1949. This spirit is the crucial factor in the growth of the Chinese church. Another important factor affecting the growth of house churches in China has been the strong eschatological obligation of evangelism. Under severe hardship and persecution, they sensed that they were in the last days and subsequently felt pressed to spread the gospel to save the lost before Jesus' second coming.[178] The seeds of the gospel sown in China have never been withered by the harsh winds of persecution. As a small mustard seed grows into a large tree so that many birds can make their nests, so too has the Chinese church, with its members' love of Jesus, become a resting place for those who seek comfort for the soul from God.

Chinese church history reveals that socio-political factors have affected the churches in China, where Christianity has become one of the five major religions. It has been growing steadily. Nevertheless, it is now facing challenges from non-governmental societal factors, specifically the unprecedented social changes brought about by economic development. Ying Fuk-tsang, a Hong Kong scholar, states that the prospects for

176. Lambert, *Resurrection of Chinese Church*, 282–83.

177. Lambert, *China's Christian Millions*, 196.

178. Lambert, *China's Christian Millions*, 200.

Christianity in China depend on such factors as political constraints, the socio-economic development of China, and the internal conditions of the Chinese church.[179] One of the significant contingent factors is government policy. Currently, the Chinese government is concentrating more on the stability of the society through economic development rather than through political struggle. This trend gives more freedom to religions, unlike during the last three decades. It seems that the Chinese government is not restricting religious activities if people abide by the law. If the CCP maintains the present religious policy, churches in China will keep growing in number and quality. The church in China needs to provide theological education to those dedicated to evangelism.

The economic reforms have resulted in industrialization, urbanization, and structural changes in Chinese society, just as in other countries. The swift, social changes have caused disparities in economic conditions among the people, especially between urban residents and the rural poor. The churches in China have more opportunities to serve the poor and alienated with the sacrificial love of Christ. In so doing, the Chinese church will be accepted by the people and become deeply rooted in the society. A great influx of people from the rural areas to the cities has resulted not only in social problems, but also in a vacuum of young people in the rural churches. The churches in China should address these issues in order to have an enduring and nationwide influence.

The churches in China also face the challenge of meeting the current needs caused by rapid socio-economic development. Before the society was economically developed, the church focused its ministries on simpler areas, such as worship and evangelism. Now, however, the churches need to meet the diverse needs of the people, which are mostly new needs arising from a complex society. Therefore, the churches in China need to invest their resources to train qualified seminary teachers and pastoral workers. Chinese church leaders may learn lessons from other churches in developed countries, especially that church buildings become empty when the people and churches are secularized.

In 2005, although Lambert shared his worry that materialism might be a strong obstacle that would prevent intellectuals from meeting Christ, to his surprise, a full-time campus worker among university graduates said that:

179. Ying, "Mainland China," 167.

Many intellectuals have a profoundly pessimistic outlook on life. They are under no illusions about the negative trends in society and the pressures they are under to get good jobs after graduation. As a result, many are still extremely open to the gospel message. In the east China region centered on Shanghai, there are some 60 universities—I reckon about two-thirds now have student Christian fellowships.[180]

Many Chinese students studying in the freer atmosphere overseas attend church out of curiosity and become Christian by meeting local Christians who befriend them, invite them home, and share the gospel. Many Chinese churches in the United States, for example, systematically organize activities for students and intellectuals from China, inviting them to people's homes and presenting the gospel. I myself have been invited to share the gospel to the Chinese students and intellectuals in the United States, Singapore, and now, Korea.

## Summary

Chinese people have experienced the rise and fall of ideologies throughout the latter half of the twentieth century. The Christian faith has now become a faith that is present in almost all levels of Chinese society and is one of the major bases of moral order. Along with Lambert, we might say that "there are reasons for hope of a continuing spiritual and social transformation."[181] Daniel H. Bays has evaluated Chinese Christianity appropriately, as follows:

> China has been part of this phenomenon, which has transformed the face and identity of Christianity globally. From being Christendom, the religion mainly of the North and West, Christianity has become a religion of the East and South—Chinese Christianity is already one of the most interesting and important examples of enculturation of the essential doctrines and ritual of world Christianity into an originally non-Christian West.[182]

The next section will present analysis of major Chinese traditional religions and culture from the perspective of Christianity.

180. Lambert, *China's Christian Millions*, 173.
181. Lambert, *China's Christian Millions*, 178.
182. Bays, *Christianity in China*, 206.

## Understanding Chinese Traditional Religions and Culture from the Perspective of Christianity

Judith A. Berling, in her book *A Pilgrim in Chinese Culture*, states that China, as with other countries, has generated a civilization rich in religious beliefs and practices—"mythological images, symbols, and stories; divination arts; elaborate burial and funerary practices; shamanistic and demon-exorcising rites; schema for understanding and ordering the cosmos."[183] These religious ideas and practices developed into multiple streams that later came to be labeled as Confucian, Taoist, or Buddhist.[184] Maurice Freedman argues that though there is order in Chinese religion "both at the level of ideas (beliefs, representations, classifying principles and so on) and at that of practice and organization (ritual, grouping, hierarchy, etc.)," there is no thoroughgoing unity and tightness in its religious system.[185] Chinese people have adjusted philosophies and religions to fit their worldly needs. According to Thomas A. Robinson and Hillary P. Rodrigues, "the religions of East Asia focus more on ethical behavior, social relationships, and individual self-realization than on such notions as god, sin, and salvation."[186]

This section treats the major traditional religions in China—Confucianism, Daoism (Taoism), and Buddhism—and Chinese culture in Chinese history from the perspective of Christianity. Lizhu Fan and Na Chen studied the recent situation of traditional religions related with conversion and the resurgence of indigenous religion in China. In the study, they found that the earlier religious and ritual practice are revitalized among the people in China.[187]

### Confucianism

Confucianism has had an immense influence on the lives of Chinese people in areas such as education, ethics, politics, philosophy, ritual, and daily life. In *Religion in Chinese Society*, C. K. Yang, in describing the significant influence of Confucianism, states that "Confucianism has been a determining fact in Chinese culture. It laid down the structural principles and supplied the

183. Berling, *Chinese Culture*, 43.
184. Berling, *Chinese Culture*, 43.
185. Freedman, "Chinese Religion," 20.
186. Robinson and Hillary, *World Religions*, 266.
187. Fan and Chen, "Religion in China," 556.

key operational values of the basic Chinese institutions from the family to the state."[188] Confucius (551–479 BCE) is the most influential philosopher in Chinese history. His teaching centers on the modification of appropriate human relationships in order to secure social harmony. Though his teachings did not have much influence on society and politics during his lifetime, they developed in the following centuries into religious rituals.

Confucius' most influential followers, Mengzi (also known as Mencius, 372–289 BCE) and Xunzi (312–238 BCE), articulated his teachings more directly and in a more organized manner than Confucius himself. Since the Han dynasty, bureaucrats and scholars mastered the Confucian classics, which raised the Confucian/literati tradition to a preeminent position in China.[189] Neo-Confucianism developed in response to Buddhism and Daoism in the eleventh century. Zhu Xi is the most prominent Neo-Confucian philosopher. He wrote commentaries on Confucian classics that became major textbooks for the national examinations for government officers for the next six hundred years. Neo-Confucians see the cosmos as the *taiji* ("supreme ultimate").

Confucius emphasized proper relationships among people—both respect and responsibility are of crucial importance in the constitution of society. He also established the ancient Eastern principle of filial piety. His teaching has hierarchical characteristics. That is, one must revere one's superiors, and superiors are obligated to care for their inferiors. Confucius also elaborated on propriety (*li*), righteousness (*yi*), and human-heartedness (*ren*). *Li* is the performance of ritual and ceremony, a complex of social behaviors (such as greetings) and ceremonial rites (such as ancestral veneration with sacrificial offerings).[190] *Yi* is the sense of righteousness that can be internalized through the practice of *li*. *Ren* is the highest Confucian principle of deep empathy towards other people, which surpasses the external practice of *li* and *yi* and resides intrinsically in people's hearts. Therefore, Confucius argued that human beings are born to be good and empathetic to others. The golden rule of Confucius is from *ren*: "Do not do to others what you do not want done to yourself."[191] A *junzi* is a man who has fully cultivated and developed these principles. Though Confucius was critical of

188. Yang, *Religion in Chinese Society*, 244.

189. Robinson and Rodrigues, *World Religions*, 252.

190. Robinson and Rodrigues, *World Religions*, 255.

191. Robinson and Rodrigues, *World Religions*, 255.

rituals without the faculty of *ren*, he emphasized that propriety (*li*) is associated with the promotion of ceremonies and rites.

Julia Ching regards Confucianism as religious humanism, describing Confucianism as a humanism that is open to religious values.[192] C. K. Yang recognizes Confucianism as a faith in the sense that "through centuries of enforcement and practice as a social doctrine, it won uncritical acceptance by the people and became an emotional attitude as well as a body of rational teaching."[193] Regarding the process of Confucianism becoming a religion, Yang explains that in a superstitious society, Confucianism "adopted many religious elements that helped it to function effectively in the traditional social milieu."[194] Although Confucianism has a religious form, it does not have a theistic doctrine that teaches of a transcendent god and explains the relationship between human beings and god. Confucianism is in its essence this-worldly and rationalistic. Many Confucian scholars in the Ming and Ching dynasties believed that Confucian teachings did not involve spirits and miracles.

The eventual aim of Confucian morality is to cultivate the self and to develop every potentiality of human nature (*jin xing*) from the seeds of goodness inherent in the person.[195] Buddhism teaches that every person inherently has part of Buddha's nature. This teaching affected the Neo-Confucians, who sought to rediscover the heavenly principle within oneself and develop it while overcoming desires that obstruct the five principal virtues of humanity, righteousness, propriety, wisdom, and sincerity.[196] As Jacques Gernet asserts, there is evidence that this parallels the moral attitude of the Christian world, though it stems from different concepts. Chinese intellectuals also emphasized the examination of conscience to take control of themselves according to "the principle of the heavenly order" (*tian li*), whereas Christians humble themselves before God for salvation. Christians believe that human nature is corrupt and needs to be healed by the salvific grace of God. The Confucian tradition perceived human beings as possessing naturally good dispositions. This perception completely contradicts the understanding of Christianity, which sees human beings as fully corrupt and having no goodness.

192. Ching, *Chinese Religions*, 51–52.
193. Yang, *Religion in Chinese Society*, 244.
194. Yang, *Religion in Chinese Society*, 245.
195. Gernet, *China and Christian Impact*, 157.
196. Gernet, *China and Christian Impact*, 143.

## Daoism (Taoism)

According to Ching, Daoism (Taoism) existed early on, from the time of oracle bones and divination.[197] Before it became an organized religion, Daoism in the early Han period was known as the cult of the Yellow Emperor and Lao Zi, or Huang-Lao. Later on, Daoism developed as a religion of salvation, healing the sick and guiding people to a happy eternity through their relying on supernatural powers for help and protection.[198] Daoism was developed by Chinese recluses who revered nature and is sometimes viewed as a form of natural mysticism. Daoism, as a trend of Chinese philosophy led by Laozi in the early sixth century and Zhuangzi, is known as *daojia*, and as a trend of religion, is known as *daojiao*. Laozi was greatly influenced by the book *Dao De Jing*, which has two parts: exploration of the *dao* ("way") and the concept of *de* ("virtues").[199] Although the former was a theoretical, metaphysical exploration of the *dao*, the latter treated the practical and political dimensions of philosophy. Zhuangzi was not keen on politics and bureaucratic use of his philosophy. He espoused union with the *dao*, the mysterious principle of nature. Subsequently, Neo-Daoism emerged in the social upheavals between the third and sixth centuries CE, particularly following the collapse of the Han dynasty. Various factions in the Neo-Daoist movement promoted a naturalistic lifestyle free from traditional constraints.

Daoist religion (*daojiao*) has practiced divination, older magical and ritual-based traditions, and the worship of nature spirits, all of which can be found in the ancient Chinese religions. Religious Daoism is characterized by "alchemy, a belief in a pantheon of immortal sages, and search for bodily immortality."[200] In Daoism, *dao* is understood as the mystery of mysteries, the mysterious way that cannot be easily explained. *Dao* is the source of creation, of heaven and earth. All things are created by *dao*. Thus, the way of expressing its philosophy is somewhat enigmatic. Unlike other Chinese philosophers, such as Mozi, Confucius, and the Legalists, who support civilization by maintaining society through orderly manners, Daoists seek freedom from human conventions and structures. When one

---

197. Ching, *Chinese Religions*, 102.
198. Ching, *Chinese Religions*, 103.
199. Robinson and Rodrigues, *World Religions*, 257.
200. Robinson and Rodrigues, *World Religions*, 258.

returns to one's original state and thus abides with or becomes one with the *dao*, then one becomes a sage (*sheng zhe* or *sheng ren*).

The simple lifestyle, meditation, and contemplation of the recluse are ways to become one with the *dao* and receive mysterious powers within nature. The sages seek to live harmonious lives according to the principles of *yin* and *yang*, which constitute the *dao*. The natural principle of *wuwei* of the sage and the Daoists means not acting in a contrived or planned manner. *Shunqi ziran* is an expression that Chinese people frequently use, which means "to follow nature" or to avoid reversing the natural way or natural flow of situations or works. This is one of the examples of the deep impact of Daoism among the Chinese people.

Laozi comprehends heaven as "an unfathomable mechanism devoid of any personality or moral meaning."[201] The belief associated with the supernatural concept of heaven is the belief in predetermination or fate (*ming*, meaning "determined appointment" or "so ordered") that is deeply embedded in Confucianism. Although Confucius and Mencius' thinking has a tendency towards a this-worldly and rationalistic orientation to the problems of life, they also hold the idea of the supernatural, anthropomorphic notion of heaven as the governor of man's fate.[202]

The Chinese, influenced by Daoism, had a tendency to consider the unity of substance and spirit and not to separate the creator spirit and his creation. For instance, Cheng Hao (1032–1085) states that heaven, earth and the Ten Thousand Beings are a single and unique substance (*tiandi wanwu yiti*). They also think the spirit of human beings is one with the universe. Therefore, the Chinese have an inclination "to deny any opposition between the self and the world, the mind and the body, the divine and the cosmic."[203] These Chinese ideas were fundamentally different from those of missionaries who were influenced by Greek dualism and medieval scholasticism.

Consequently, Matteo Ricci, a sixteenth-century missionary to the Chinese people, tried to demonstrate the existence of purely spiritual substances. In 1607, Father Sabatino de Ursis also pointed out the problem of the Chinese perception of the spiritual substance and material, saying that "the Chinese have never known any spiritual substance distinct from

---

201. Yang, *Religion in Chinese Society*, 248.

202. Yang, *Religion in Chinese Society*, 249.

203. Gernet, *China and Christian Impact*, 201.

matter."[204] Father Adam Schall von Bell, in *The Countless Proofs That the Master of Heaven Governs the World* (*zhu zhi quan zheng*, 1626), stressed the radical difference between the substance of God and the material world of heaven, earth, and the Ten Thousand Beings. He stated that "[God] does not proceed from the *Taiji* (the cosmic origin), nor *yin* and *yang*, too. God created everything including *taiji, yin* and *yang*."[205]

The Chinese thought that an omnipresent, uncreated primordial energy, or natural and spontaneous mechanism, was the origin of the universe and all the beings in the world. Father Aleni, in *On the True Origin of the Ten Thousand Beings* (*wanwu zhenyuan*) disputes this Chinese perception, saying that "Heaven and Earth cannot create men and other beings on their own. The primordial energy cannot have separated Heaven and Earth on its own."[206] Ricci stressed the existence of a Creator God who created the universe in perfection and order, saying that "houses do not build themselves; they are not constructed by themselves."[207]

Unlike Christians, who see no hope for their salvation without the saving act of the transcendent God, Daoists do not think that they need to deny the self to get salvation from God. Daoists have no concept of a transcendent God except for the cosmic origin, which they try to be united to through their own efforts. As Ricci and his contemporary missionaries found, teaching them the existence of God and the limits of human beings in saving themselves is of utmost important to win them for Christ.

## Buddhism

Buddhism entered China around the first century CE through the Silk Road, becoming established after the collapse of the Han dynasty and flourishing during the dynasties of Sui (581–618 CE) and Tang (618–907 CE). Later on, as Neo-Confucianism grew, Buddhists faced persecution. Though both the *Theravada* and *Mahayana* forms of Buddhism entered China, only the latter form survived. Buddhists tacitly accepted some of the dominant secular values that contradicted their creeds.

Berling argues that "the Buddhist accommodated most fully to the rule of the Chinese religious field, establishing a strong and lasting

204. Gernet, *China and Christian Impact*, 203.

205. Gernet, *China and Christian Impact*, 202.

206. Gernet, *China and Christian Impact*, 208.

207. Gernet, *China and Christian Impact*, 208.

position."[208] She further states that "[it] was they who borrowed most extensively from the common pool of deities and practices, who emulated native genres of writing, and who cast Buddhist teachings in the practical this-worldly vein so attractive to the Chinese."[209] Ching also analyses the encounter of Buddhism with Chinese culture as a process of adaptation to a new context, writing that "Buddhism adjusted itself to the Chinese environment, taking account of Confucian moral values, such as filial piety, while making use of Taoist ideas and terminology for its own survival and advancement."[210] Buddhism introduced new ideas such as rebirth, transmigration, and monastic life to the Chinese society in which descendants venerated their ancestors. Ching argues that "Chinese realism and pragmatism also influenced Buddhism, affirming this life and this world, including the values of family, longevity, and posterity."[211]

The *Chan* ("meditation") school stresses the attainment of experiences that the Buddha himself achieved. Other schools emphasize a devotional attitude to the salvific power of celestial *bodhisattvas*. *Jingtu* ("pure land") Buddhism prospered even after other schools of Buddhism declined. It attracted people who found self-reliant meditation too burdensome. *Jingtu* is one of the most popular forms of Buddhism in East Asia. A specific characteristic of Chinese Buddhism is that it transformed other-worldly characteristics of Indian Buddhism into this-worldly ones. In other words, it applied many figures of Indian Buddhism to this-worldly ends than to achieving *nirvana*. For example, *Avalokiteshvara* (the *bodhisattava* of compassion) became the goddess of *Guanyin*, while *Maitreya* (the Buddha-to-come) was associated with *Budai*, known as the Laughing Buddha, who is widely worshiped for secular prosperity in Japan and East Asia.

The remission of sins in Christianity has nothing in common with the "elimination of sins" (*chu zui*) in Chinese Buddhism. In Buddhism, reducing one's stock of bad *karma* is the way to eliminate sins, requiring pious actions. For Christians, good behavior can be a merit only if done by faith. Gernet clearly states that "whoever is unaware of God cannot act well whatever he does, for there is no good without him."[212]

---

208. Berling, *Chinese Culture*, 55.
209. Berling, *Chinese Culture*, 55.
210. Ching, *Chinese Religions*, 125.
211. Ching, *Chinese Religions*, 125.
212. Gernet, *China and Christian Impact*, 167.

Buddhists see the world as temporary aggregates. Ricci, in *The True Meaning of the Master of Heaven*, criticized the Buddhist idea that everything emerged from nothingness and is aimed for nothingness. He argued that nothing in the world can develop out of the void (*kong*), as the Buddhists had thought, or out of nothingness (*wu*), as the Taoists had believed.[213] The Buddhists perceived that there exists tension between the self and the world. That is, the self has the nature of Buddha, the awakened one, while "the world was the cause of the attachment which kept being in a state of illusion and confined them to the sufferings of their successive existences."[214] The Buddhist ideas that every human being is an unrecognized Buddha, and that the absolute constitutes one's fundamental nature was regarded as heresy by the missionaries.

## The Gospel and Culture in Chinese History

The historical interaction between the gospel and Chinese culture has been quite complicated and remains so. According to Jonathan Chao, there were four entries of Christianity into China: the entry of the Nestorians during the Tang Dynasty (618–907), the return of the Nestorians and the entry of Catholicism during the Yuan Dynasty (1279–1368), the entry of the Jesuits during the Ming Dynasty (1369–1644), and the entry of Protestant and Catholic missionaries following the Opium War (1839–1842).[215]

Chao points out seven key factors leading to the success or failure of the gospel to penetrate Chinese people's mind and society: the nature of the dominant Chinese culture, the political ideology of the governing authority, the kind of gospel messages presented, the missionary's view of Chinese culture, the receptivity of the Chinese people and the nature of resistance, the perception of the Chinese people of the gospel bearers and their message, and missionary efforts to overcome Chinese resistance to the gospel.[216] Chao's analysis from an emic perspective still sheds great light on developing appropriate and effective evangelistic approaches in this complex, changing world.

After analyzing the history of the encounter of Christianity with the Chinese people, Chao summarizes some of the culturally important

213. Gernet, *China and Christian Impact*, 214.

214. Gernet, *China and Christian Impact*, 215.

215. Chao, "Gospel and Culture," 10.

216. Chao, "Gospel and Culture," 9.

factors for mission. First, it is the political factors, rather than cultural ones, that govern the receptivity of the Chinese people toward the gospel. Second, Confucian literati used political power to promote Confucian state orthodoxy during the Tang, Ming, and Qing Dynasties. Marxist-Maoist orthodoxy similarly tries to control other ideologies and religions. Third, in order to be effective, the gospel bearer should respect rather than confront the dominant culture advocated by the state. Fourth, Christians tried four different approaches in the context of Chinese culture and political power prior to 1949: (1) the Nestorians and Catholics during the Yuan Dynasty and Protestant Christians during the early republican era after 1911 were able to *independently* proceed in evangelistic work without being forced to reckon with Chinese cultural factors; (2) *accommodation* was practiced by Jesuits in the Ming Dynasty and by some missionaries in the nineteenth century (they made concessions to Chinese cultural demands without committing doctrinal syncretism); (3) *adaptation* was practiced by the Nestorians, the liberal Protestants during the New Culture Movement (1919–1927), and the state church under the Three-Self Patriotic Movement (1949–present), but this involved critical changes in the doctrine of salvation in the first two instances and was ultimately ineffective; (4) *transformation* was practiced by Protestant missionaries in the late nineteenth century as well as during the republican era (1928–1949) and is the approach used in the house church movement today (by seeking to change Chinese culture to a form of Christian culture through evangelism, education, and social reconstruction).[217]

After 1949, the monolithic socialist culture of the Marxist-Leninist and Maoist model took over the pluralistic character of modern Chinese culture on the mainland. Marxism became the leading official orthodoxy. Christianity, along with other religions, was tolerated as long as it was under state control under the Three-Self Patriotic Movement, except for the duration of the Cultural Revolution (1966–1976).[218]

A group of Chinese Christian intellectuals tried to integrate Christianity with Chinese culture through academic work during the decade of reform leading up to spring 1989, under the open atmosphere of exploration under the tutelage of Zhao Ziyang and other leaders in the 1980s. Their group was called Research on Christianity (*ji du jiao yan jiu*) and was based in Chengdu, and its members firmly believed that Christianity was

217. Chao, "Gospel and Culture," 21.
218. Chao, "Gospel and Culture," 19.

benevolent for China. According to Liu Xiaofeng, "their concern is how Christianity can be a concrete social and cultural experience in China."[219] In order to do so, they attempted to firmly root Christianity in Chinese culture through literature, philosophy, and sociology by means of scholarly work and translations of certain Western books.[220] For the Christian faith to be a more influential and enduring religion in China, which has a rich cultural heritage, it is important for a ministry to evangelize and equip intellectuals to enhance the cultural receptivity to Christianity in China.[221]

Chao points out some of the more important components of modern Chinese culture, which include legacies from Confucianism, Buddhism, Daoism, rationalism, scientism, evolution, Marxism-Leninism and Mao Zedong thought, as well as contemporary capitalism, consumerism, and nihilism.[222] He recommends that "communicators of the gospel today must realize that the Chinese mind is complex, and that the Chinese people live in a complex cultural context in a process of rapid change."[223]

## Summary

In summary, the traditional Chinese religions, especially Confucianism, do not perceive human beings as totally corrupt and requiring salvation from an omnipotent God who does not belong to this world. The Daoists do not have a concept of a transcendent God and only emphasize the unification with the cosmic unison through their own efforts. The Buddhists see human beings as being able to awaken the nature of Buddha when they discard all their earthly desires, the cause of suffering. To effectively confer the gospel to those believing such traditional religions, the essence and the limitedness of human beings and the transcendent nature of God and his way of saving the people of the world should be presented with the understanding of the thoughts and culture of Chinese people. The next section presents literature on research methodology, covering the topics of qualitative research methodology, phenomenology and conversion study, and grounded theory.

219. Xiaofeng, "From Enlightenment to Exile," 61.
220. Xiaofeng, "From Enlightenment to Exile," 61.
221. Xiaofeng, "From Enlightenment to Exile," 57.
222. Chao, "Gospel and Culture," 19.
223. Chao, "Gospel and Culture," 20.

## Literature on Research Methodology

This section will present qualitative research methodology, phenomenology and conversion study, and grounded theory.

## Qualitative Research Methodology

John W. Creswell states that a researcher conducts qualitative research methodology when he or she needs to explore a problem or issue, in order to achieve a complex and detailed understanding of it or to test or develop a theory.[224] Since the goal of this study is to explore the lived experiences of the conversion of Chinese students in Korea within a cross-cultural context, a qualitative research paradigm will be used for this study. Within this paradigm, however, this research is based on an interpretive (versus positivistic or critical theory) research orientation, with the addition of a philosophical commitment to critical realism. This philosophical orientation acknowledges that there are multiple realities constructed by individuals but that underlying (or transcending) these diverse experiences of reality are core realities that are common to humankind and can be described in the construction of theories and laws.[225]

The main paradigm of qualitative research is the assumption that "reality is constructed by individuals interacting with their world."[226] Qualitative researchers explore the meanings people have constructed and bring to their experiences.[227] According to Creswell, the characteristics of qualitative study is as follows: natural settings, collecting data in the field, researcher as a key instrument, multiple sources of data, inductive data analysis, participants' meaning, interpretive inquiry, and holistic account.[228] He defines qualitative research as "a form of inquiry in which researchers make an interpretation of what they see, hear, and understand."[229] The emphasis in qualitative research is holistic, that is, "qualitative research identifies the complex interactions of factors in any

---

224. Creswell, *Research Design*, 39.

225. Hiebert, *Anthropological Insights*, 38–42.

226. Merriam, *Qualitative Research*, 6.

227. Merriam, *Qualitative Research*, 6.

228. Creswell, *Research Design*, 37–38.

229. Creswell, *Research Design*, 38.

situation."[230] The methodology of this study is not designed to take apart a phenomenon and look at its individual parts. Instead, its aim is to see how all the parts and factors of conversion work together as a whole in its cross-cultural contexts. The main characteristic of this kind of research is to obtain an *emic* or insider perspective and understanding, as opposed to the *etic* or outsider perspective belonging to the researcher.

It is important to consider the emic and etic perspectives on conversion. Rambo recommends that researchers need to consider and adopt an emic perspective, in which the experience of converts is appreciated phenomenologically.[231] In order to properly analyze the conversion experiences of foreigners who have a different socio-cultural background, language, and religious understanding, researchers should have the ability to comprehend the convert's worldview and should also have linguistic competence.

Researchers also need to consider the theological rationale used by converts to tell their experience, because theology is deeply embedded in "the structures that serve as the foundation, infrastructure, and motivation of the conversion experience."[232] Therefore, it is desirable, if possible, to consult with religious experts or leaders who have the emic perspective of a convert. For this reason, I consulted with Chinese pastors who serve Chinese students in Korea, even though I have served Chinese people as a missionary since 1991.

## Phenomenology and Conversion Study

I do not utilize phenomenology for this study, because it is not appropriate for the purpose of developing a theory. Nevertheless, it is worthwhile to review the possibilities of the phenomenological study of conversion. The phenomenological methodology can be an alternative way of doing conversion study for researchers who want to describe or interpret the meaning of the conversion experience rather than the factors, processes, and types—my main interest.

In his book, *The Phenomenology of Practice*, Max van Manen states, "Phenomenology aims at description and interpretation."[233] Phenomenology is oriented toward finding the meaning of the lived experience. Manen

230. Creswell, *Research Design*, 38.

231. Rambo, "Anthropology and Conversion," 214.

232. Rambo, "Anthropology and Conversion," 215.

233. Manen, *Phenomenology of Practice*, 43.

argues that "phenomenology is best suited to investigate the meaning aspects of terms that clearly correlate with lived experience."[234] Therefore, the conversion experience, which is highly meaningful for the converts who are transformed into such a new person that they are born again, is an appropriate subject for phenomenological study.

The conversion experience is always filled with a wondrous story that includes how one encounters God cognitively, affectively, and physically in a specific context. It is therefore significant to describe or interpret the wondrous experience of conversion that is distinctive to each convert. When Manen states that "phenomenology is about wonder, words, and world," he seems to be describing how the method of phenomenology explores the lived experience in a specific context, using the words of the both the researcher and the participants, which may be a wonderful experience for both the researcher and the reader.[235] Manen's statement is true in the case of conversion study using phenomenology. The act of sharing in the restatement of the conversion experience may reinforce the faith of the participants, who share conversion experience, and that of the readers.

The phenomenological study of conversion may give a new and fresh understanding of the work of God in saving people and of individuals' distinctive ways of turning to God, rather than a doctrinal understanding of conversion, because phenomenology fundamentally seeks to capture the "primal impression," to borrow Husserl's expression.[236] The phenomenologist also tries to find not a named concept but the existent, which is the raw moment or aspect of existence itself, that is, the raw dimension of prereflective experience.[237] Prereflective experience is the *ordinary experience* that we experience in our day-to-day existence.[238]

Husserl emphasizes description rather than interpretation, but Heidegger doubted the possibility of any knowledge without an interpretation of the lived world.[239] Max van Manen and Jonathan A. Smith prefer the interpretative aspect of phenomenological analysis. Smith developed interpretative phenomenological analysis, and Manen developed hermeneutic phenomenology. Manen states that "phenomenology is, in some sense,

234. Manen, *Phenomenology of Practice*, 44.

235. Manen, *Phenomenology of Practice*, 13.

236. Manen, *Phenomenology of Practice*, 52.

237. Manen, *Phenomenology of Practice*, 52.

238. Manen, *Phenomenology of Practice*, 28.

239. Smith et al., *Interpretative Phenomenological Analysis*, 16.

always descriptive and interpretive, linguistic and hermeneutic.[240] He defines hermeneutic phenomenology as "a method of abstemious reflection on the basic structures of the lived experience of human existence."[241] Manen explains this as follows:

> Abstemious means that reflecting on experience is to abstain from theoretical, polemical, suppositional, and emotional intoxications. Hermeneutic means that reflecting on experience must aim for discursive language and sensitive interpretive devices that make phenomenological analysis, explication, and description possible and intelligible. Lived experience means that phenomenology reflects on the prereflective or prepredicative life of human existence as living through it.[242]

Because of these factors, interpretive and hermeneutic phenomenology is appropriate for studying the conversion experience. The conversion experience needs to be interpretively described by a person who has an authentic understanding of the biblical teaching in order to make the conversion story more understandable through the commonalities in Christian conversion stories.

"The main task of phenomenological research," according to Manen, "is an interpretive description of the primordial meaning structures of lived experience—a graphic depiction of phenomena just as they give and show themselves in what appears or gives itself."[243] Examining *the lived experience* as expressed by Dilthey, Husserl, and Merleau-Ponty implies "the intent to explore directly the originary or prereflective dimensions of human existence: life as we live."[244] Phenomenologists like Hans-Georg Gadamer and Maurice Merleau-Ponty stress the importance of lived experience, which is regarded as the starting point of inquiry. Merleau-Ponty states, "The world is not what I think, but what I live through."[245] Regarding the characteristics of phenomenological writing, Manen, states that "writing a phenomenological text is a reflective process of attempting to recover and express the ways we experience our life as we live it."[246]

240. Manen, *Phenomenology of Practice*, 26.

241. Manen, *Phenomenology of Practice*, 26.

242. Manen, *Phenomenology of Practice*, 26.

243. Manen, *Phenomenology of Practice*, 61.

244. Manen, *Phenomenology of Practice*, 39.

245. Merleau-Ponty, *Phenomenology of Perception*, xvi–xvii.

246. Manen, *Phenomenology of Practice*, 20.

Smith et al. have recently developed interpretative phenomenological analysis, which is in alignment with Heidegger's stance that "phenomenological inquiry is from the outset an interpretative process."[247] In their book *Interpretative Phenomenological Analysis: Theory, Method and Research*, Smith and his colleagues state that "the IPA [Interpretative Phenomenological Analysis] researcher is engaged in a double hermeneutic because the researcher is trying to make sense of the participant trying to make sense of what is happening to them. . . . [T]he IPA researcher has only access to the participant's experience through the participant's own account of it."[248]

Phenomenologists fundamentally try to discover the meanings that arise in experiences. Manen states, "Wondering about the meaning of a certain moment of our lived life may turn into the phenomenological question: we may then wonder and ask, what is this experience like?"[249] Then, he asks the following questions: What is the nature, meaning, significance, uniqueness, or singularity of this or that experience as we live through it or as it is given in our experience or consciousness? How does this experience present itself as a distinguishable phenomenon or event? The phenomenological interest is focused on the phenomenon as an aspect of our prereflective existence. It tries to grasp attentively the living sense of the experience before we have lifted it up into cognitive, conceptual, or theoretical determination or clarity.[250]

Manen understands phenomenology basically as a method for questioning, not a method of answering or discovering or drawing determinate conclusions. He holds that there are possibilities in the questioning for experiencing openings, understandings, insights—producing cognitive and non-cognitive or pathic perceptions of existentialities.[251] He explains how a phenomenological question arises with a question as follows: What is the experience like? How does the meaning of this experience arise? How do we live through an experience like this? What is that experience like? What makes the experience so meaningful and unique? How does the phenomenon originate? How can we grasp the phenomenon in its inception and existence?[252] Considering these issues and questions, we may ask the following questions

247. Smith et al., *Interpretative Phenomenological Analysis*, 3.
248. Smith et al., *Interpretative Phenomenological Analysis*, 3.
249. Manen, *Phenomenology of Practice*, 38.
250. Manen, *Phenomenology of Practice*, 39.
251. Manen, *Phenomenology of Practice*, 29.
252. Manen, *Phenomenology of Practice*, 32–36.

related to the study of conversion with the phenomenological methodology. The main question could be something like this: What meaning do the converts confer to their conversion experience?

Manen argues that there is no common methodology of phenomenology that can be applied as a model for doing phenomenological research, and phenomenological inquiry cannot be reduced to procedural schemes or a series of steps. He accepts Gadamer's stand that "any method, in a procedural sense, inevitably technologizes and objectifies what it studies and thus fails to grasp what is singular, subtle, or what can only be grasped with inventive and vocative means of reflective writing."[253] The phenomenological method of inquiry does not have a general set of strategies or research techniques. Heidegger and Merleau-Ponty warn against any notion of a unified set of standards or sets of methodology for doing phenomenology that might block the researcher from capturing the meaning of the prereflective experience.[254] Nevertheless, Smith et al. present the process of conducting an interpretative phenomenological analysis study. It is not prescriptive but offers an acceptable guide to practice. Regarding the method of writing, Manen strongly suggests using poetic language and indirect description such as anecdotes, examples, or stories in order to describe the subtle meaning of human experience, since conceptual thinking cannot easily convey the felt meaning.[255]

## Grounded Theory

In my research, I have utilized the method of grounded theory, which originally was developed by Barney G. Glaser and Anselm L. Strauss. In 1967, Glaser and Strauss co-authored *The Discovery of Grounded Theory*, which established the methodology of grounded theory in order to develop theories from research, grounded in data rather than deducing testable hypotheses from existing theories. Later on, their ideas on grounded theory diverged. Glaser's views remained consistent, but Strauss and Juliet Corbin developed new technical procedures rather than emphasizing comparative methods. Kathy Charmaz views grounded theory methods as flexible rather than rigid, as "a set of principles and practices not as prescriptions or packages," stating that "grounded theory methods consist of systematic, yet

253. Manen, *Phenomenology of Practice*, 30.
254. Manen, *Phenomenology of Practice*, 41.
255. Manen, *Phenomenology of Practice*, 46.

flexible guidelines for collecting and analyzing qualitative data to construct theories *grounded* in the data themselves."[256]

In her book *Constructing Grounded Theory*, Charmaz argues that the researcher is an inseparable part of the entire research process. Glaser and Strauss differ from Charmaz in that Glaser and Strauss see the researcher as neutral and separate from the data in discovering theories, but Charmaz views the researcher as part of the world rather than separate from it. Charmaz states, "We construct our grounded theories through our past and present involvements and interactions with people, perspectives, and research practices."[257] Thus, she takes a pragmatic stance and advances interpretive analyses that acknowledge the researcher's experiences and views as a part of reality. In this vein, I view the experience of the researcher as significant not only in conducting the research, but also in interpreting the data.

According to Strauss and Corbin, qualitative analysis is carried out for the purpose of discovering concepts and relationships in raw data and then organizing these into a theoretical explanatory scheme.[258] In this method, data collection, analysis, and the eventual theory stand in close relationship to one another. The researcher begins with an area of study and allows the theory to emerge from the data. Grounded theories, because they are drawn from data, are likely to offer insight, enhance understanding, and provide a meaningful guide to action.[259] This aspect of the methodology is congruent with the purpose of this study in terms of helping missionary personnel to understand the factors, process, and types of conversion in a way that might give them insight into and help guide their ministry.

Strauss and Corbin define theory as "a set of well-developed concepts related through statements of relationship, which together constitute an integrated framework that can be used to explain or predict phenomena."[260] Conceptual ordering is a major part of the process of building theory. This refers to classifying events and objects along various explicitly stated dimensions, without necessarily relating the classifications to each other to form an overarching explanatory scheme. Theorizing is the act of constructing from data an explanatory scheme that systematically integrates various concepts through statements of relationship. In this methodology,

256. Charmaz, *Constructing Grounded Theory*, 2.
257. Charmaz, *Constructing Grounded Theory*, 10.
258. Strauss and Corbin, *Qualitative Research*, 11.
259. Strauss and Corbin, *Qualitative Research*, 11.
260. Strauss and Corbin, *Qualitative Research*, 12–22.

data collection and analysis occur in alternating sequences. Analysis begins with the first interview and observation, which leads to the next interview or observation, followed by more analysis, more interviews or fieldwork, and so on.

## Theoretical Frameworks in Research and Grounded Theory

In *The Basics of Qualitative Research 3e*, Corbin and Strauss use the term grounded theory in a more generic sense to indicate theoretical constructs derived from qualitative analysis of data.[261] Theoretical frameworks are generally used in quantitative research, and they provide a conceptual guide and framework for the research. Using such a theoretical framework to frame the research itself and its findings in a study conducted with grounded theory is controversial. Strauss and Corbin do not support beginning the research with "a predefined theoretical framework or set of concepts."[262] Nevertheless, they acknowledge the possibility of using a theoretical framework in some instances, as follows:

1. It can be used "to complement, extend, and verify the findings" when a "previously developed framework is closely aligned to what is being discovered in the researcher's present study."

2. "It can also be used to offer alternative explanations for findings."

3. "If the researcher is building upon a program of research or wants to develop middle-range theory, a previously identified theoretical framework can provide insight, direction, and a useful list of initial concepts" while the researcher remains open to new ideas and concepts.

4. It can help "the researcher determine the methodology to be used."[263]

Although the researcher may recognize the sensitizing concepts and disciplinary perspectives at the start of a study, not the end, it is necessary not only to remain as open as possible in the early stage of the research, but also not to limit his or her ideas.[264]

261. Corbin and Strauss, *Qualitative Research 3e*, 1.
262. Corbin and Strauss, *Qualitative Research 3e*, 39.
263. Corbin and Strauss, *Qualitative Research 3e*, 40.
264. Charmaz, *Constructing Grounded Theory*, 17.

*Strategies for Qualitative Data Analysis*

Grounded theory methodology utilizes some analytic tools and techniques to facilitate the coding process and stimulate the analytic process, such as the use of questioning, making constant comparisons, and making theoretical comparisons.[265] The use of questioning is the fundamental analytic tool of analysis that enhances the discovery of new knowledge, especially in terms of probing and developing provisional answers.

Making comparisons is an essential feature of the methodology of grounded theory. Strauss and Corbin suggest two different types of comparison-making: constant comparisons and theoretical comparisons. Constant comparisons are a fundamental analytic tool for discovering the similarities and differences between concepts, categories, and events by comparing. Theoretical comparisons help the analyst to identify the significance and meaning of an incident or object by looking at its properties and dimensions.

*Concepts for Theorizing*

Strauss and Corbin define the aim of research as attempting "to make sense out of [the] data by organizing them according to a classificatory scheme, such as types or stages."[266] In this process, theorizing is crucial. According to Strauss and Corbin, "Theorizing is interpretive and entails not only condensing raw data into concepts but also arranging the concepts into a logical, systematic explanatory scheme."[267] Conceptual ordering is an essential part of theorizing because of its development of properties and dimensions. The ordering of concepts with levels can help to structure the events or phenomena that a researcher is exploring. Whether it is a classificatory scheme or a core concept that overarches the phenomena, concepts are the foundation. Concepts/themes are foundational and play a central role in the analytic method of grounded theory presented by Corbin and Strauss. Theorizing necessitates inductions and deductions—inductions for deriving concepts, their properties, and dimensions from the data and deductions for hypothesizing about the relationships between concepts.

---

265. Corbin and Strauss, *Qualitative Research 3e*, 65.

266. Corbin and Strauss, *Qualitative Research 3e*, 55.

267. Corbin and Strauss, *Qualitative Research 3e*, 56.

## Analyzing Data for Process

Analyzing data for process allows the researcher to incorporate variation into the findings. Corbin and Strauss point out the crucial point of variation related to the process as follows: "Along with variation, process can lead to the identification of patterns as one looks for similarities in the way persons define situations and handle them. And, if one's final goal is theory building, analyzing data for process is an essential step along the way."[268] As mentioned earlier, in this study I explore factors affecting conversion, the process of conversion, and the types of conversion. Variations in factors and process lead to different patterns or types of conversion.

## Summary

In summary, this chapter presented literature on understanding conversion from various perspectives. Then, the topics of diasporas and international students, the ministry of Chinese students in Korea, as well as the state of ministry to Chinese students in Korea were reviewed. Next was an overview of the Chinese church in Communist China since 1949, followed by an understanding Chinese traditional religions and culture from the perspective of Christianity. Finally, literature on research methodology was discussed. The next chapter presents research methodology.

---

268. Corbin and Strauss, *Qualitative Research 3e*, 100.

# 3

## Research Methodology

BECAUSE THE PURPOSE OF this study is to develop a theory about conversion, I have chosen to use qualitative methodology. I also utilize the methodology of grounded theory and consult Strauss and Corbin's two books, *Basics of Qualitative Research 3e: Techniques and Procedures for Developing Grounded Theory* and *Basics of Qualitative Research: Techniques and Procedures for Developing Grounded Theory*. Also, I draw on Kathy Charmaz's book, *Constructing Grounded Theory: A Practical Guide through Qualitative Analysis*. I initially familiarized myself with the two books by Strauss and Corbin, in order to grasp the process of data analysis and the method of using grounded theory. After reading Charmaz's book, I adopted her flexible stance and understanding of grounded theory. She sees grounded theory methods as guidelines suggesting general principles and heuristic devices, rather than as rigid prescriptions. This chapter will present data collection process, population, sampling, written data, interview procedures, and data analysis.

### Data Collection

The literature used in the research for this study was gathered from the following sources: (1) libraries of Torch Trinity Graduate University, other universities and seminaries; (2) electronic resources supported by Torch Trinity Graduate University and the Research Information Sharing Service; (3) dissertations through ProQuest; (4) books through online bookstores; (5) books, articles, and other publications from mission organizations; and (6) Internet resources. While writing the literature review, I contacted the leaders of two leading mission organizations for China, China to God and CHISTA Busan, sharing my research plan and asking for resources about Chinese students. They gave me magazines and access to resources on their websites related to ministry for Chinese students in Korea. I also met the director of CHISTA Seoul, who sent me resources by email. In addition, I spoke on the phone with the president of the KOWSMA about resources concerning ministries for international students in Korea, and he emailed me articles. I observed C Chinese Church, which was founded to target Chinese students at I University, and attended its Sunday services to preach and lead Bible study once a month.

## Population

The population of this study is Chinese students living in Korea who converted to Christianity while studying in a Korean university. Their academic focus is varied and includes Korean language courses, undergraduate courses in universities, master's degree courses in graduate school, and doctoral courses. Some students started their studies at a Korean language school after graduating from high school in China, and some students came to Korea as university exchange students. Graduate students are composed of two types: students who came to Korea after graduating from college in China and students who are continuing their studies after graduating from college in Korea. In 2019, the total number of Chinese students in Korea was 71,067 (44.4 percent of international students). Of these, 13,572 were in non-degree programs, and 57,495 were in degree programs.[1]

## Sampling

In grounded research methodology, specific sampling decisions evolve during the research process. That is, sampling decisions are based on concepts that emerge from the analysis and appear to have relevance to the evolving theory. By means of theoretical sampling, the researcher not only seeks data that is pertinent to developing the emerging theory, but also endeavors to elaborate and refine the categories constituting the theory. I used purposeful sampling to find appropriate subjects based on what they could contribute to the study. Because this study was on Christian conversion, I chose subjects who were identified as having a reliable and sustained Christian conversion experience by their pastors. Furthermore, since the subject of this study is bounded by time and culture, subjects were chosen

---

1. Korean Ministry of Education, "Statistics of Foreign Students."

who claimed to have been converted since coming to Korea and who are from mainland China. The researcher interviewed thirty Chinese students, women and men, who converted to Christianity while studying in universities in Incheon or Seoul, Korea. They have all been baptized and have been actively participating in evangelical Christian churches.

I asked thirteen pastors and missionaries to introduce me to suitable interview participants. Since I have been serving as a missionary for twenty-five years, I am acquainted with many of these church leaders, some of them as coworkers. Since 2011, I have been attending the annual four-day retreat held by CHISTA. In 2015, about one thousand Chinese students attended this retreat.

I have also attended the forums for the Chinese students' mission held in seminaries and churches and have attended meetings of CHISTA to observe and become acquainted with pastors working with Chinese students. I had the opportunity to discuss matters related to student ministry with them during these events. During the retreat in 2015, the pastors of Chinese churches who were present promised to introduce me to potential participants for my study. I then selected twenty-six participants who attend nine churches located in Seoul and four located in Incheon. I also interviewed seven pastors and missionaries serving Chinese students in Incheon and Seoul in order to gain useful information from their experiences and for the purpose of triangulation.

## Interview Procedures

To conduct the interviews with participants, I obtained ethical approval from the Korean Institutional Review Board (approval number: P01-201503-22-001). To establish a climate of trust and rapport with the participants, I attended services and meetings held at each of the participants' churches and had informal meetings with them, accompanied by their pastors. Some of the pastors asked me to preach during worship at their churches. The interviews were held at the participants' churches and in places out of church where the participants felt comfortable. Participants were told that the objective of the research was to study the conversion of Chinese students in Korea, with particular focus on the factors, process, and types of conversion. Before starting each interview, I gave the participant a form that informed them of the purpose and methods of the research and their rights as a participant in the study. I also provided an informed consent form that explained their right to refuse to participate without any negative consequences, as well as the possibility of being requested to participate in further interviews.

I used in-depth interviews of about fifty minutes to one hour. Initially, I adopted a flexible approach, asking a few broad and open-ended questions that were also directed and emergent, followed by focused questions inviting detailed responses.[2] In-depth interviewing is said to be the hallmark of qualitative research.[3] Deeper understandings may develop through in-depth interviews as the interviewer and participant *construct* meaning. I identified the regularities and patterns that emerged from the data as major themes that I then used to direct further interviews. As Rossman et al. state, as the researcher develops categories or topics to explore, one needs to remain open to pursuing topics that the participant brings up.[4]

Initially, pilot interviews were conducted in semi-structured format, asking the following questions:

1. What was your life like before you became a Christian?

2. What made you decide to become a Christian?

3. What were the difficulties for you in becoming a Christian?

4. How did you overcome these difficulties?

During the pilot interviews, further questions emerged, focusing on two key aspects of the research question, the factors and processes of conversion. The questions that gradually emerged could broadly be organized into three phases of the conversion process:

1. Background and life before conversion,

2. Initial contact (encounter) with the gospel, as well as action/interaction, and making the decision to believe, and

3. Consequences of conversion.

In doing research with the methodology of grounded theory, sampling evolves during the process and theoretical sampling guides the whole process of data gathering. In order to follow the principle of theoretical sampling, I not only sought pertinent data for developing the emerging theory, but also

2. Charmaz, *Constructing Grounded Theory*, 26, 28.

3. Marshall and Rossman, *Designing Qualitative Research*, 180.

4. Marshall and Rossman, *Designing Qualitative Research*, 181.

elaborated and refined the categories that constituted a theory. The process of completing interviews and gathering other data is gradual in grounded theory. I gathered data until each category was saturated. That is, no new or significant data was emerging (additional information was shedding little or no new light on the subject of this study) and the categories were well developed in terms of properties and dimensions.[5]

## Data Analysis

As I collected and analyzed data from the interviews, research materials, and observations, I found issues to explore, and questions arose that created the need for further observing or interviewing. Using Glaser and Strauss' constant comparative method of analysis which is central to grounded theory research, I collected data and looked for emerging themes and categories.[6] As I collected more data, I wrote analytic memos about the data and reevaluated the previous analysis by comparing the old data with the new. The preliminary factors and processes of conversion of Chinese students, generated by the pilot interviews, continued to expand in depth and breadth throughout the process, and this generated more themes that guided the development of the study.

For example, I interviewed a Chinese student for the pilot study who had become a Christian when he was experiencing a kind of crisis caused by complex reasons in Korea. His friends had stolen his money, he felt lonely, and he had failed the college entrance exam. Because all of these hardships were too heavy for him to endure, he had considered suicide. During that period, one of his friends asked him to go to a Chinese church. Soon after his first attendance, he experienced something unexpected—he received an admission letter from the same university he had applied to earlier. Later, he found out that the professors had reevaluated his work of art and decided to accept him. He confessed that God had answered his own and his church friends' prayers. Another student I interviewed had become a Christian without experiencing any crisis or difficulties. She just followed her Korean friend, who had asked her to go to a church on her campus. From the first day, she liked the atmosphere of the service, feeling relaxed when hearing hymns in the church. She believed God answered her prayer of finding students to teach Chinese in order to improve her financial situation. She asked

5. Strauss and Corbin, *Qualitative Research*, 212, 215.
6. Leedy and Ormrod, *Practical Research*, 168.

her mother, an intellectual, to believe in Jesus over the phone, and surprisingly, her mother accepted her request, became a believer, and currently serves at a church in China.

In regard to the above two examples, the former case led me to look for the existence of a crisis during the process of conversion and to examine whether students had overcome a crisis with faith. The latter case led me to look for factors other than crisis or difficulties, such as affection and answer to prayers. Thus, the early data codes were Frustration, Failure, Loneliness, Desperation, Miraculous answering of a prayer, Affection, Warmth, Friendliness, Answer to prayer, and Love. The concepts found in the open coding were used for both theoretical sampling for guiding new interviews and for axial coding and selective coding for comparing and developing a theory.

After each interview, the recorded responses were transcribed. I embedded observer comments in the transcribed texts as I reviewed them throughout several levels of coding. The first level is open coding, which was descriptive, that is, I assigned descriptive tags to parts of the text. The second level is axial coding, which is the formation of concepts, categories, and themes from the transcribed text. The third level is selective coding (or theoretical coding), in which I integrated themes from which a substantive theory could be developed.

In axial coding, I related categories to their subcategories to form more precise and complete explanations of the phenomena. Each of the highest level of categories was defined by an interview question, because these questions were considered to be crucial markers of the factors and phases in the conversion process, as mentioned in the previous section. Thus, the highest-level categories reflect a process-oriented categorization. The procedure of axial coding involved the following tasks: (1) laying out the properties of a category and their dimensions, a task that began during open coding, (2) identifying the variety of conditions, actions/interactions, and consequences associated with the phenomenon, (3) relating a category to its subcategories through statements denoting how they were related to each other, and (4) looking for clues in the data that denoted how the major categories were related to each other.[7]

7. Strauss and Corbin, *Qualitative Research*, 123.

Selective coding is the process of integrating and refining the theory.[8] Kathy Charmaz calls this theoretical coding.[9] In integration, categories are organized around a central explanatory concept. The central or core category represents the main theme of the research. In this methodology, integration takes place over time during the process of research. Once a central idea is set, major categories are related to it through explanatory statements of relationships. I used several techniques to facilitate the integration process, such as writing the storyline, using diagrams and figures, sorting and reviewing memos. Once I had outlined the overarching theoretical scheme, I then proceeded to refine the theory, which consisted of reviewing the scheme for internal consistency and gaps in logic, filling in poorly developed categories, trimming excess ones, and validating the scheme.

The purpose of this study was not only to identify the factors affecting conversion, but also to explore the process of conversion—how the factors result in conversion through the process. According to Corbin and Strauss, "if one's final goal is theory building, analyzing data for process is an essential step along the way."[10] Corbin and Strauss define process as "ongoing action/interaction/emotion taken in response to situation, or problems, often with the purpose of reaching a goal or handling a problem."[11] They also pay attention to the individual variations in any action, interaction, or emotion in relation to goal accomplishment, the situation, the event, or the set of circumstances. I gave special heed to group-specific factors, that is, how the students responded to particular situations or circumstances. I wanted to capture the dynamic quality of (inter)action and emotions when analyzing data for process.

In order to accurately understand the phenomenon under investigation, I used tables to show its categories and themes.[12] After the categories were well developed, I made diagrams that were visual representations of the relationships between the analytic concepts. These diagrams helped me to think beyond the level of facts, organize the data, illustrate conceptual relationships between the data, and integrate the data.

The final analytic process of this research was theoretical integration. The purpose of doing the research by means of the methodology of

8. Strauss and Corbin, *Qualitative Research*, 143.

9. Charmaz, *Constructing Grounded Theory*, 63.

10. Corbin and Strauss, *Qualitative Research 3e*, 100.

11. Corbin and Strauss, *Qualitative Research 3e*, 96.

12. Strauss and Corbin, *Qualitative Research*, 191.

grounded theory was to build a theory through the theoretical integration of the data. Concepts are the foundation of theory building. In order to build a theory, as Strauss and Corbin point out, "concepts must be linked and filled in with detail to construct theory out of data."[13] In addition, concepts are related to explanations, meaning the interpretation of the researcher. Generally speaking, a concept that reaches the level of categories that overarch the process should have general applicability to all the cases in the study (that is, the overall unifying scheme).[14] I also tried to identify the types or patterns of conversion together with the factors and process of conversion of the participants. The variation of categories might lead to types or patterns.

The central or core category is what all the other categories or concepts are geared towards or converge on, so it represents the main theme and also holds great explanatory power. The core category enables the reader to determine *theoretically* what the research is all about. Therefore, I endeavored to develop a central or core category that could link all of the other categories together. Strauss and Corbin describe several techniques for facilitating identification of the central category, such as writing the storyline, making use of matrices and figures, and reviewing and sorting memos either by hand or with computer software.

I used QSR International's NVivo 11, a computer software, to code the data that was specifically designed to analyze qualitative research. This program enabled me to (1) import and analyze interview transcripts and other text, (2) keep data organized, (3) bring different themes together in a single category, (4) look for emerging themes, and (5) visually explore connections, similarities, and differences between categories and themes. The next section will present the analysis process.

## The Analysis Process

I conducted the interviews in Chinese and translated and transcribed them into English, which totaled 314 pages. After each interview was completed, I summarized it in order to sketch the specific features of the conversion of the participant. A sample summary of an interview is presented below.

---

13. Corbin and Strauss, *Qualitative Research 3e*, 103.
14. Corbin and Strauss, *Qualitative Research 3e*, 103.

L came to Korea after graduating from high school, even though he could have been admitted to a high-ranking university in China. He left China because he was very dismayed by his parents' divorce. He even thought of suicide. He got a full scholarship and a stipend for living expenses. L went to church through a Korean friend. He received much help from a pastor of his church. He felt this pastor was like God to him in the sense that "God helps with everything," which is also how his pastor had described God. He recently experienced a very special spiritual event. When he attended a retreat, he saw a cross while praying. This experience enhanced his faith greatly with a new understanding of the meaning of the cross. He clearly explained the grace of Jesus' sacrifice. He faced the objections of friends and parents, as well as a struggle caused by brothers in his church who asked him to do things that Christians should not do, but he decided to believe in Jesus. He was greatly moved by his senior pastor. Although he could understand only a third of the sermons in Korean, he often shed tears while listening to them. He came to have hope since believing in Jesus, and this is also why he decided to be baptized. He likes Christianity's honest perspective on life compared to other religions and philosophies. He believes that he can be a better person because he believes in Jesus. He thinks the most important teaching is to obey God's commandments.

Using the software program mentioned above, I prepared detailed memos for axial coding, selective coding, and theory making. Examples are given in Table 2.

Table 2. Example of Memos

| Type of Memo | Text of Memo |
| --- | --- |
| Coding | Q was not used to opening her heart to others, not even to Jesus, because she was not used to relying on others. He had been a "bad student" who did not study at all but spent time drinking and playing with friends at night and going to school in the afternoon to play and sleep. He became a Christian when he learned about the "existence of God" through listening to sermons and reading spiritual books. The Holy Spirit moved him during prayer. The Holy Spirit "convicted" him of his faults and "answered" his questions while praying. He also experienced that the Bible is "the truth that can guide my life" and make him a "better person." He wants to study at seminary to become a pastor. |

| Type of Memo | Text of Memo |
| --- | --- |
| Analytic | L thinks God is powerful. This is because he experienced the power of God when he was admitted to university after failing a course. He also said, "You can experience God's power when you pray." |
| | Need to check when in the conversion process W was baptized. Was it after making the decision to convert or not? Decision/baptism/ growth in faith or baptism/decision/growth in faith? |
| Theoretical | Analyze the relationship between the obstacles to believing and how they were solved and visually present it with a matrix if possible. |
| | Need to compare the cognitive perspective and experiential perspective in terms of decision-making, in order to find the factors that are most influential in conversion. |

The regularities and patterns that emerged from the data were identified as major themes and categories and illustrated as tables with descriptive analysis. These categories were compared as a part of selective coding. I used the constant comparison method to help analyze the relationships between the categories (which include factors) in the process of conversion during the stage of selective coding.

During the coding stage, I used NVivo 11 for the following: (1) open coding to name the concepts found in the data, (2) axial coding to identify the patterns emerging from more than one reference, and (3) comparative analysis of the open and axial coding. Figures 3 and 4 show examples of using NVivo 11 for open coding and axial coding, respectively. Figure 5 gives an example of a comparison made after the axial coding, using NVivo 11.

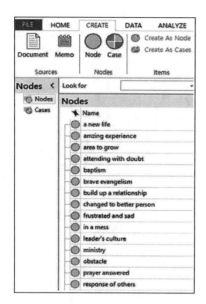

Figure 3. Example of Open Coding
with NVivo 11

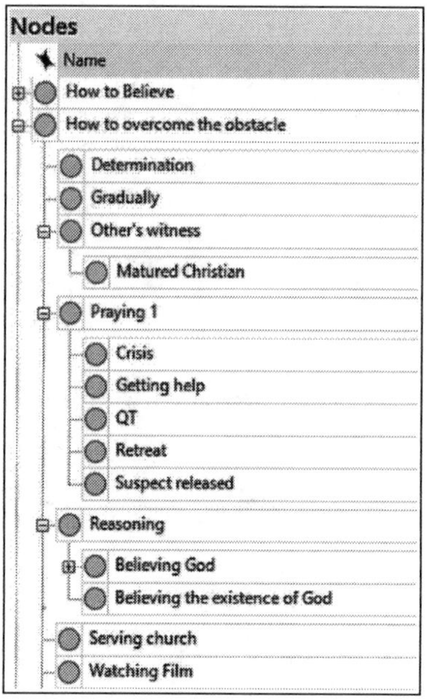

Figure 4. Example of Axial Coding
with NVivo 11

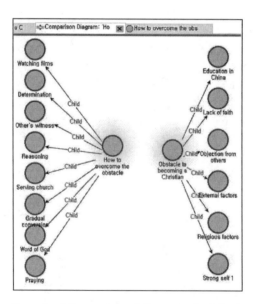

Figure 5. Example of Comparison of Categories for Selective Coding

During the last stage of coding, I did selective coding by making a figure to theoretically integrate all the themes. Then, I wrote a storyline to show the overall schema of conversion, focusing on the factors, process, and types of conversion of these Chinese students in Korea. Finally, I delineated a theory and model of conversion created as a result of the study.

In summary, this chapter presented the research methodology used in this research, in terms of data collection, population, sampling, written data, interview procedures, data analysis, and the analysis process. The next chapter will present the findings of this study.

# 4

# Findings

THIS STUDY REGARDS AN investigation into the conversion of Chinese students in Korea to Evangelical Christianity. The qualitative study was intended to explore the factors, process, and types of conversion and develop a theory of conversion of Chinese students in Korea. The primary purpose of this chapter is to present the analysis of the transcribed data and the findings derived from the analysis.

## Demographic Findings

The participants involved in this study consisted of a purposeful criteria sample of Chinese students studying in Korea. A total of thirty students participated in this research. The thirty participants included thirteen male and seventeen female students, ranging in age from nineteen to thirty. All participants fit the criteria set for this research study, and all but two of the participants were married. The number of years since the participants had converted ranged from one to six years at the time of the study. Regarding the composition of the participants' course of study, there were eleven college students, fourteen graduate students, and five doctoral students. The duration of the participants' stay in Korea varied as follows: one year (one), two years (six), three years (eight), and over four years (fifteen). Twenty-three of the participants were studying in Seoul and seven in Incheon. The ethnicities of the participants' pastors were Korean (five), Chinese (four), and Korean-Chinese (five). Table 3 gives detailed results of the demographic questionnaire.

Table 3. Demographic Overview of Research Study Participants

| Characteristics | Participants (*n*=30) | Characteristics | Participants (*n*=30) |
|---|---|---|---|
| Level of Coursework | | Gender | |
| *Undergraduate* | 11 | *Male* | 13 |
| *Graduate* | 14 | *Female* | 17 |
| *Doctorate* | 5 | Age | |
| City | | *19–20* | 2 |
| *Incheon* | 7 | *21–24* | 8 |
| *Seoul* | 23 | *Over 25* | 20 |
| Ethnicity of their pastors | | Years in Korea | |
| *Korean* | 5 | *1 Year* | 1 |
| *Chinese* | 4 | *2 Years* | 6 |
| *Korean-Chinese* | 5 | *3 Years* | 8 |
| | | *Over 4 Years* | 15 |

To preserve the anonymity of the interviewees, participants are referred to by their code names used in this study. For instance, for the code name D/F, D refers to the participant, while F stands for female. The next section presents the participants' lives before contact with the gospel.

## Participants' Lives Prior to Contact with the Gospel

This section treats the lives of the participants before they contacted the gospel, in order to understand their situations and lifestyles. Several themes emerged from the data analysis, which utilized axial coding to extract and cluster into categories the pertinent statements from the initially prepared question, "How was your life before you became a Christian?" The result of the axial coding rendered 171 references that were then categorized into twenty-four themes. The themes were re-categorized into the following five themes: Ordinary Life, Self-Centered life, Insecure Life, Crisis, and Religious Background. These themes elucidate the contextual influences and the situation of the converts before conversion. The emergent themes and their subthemes for this section are illustrated in Table 4.

Table 4. Themes Related to Participants' Lives Prior to Contact with the Gospel

| Category | Themes and Subthemes | Participants* (n=30) |
|---|---|---|
| Life Prior to Contact with the Gospel: What was the participant's life like before conversion? | Ordinary Life | 14 |
| | Self-Complacent | 7 |
| | No Goal | 4 |
| | Ordinary Life | 3 |
| | Meaninglessness | 2 |
| | Self-Centered Life | 19 |
| | No Standards | 10 |
| | Success-Oriented | 6 |
| | Competitive | 4 |
| | Enjoying Life | 4 |
| | Empty | 4 |
| | Self-Reliant | 2 |
| | Insecure Life | 15 |
| | No Confidence | 6 |
| | Living Blindly | 5 |
| | Lonely | 5 |
| | Wanting Love | 3 |
| | Depressed | 2 |
| | Crisis | 9 |
| | No Hope | 3 |
| | Family Problems | 1 |
| | Complex Crisis | 2 |
| | Bad Grades | 2 |

* Some participants reported multiple (sub)themes.

96

| Category | Themes and Subthemes | Participants*<br>($n=30$) |
|---|---|---|
| | *Financial Problems* | 1 |
| | *Religious Background* | 15 |
| | *Contact with Christians in China* | 7 |
| | *Buddhist* | 4 |
| | *Atheist* | 3 |
| | *Praying to an Unknown God* | 1 |

\* Some participants reported multiple (sub)themes.

## Ordinary Life

The theme Ordinary Life has four subordinate themes: Self-Complacent, No Goal, Ordinary Life, and Meaninglessness. Fourteen out of thirty participants described the idea of an ordinary life when they were asked to elaborate their life before conversion. I expand on this theme below by discussing the emergent four subthemes.

### Self-Complacent

Seven participants reported living satisfying lives before conversion. Some thought they were satisfied because they worked hard:

> I thought that I could do anything by doing my best. I thought that I could get admitted to Y University with a scholarship because I worked hard. Also, I thought I was working hard for my future life. . . . I tried hard so that I might have a stable life in the future.[1]

> No, I did not feel discontent with my life. I just got used to many things, and life conditions are diverse, so that I didn't feel dissatisfied or that anything was unfair.[2]

1. L1, Transcripts of Converts, 97.
2. Z4/F, Transcripts of Converts, 318.

One participant recalled that she was very happy because her mother loved her very much and had raised her with traditional Chinese wisdom:

> To recall my life, I was cheerful under the protection and love of my mom. . . . My mom often said that there must be a way [in this world] under the heaven. Though you reach a dead end, there must be a way to get out. My mom also often said that though heaven falls down, you cannot hold out, so you do not need to worry about anything. . . . If I achieved well, it was because of what I learned from my mom.[3]

## No Goal

Some participants whose parents were highly demanding and made arrangements for them did not have goals for their lives. Some also articulated that they did not have a clear purpose of life or a goal, so that they did not know what to do or what was right.

> Before becoming a Christian, I felt a kind of emptiness. I lived a hollow life. Also, I did not have a clear goal for my life, and I did not have a clear view on values. People think that something is right, the things of the world, but I did not know what is really right, which made me confused.[4]

## Ordinary Life

Some participants noted that they lived an "ordinary life" without any major crisis as students:

> I was a student and studied, so I did not experience that much of society. I lived a simple life and was busy thinking of my future plan of study and a job after finishing school.[5]

> I lived a plain life—eating, going to school, sleeping, doing sports, and playing computer games. I lived an ordinary life.[6]

3. N1/F, Transcripts of Converts, 128.
4. Q, Transcripts of Converts, 150.
5. C3/F, Transcripts of Converts, 26.
6. Z1, Transcripts of Converts, 276.

## Meaninglessness

One participant who followed his parent's arrangements for his daily life felt that his life was meaningless. Generally, Chinese parents have only one child due to the policy implemented until recently, which may have led them towards excessive care and attention. This participant described his experience as follows:

> Before becoming a Christian, I grew up in a family in which my parents arranged almost everything for me. So, I did not have my own ideas. Almost everything was arranged by my parents until I came to Korea to study in the college. I just needed to listen to my parents for everything, and then everything was okay. I just followed the guidance of my parents, even about how to have relationships with other people. I did not know what to do in the future, and I had no possibility to choose for myself, except for listening to my parents. I felt I lived a meaningless life day by day.[7]

In summary, almost half of the participants noted that they had lived ordinary lives before converting to Christianity. Some participants lived a self-complacent or ordinary life, while others lived without goals or meaning.

## Self-Centered Life

Nineteen out of thirty participants stated that they had lived self-centered lives. The theme Self-Centered Life has six subthemes, with a total of sixty-seven comments categorized as No Standards, Success-Oriented, Competitive, Enjoying Life, Empty, and Self-Reliant.

## No Standards

Ten participants stated that they had lived "without standards," "without knowing what to do," or "what is really right," so they just followed their desires, their parents' expectations, or others' opinions.

> I felt good about what other people said was good, though they were worldly things. . . . Sometimes I felt it shouldn't be like that. If

---

7. W2, Transcripts of Converts, 196.

others all said the same, though, I also gradually did follow them in their way of thinking.[8]

Before having faith, I had no standard for living a good life. I had my way or lived by my parents' expectations. Now, after having faith, I think the Bible is the standard, and compared to before, I don't lie, even if it is a small thing. Now, I would rather just be honest.[9]

One participant felt conflicted when she found a discrepancy between what she knew from books and reality. She felt that if she followed this world, then she would be "lost," so she wanted some truth that could guide her towards a steady and safe life.[10] Another student who was strongly motivated and had excellent grades at a renowned university described her life as a "mess," because she did not know what she "truly wanted" and "wanted a lot but did not know what to do."[11]

## Success-Oriented

Almost all of the success-oriented participants stated they "worked hard" or did their best for their "success," "future," "job," or "fame and fortune." For instance, one participant was dedicated to the point of risking her life, and Koreans around her called her a "*dok-han* ("iron-willed") woman."[12] For most of these participants, their core value was academic achievement for securing their future:

Before I became a Christian, I hoped to have a good job after I graduated and to live a very stable life. At that time, I was busy preparing for further studies. I was working hard for my future life.[13]

Before becoming a Christian, I was following the world. I mean, I worked hard for fame and fortune. Also, the message that the world gave me was that you should make money and have money.[14]

8. Q, Transcripts of Converts, 157.

9. W3/F, Transcripts of Converts, 221.

10. Z3/F, Transcripts of Converts, 302.

11. W5/F, Transcripts of Converts, 241.

12. W4/F, Transcripts of Converts, 225.

13. L1, Transcripts of Converts, 97.

14. X/F, Transcripts of Converts, 260.

A representative example of the self-centered life is found in a doctoral student's comment: "The most different thing is that I did what I wanted to do, got drunk, and slept whenever I wanted. I did not control time. I did not care about other people, and I lived a self-centered life. Whatever I wanted to do, I did without any standard."[15] Though she lived to cater to herself and one goal after the next, she admitted that she "was not really satisfied" with her life.[16]

## Competitive

Competitive participants were hardworking students who had confidence in themselves and performed well in school. One participant was not only proud of what she achieved, but also judgmental because she always thought she was right. Others also mentioned their pride in achievements.

> Right, right! I was very proud of myself. . . . I thought like that, because I thought I was an outstanding person, and others envied me, so they hurt me. . . . So, I worked much harder! I could not rely upon people. The driving force of trying to do my best was my jealousy. If someone was better than me, I felt I must get ahead of her, so I could not be a good friend of hers.[17]

> Before I became a Christian, I was [pause] perhaps rather self-confident, so confident that I was rather proud of myself. I felt that as long as I worked hard, I could rank among the top in the class, that kind of pride.[18]

## Enjoying Life

Unlike most of the participants, who studied hard for success and the betterment of their future lives, some participants did not care for their studies and only wanted to enjoy their life. They confessed that though they tried hard to find pleasure, they felt "lonely," "hollow," "worried," and "hopeless."

15. K/F, Transcripts of Converts, 85.
16. K/F, Transcripts of Converts, 85.
17. W4/F, Transcripts of Converts, 225.
18. T/F, Transcripts of Converts, 180.

Before I converted to Jesus Christ, I was quite a terrible person. I didn't want to listen to my parents, and I also often skipped classes, then stole money, and went to a nightclub, stayed with bad friends, and had love affairs at random. And then I found my whole life was totally in a mess. I often felt very lonely and hollow.[19]

When I studied in high school in China, I did not study. I slept until noon and went to school to play games with some of my friends, and we played, drank, and went to karaoke to sing until midnight. I was a bad student. . . . I enjoyed my life.

## Empty

Though some participants wanted to fill the void in their heart with worldly things, they felt empty instead. They recalled their experience of an empty life as follows:

We went to school after lunch. In the afternoon, when the teachers were teaching, we were playing poker [laughs]. And, in the evening we went to karaoke and sang and drank there. After that, we went to the Internet cafe and played computer games all night [laughs], and then we went home in the morning to sleep . . . but I was not happy at all in my heart. I felt empty and did not know what to do.[20]

I found my life was really disorderly and unsystematic and did not have any principles. Such a terrible life continued for almost twenty-one years. Yes, it was such a long time and I often felt so lonely and hollow.[21]

I felt that my life was very dark, a bit worrisome, often not happy, no hope, always depending on the relationship with my boyfriend and loving shopping to satisfy my empty heart. Before becoming a Christian, my relationship with my father was not solid, so I felt a shortage of love in my heart.[22]

19. C2/F, Transcripts of Converts, 13.
20. Z5, Transcripts of Converts, 325.
21. C2/F, Transcripts of Converts, 13.
22. J3/F, Transcripts of Converts, 78.

## Self-Reliant

The Chinese students had no opportunity to think about religion. One participant related her self-reliance to her atheism. She relied upon herself and believed in herself and her own power, but she confessed such a life made her very tired. Another participant also said that relying on herself was exhausting. One felt tired because he had to solve his problems by himself, without sharing them with other people, and another felt exhausted because he did not know what to do. They described their self-reliant lives as follows:

> Before becoming a Christian, I was an atheist, and I was not taught about anything related to faith. . . . As an atheist, I felt that I should rely on myself and believe in myself. And then, I thought that there are many things that I could do, so I would do whatever I'd like to do through my power. . . . I really didn't like to tell my difficulties to other people. I felt I should solve them by myself.[23]

> In short, I just relied on myself to deal with things, whether I succeeded or I failed. However, I was exhausted. My heart was particularly exhausted. I didn't know what I was doing.[24]

In summary, a majority of the participants said they lived a self-centered life before their conversion. Although most of them worked hard academically to secure their future lives, some participants just enjoyed their youth without studying. Most of them noted living a life without standards and relying on themselves. Though they lived a self-centered life based on the desires, passions, and expectations of their parents, they confessed that they felt tired, exhausted, frustrated, empty, and unhappy.

## Insecure Life

Half of the participants described their lives before their conversion as insecure. Common descriptors that participants employed during the interviews included having "no confidence," "living blindly," being "lonely," "wanting love," and being "depressed." These descriptors are treated as the subthemes of Insecure Life and are described more fully below.

---

23. Y, Transcripts of Converts, 271.
24. W5, Transcripts of Converts, 240.

## No Confidence

Many participants mentioned the pressure to study, though they did not study hard. Chinese society as a whole emphasizes entering a renowned university to secure success. Students with low grades may not easily have confidence in such an environment. A female participant stated that she had no confidence, even though she was a high-ranking student. She also felt insecure, saying, "I did not have a sense of security. I had no confidence to do anything. So, I worked very hard! . . . If someone was better than me, I had to get ahead of her."[25]

Moreover, lacking a sense of security and confidence might come from thinking that there is nobody to rely upon, especially in a society that operates by relationship (*guan xi*). One such participant confessed, "I felt that I should rely on myself in whatever I did. So, if I could not manage to do it, I would fail."[26]

## Living Blindly

Some participants did not know what to do after finishing their studies and did not have a clear goal in life. Although they had decided to go to Korea to study, they "did not have any idea what I would do after."[27] One participant recalled such uncertainty:

> Before becoming a Christian, I did not have a clear goal for my life. I was in a foggy and vague state. I just wanted to have a degree in Korea. Then, I would think about the rest later [*laughs*]. . . . I did not have a plan for my life. I did not know how I would live in the future.[28]

## Lonely

Feeling lonely was also a factor of insecurity. One doctoral student who had difficulty making friends in a new place. She felt desperate and "did not have

---

25. W4/F, Transcripts of Converts, 225.

26. C1, Transcripts of Converts, 2.

27. C1, Transcripts of Converts, 2.

28. L2/F, Transcripts of Converts, 104.

any hope," living in Korea without her friends.[29] Another doctoral student shared his loneliness studying in Korea: "I felt empty, lonely, not because I didn't have any friends, but because I felt that I had no strength.[30]

## Wanting Love

Three female participants mentioned they needed love from their parents. One participant who often felt lonely chose to study abroad to feel better, but "did not realize that actually [she] just needed love."[31] Another wanted to compensate for the lack of love through "a boyfriend and shopping," but to no avail.[32] Yet another participant whose parents had divorced recalled, "I could not get love from my parents. So, I kept hoping that I could get love from my family and be cared for by my parents. Whenever I saw some families going shopping, I felt kind of dejected."[33]

## Depressed

When students' academic achievement was not good, they could become depressed due to the heavy pressure from their parents and society. One participant noted that he could not have friends due to his bad grades:

> I lived a very depressed life, because when I studied in my hometown my grades were very bad. In China, if your grades are not good, you will be under heavy pressure. . . . Also, I felt that I had no hope for the future . . . because my grades were not good, I had no friends, and was very lonely. This caused me to hide myself. At that time, my life was very unhappy.[34]

In summary, fifteen participants felt insecure when they recalled their lives before they converted. The major reasons for their insecurity were related to academic achievement and their relationships with their parents, their personal character, their uncertainty about the future, and the discrepancy between knowledge and reality. As a result, the participants

29. K/F, Transcripts of Converts, 86.
30. W1, Transcripts of Converts, 196.
31. C2/F, Transcripts of Converts, 13.
32. J3/F, Transcripts of Converts, 78.
33. X/F, Transcripts of Converts, 260.
34. L3, Transcripts of Converts, 114.

felt blind, conflicted, depressed, lonely, destitute of love, depressed, and had no confidence.

## Crisis

The transcripts of nine participant interviews yielded nineteen comments related to the theme of Crisis. Five subthemes were identified: No Hope, Family Problems, Complex Crisis (a crisis of multiple causes), Bad Grades, and Financial Problems.

### No Hope

Under the great pressure of studying to be admitted to a good university, some participants became depressed or ill due to their bad grades and lost hopes.

> Yes, I was not satisfied, and I also had no purpose in my life. There was a great gap between my hopes and my reality. I was not satisfied with my grades, because I was taught when I was young to study hard and enter a good university, so that I might be successful. At that time, because my grades were not good, I thought that I had no hope of entering a good university in the future.[35]

### Family Problems

One male participant could not endure the painful reality of his parents' divorce and his grandfather's death, so he came to Korea to escape the place of painful memories:

> When I was in China, I studied very hard, but my parents divorced, and my grandfather who loved me very much passed away, so I felt a lot of pressure. After my parents divorced, they fought constantly, even at my school. I really couldn't stand it anymore. I tried to suicide without succeeding. . . . The most important reason why I came to Korea was to leave China forever, never to go back to China. So, I came to Korea in order to escape from my parents.[36]

35. W1, Transcripts of Converts, 196.
36. L3, Transcripts of Converts, 123.

## Complex Crisis

One participant experienced a crisis in Korea, caused by several kinds of problems, so he wanted to return to China:

> I experienced serious difficulties right after coming to Korea. I was deceived by my friends. And they stole my money, so it was very hurtful. It happened three months after coming to Korea. I was not good at studying the language then. Also, I had not adjusted to many things, for example, food and daily living. I didn't get help from others. Yes, I wanted to go back to my country. . . . I really hated this place. Then, I had a fight with my girlfriend because we did not meet. Um. At that time, I was helpless, helpless.[37]

## Bad Grades

Getting bad grades in a highly competitive society could also make the students desperate. A male student said that because he did not have good enough grades, he "had no hope of entering a good university in the future," and "started getting a headache" whenever he thought of studying.[38]

## Financial Problems

Financial problems were another source of crisis. One female student shared that she had no money after she arrived in Korea:

> After arriving Korea, I did not have money, and I was very lonely as well. . . . I didn't have money. My stepfather was sick. My family was with him. So, I was so hurtful, so I cried a lot. I couldn't contact my family because I didn't have a phone at that time.[39]

In summary, there were various causes for the participants' crisis before conversion. Of the two participants who could not cope with the pressures of studying for college or learning the Korean language, one got sick while in China and the other wanted to return to China. The divorce of one participant's parents led him to attempt suicide, and maladjustment to the new country made another participant want to give up studying in Korea.

37. S, Transcripts of Converts, 168.
38. W1/M, Transcripts of Converts, 179.
39. D/F, Transcripts of Converts, 34.

## Religious Background

Of the thirty participants, fifteen shared meaningful statements about their religious experiences and perspectives on religion before their conversion. While in China, seven participants had fellowships with Christians, four had Buddhist backgrounds, and three said they had been atheists. Three participants noted that they thought the ethics of Christianity were good even though they did not believe in God.

### Contact with Christians in China

Participants who had contact with Christians or went to church with their family or friends in China noted that they did not believe in the Christian faith at that time. A few of the participants studied the Korean language with Korean missionaries at school before coming to Korea, although they did not have a Christian faith.

One participant, in particular, whose grandmother was a Christian and mother was a Buddhist, was confused by what her mother said, which reflects what Chinese people often think. Her mother described that all religions would become one, although everyone has different religions. The participant herself had a perception of Christians similar to that of the majority of Chinese people:

> The Chinese church in my hometown is very big. Mostly old people like grandparents attended, but young people were very few. . . . At that time, I thought that the elderly people asked God for their family's happiness, for example, their jobs, schools, and businesses, just like people who believe in other religions. I thought that all the religions were the same, only seeking something [*laughs*].[40]

### Buddhist

Four participants had a Buddhist background. One participant did not want to be a Buddhist because she could not see any positive outcomes from her father's belief in Buddhism.[41] Another noted that he attended his family's ancestor worship in China, an annual ceremony of folk

40. C3/F, Transcripts of Converts, 27.
41. P/F, Transcripts of Converts, 147.

Buddhism.[42] One female participant became a Buddhist to seek this-worldly blessings, to become rich and get blessings:

> The place where I worked was heavily influenced by Buddhism, and there were a lot of devoted Buddhists. So, I was influenced, and so I followed them, and I let the living Buddha touch me and gave them money, hoping they would bless me and make me better. I felt that I was excessively greedy at the time, always wishing to get more. But I was not happy at all, not at all.[43]

## Atheist

Three participants noted that they had been atheists. One female participant clearly stated that she had been a strong atheist based on the core teachings of Communism, which views religion as human imagination and Christianity as feudalism.

> Before coming to Christ, I was a strong atheist, maybe also because of the education in my school from my youth. In middle school and high school, I studied politics, which included Marxism and materialist thought. And even in college I studied this, so that I naturally believed that God does not exist in this world. He is nothing more than human imagination. And I considered those who have religious faith, believing in God or Jesus, as feudalists.[44]

## Praying to an Unknown God

When a participant who lived with her grandmother was horrified at the thought of her grandmother's death, she knelt down and pled to an unknown god. She instinctively sought a god for help, without any religious knowledge:

> She was ill and coughed a lot at night. At that time, even though I was young, I was horrified when I thought of my granny passing away, like where they would go, those sort of questions. I would get really scared and burst into tears and wake up in the middle of the night. . . . So, I knelt down . . . but I had no idea who I was

42. W5/F, Transcripts of Converts, 240.

43. Y, Transcripts of Converts, 271.

44. W4/F, Transcripts of Converts, 127.

worshiping, but I would plead [sobbing] and say [pause] I didn't know what to say, that kind of feeling.[45]

In summary, most of the participants found religious faith irrelevant due to the education they had received in China, which promoted atheism, evolutionism, Marxism, dialectical materialism, and historical materialism. Except for one participant who had been a Buddhist, all of the participants declared they did not believe in any religion while in China. A few participants had been exposed to Christianity without accepting it and regarding it as a religion of old people. The majority of the participants had no opportunity to have contact with Christians in China. One participant became a Buddhist in order to be blessed materially. Two participants who were strong atheists viewed religion as feudalism. They attributed their atheism to their atheistic education in China, and they rejected all religions. Because she was afraid that her grandmother might die, one participant sought help by kneeling down and pleading to an unknown god. None of the participants sought religious faith seriously for their soul before converting to Christianity in China.

## Summary

The majority of the participants noted that they had lived a simple and self-centered life without seeking the meaning of life and religious faith. Except for a few of the participants, most studied hard to be able to enter a good school and have a good future. They relied on themselves but felt insecure and exhausted due to the endless competition. Some participants became depressed, sick, or desperate due to the pressures of their studies. Also, although some participants said they lived a simple, ordinary life, it was a meaningless life without any goal. Some of the participants just obeyed the wishes of their demanding parents, so they felt powerless and did not know what to do in the future. Though they lived without a standard of life and sought success or enjoyment in life, they often recalled that they were not happy with their lives. Some participants experienced a crisis due to their parents' disputes, financial destitution, maladjustment to Korea, poor language skills, or loneliness.

Despite such difficulties in their lives, most of the participants did not seriously seek the meaning of life or religious faith. Two participants were

45. T/F, Transcripts of Converts, 180.

strong atheists who rejected religion, viewing it as feudalism, while some regarded Christianity as a religion for old people. Only one participant tried to deal with problems religiously, appealing to an unknown god for her grandmother's health. This seems to be because they had few opportunities to encounter religion, especially since the students were educated in atheistic China, which also prohibits the dissemination of religious knowledge to anyone under the age of eighteen. The few participants who had encountered Korean missionaries or who had Christian family members did not accept the Christian faith until they came to Korea. The next section presents people who invited the participants to church initially.

## People Who Invited Participants to Church

Most of the participants went to church when they were invited, except for two participants (Korean-Chinese) who voluntarily went to church by themselves. Fourteen participants were invited by Chinese students who were acquaintances, nine by Korean Christians, and one by an American missionary. The main themes for this section are given in Table 5.

Table 5. Themes Related to People Who Invited Participants to Church

| Category | Themes | Participants (n=30) |
|---|---|---|
| People Who Invited Participants to Church: Who invited the participants to go to church? | Chinese Friend | 14 |
| | Korean Christian | 9 |
| | Missionary | 3 |
| | Family | 2 |
| | No One | 2 |

## Chinese Friend

Almost one third of the participants went to church for the first time in their life because they were invited by a Chinese friend living in the same dormitory or attending the same language school in Korea. In a representative case, one participant described that although he "did not have any knowledge of any religion, including Christianity," when invited to church by a fellow dormitory student, he "just went to church with him."[46]

## Korean Christian

Nine participants went to church because of Korean Christians—a fellow student, a deacon, a deaconess, or a missionary in Korea. One participant was invited to go to a Korean service by a group of Korean Christians, but she "could not understand and slept," so she was then invited to attend a Chinese service.[47] When another participant was invited to church by Korean Christians on campus, she accepted because her family in China were already Christians. She confessed that "God arranged all of this. I did not think that the second day after I arrived in Korea, such good Christians would tell me such good things."[48]

A male participant shared his "miraculous" experience of encountering Korean Christians and bringing fellow Chinese students to the church:

> Three days after I came to Korea, a miraculous thing happened. I met a Korean Christian who shared the gospel with me and asked me to go to church. I then met some Chinese students who had come to Korea before me at the phone store, and I asked them to go to church. They accepted my suggestion, and we went to church together. So, three days after I came to Korea, I went to church with Chinese students.[49]

## Missionary

As mentioned earlier, one participant was guided to a church by a Korean missionary in China, but she did not accept the gospel in China. Another participant was invited to the home of an American classmate who was a missionary: "He first asked me to study Korean with him in his house. Then, I started to go to his house, studying and eating together. Later on, we studied the Bible together."[50]

46. W2, Transcripts of Converts, 203.
47. X/F, Transcripts of Converts, 261.
48. Z2/F, Transcripts of Converts, 291.
49. Z5, Transcripts of Converts, 326.
50. W1, Transcripts of Converts, 195.

## Family

Two participants went to church because their spouse asked them to go with them. One female participant met her husband at graduate school, and he later invited her to the Chinese service of his church. The other participant's wife, who was not a Christian, had been attending church, and "she just said to me that the atmosphere of the church is very good, so let's go to church together."[51]

## No One

One participant, whose mother was a Christian in China, voluntarily went to church after being amazed to see so many crosses on churches in Korea. He did not believe in God yet had often complained to God about his bad grades in high school.

## Summary

Most of the Chinese students went to church in response to the invitations of their Korean and Chinese friends, missionaries, and Korean Christians. This shows us the importance of personal evangelism in approaching to the Chinese students in Korea. The next section will present personal motives for going to church.

## Personal Motives for Going to Church

For the participants, their personal motives for initially going to church were Curiosity, Loneliness, Church Activity, and Personal Problems. Table 6 outlines the emergent themes for this section.

---

51. H, Transcripts of Converts, 47.

Table 6. Themes Related to Participants' Personal Motives for Going to Church

| Category | Themes | Participants (n=30) |
|---|---|---|
| Motives for Going to Church: Why did the participants initially go to church? | Curiosity | 6 |
| | Loneliness | 5 |
| | Church Activity | 4 |
| | Personal Problems | 4 |

## Curiosity

Six participants went to church out of curiosity, wanting to know what the church and Christians were like. One male participant was so curious about church that he contacted a Christian senior student through a social network.[52]

Some participants were curious about the driving force behind Christian students and the changes in their friends who became Christians. A female participant studying in a master's program wanted to know the secret of the achievements of the Christian students, so she went to church with her husband.

> One of the great reasons for me to go to church is that some Christian friends of mine made great progress in their studies. Their grades were very good. I wondered what was supporting them to make great progress and to work hard, what the reason was. Then, I came to know that it was their religion, Christianity. So, I wanted to go to church. What supported them to make so much progress, and what gave them power to work so hard?[53]

## Loneliness

Five participants went to church due to being lonely, though they were atheists and had never been to church.

52. J1, Transcripts of Converts, 56.
53. J2/F, Transcripts of Converts, 71.

A student living next door was very friendly to me and asked me to go to church with her. She told me that I could make many friends at church. Although I was atheist, I went to church because I was so lonely, without any friends at the time.[54]

No, I was not a Christian at all, and [my friends] were not either. I told them, "We came to Korea where we don't have friends, so let's go to church and have fun."[55]

## Church Activity

Four participants went to church to join a particular activity arranged by the church, such as a tour or a dinner. One participant recalled as follows:

At the time, I had just arrived around one or two months earlier, and I had not traveled anywhere much. So, they told me we could relax together, and I thought it was a good opportunity. . . . At the time, I had a very strong impression on the first day. They organized a bus to pick us up from the school, and many people greeted us enthusiastically.[56]

## Personal Problems

Four participants went to church because of problems they were struggling with. Their problems were related to finances, health, or relationships. One female participant came to Korea without telling her parents and without any financial support. Although she "did not have money" and was "very lonely," a scholarship from her Christian college required her to attend early morning prayer meetings and receive spiritual formation, through which she "gradually came to know God."[57] Another participant went to church to pray for the healing of her back which was in pain, and she was amazed when another student prayed for her, "[knowing] what I needed at that time though I did not tell her."[58]

54. J3/F, Transcripts of Converts, 78.
55. Z5, Transcripts of Converts, 326.
56. T/F, Transcripts of Converts, 182.
57. D/F, Transcripts of Converts, 35.
58. N1/F, Transcripts of Converts, 128.

## Summary

In summary, the participants went to church with various motives. Some went to church because they were curious about Christianity and the secret to the academic excellence of Christian students. Some participants attended an activity arranged by the church and were moved by the kindness of Korean Christians. Some participants went to church because of personal problems. Others voluntarily went to church, while a few followed their friends who invited them to go to church. The next section presents the first impressions that the Chinese students felt at church.

## First Impressions of Church

Participants had both positive and negative first impressions of church. The positive responses are grouped under the subthemes of Good People, Comfortable, Peace, Enthusiastic, Like Home, Receptive Attitude, Moved by Hymns, and Good Sermons. The negative ones are grouped under the subthemes of Abnormal, Experiencing Conflict, Suspicious, Resistant, and Trying Not to Be Brainwashed. The main themes for this section are illustrated in Table 7, and the subordinate themes are discussed below.

Table 7. Themes Related to Participants' First Impressions of Church

| Category | Themes and Subthemes | Participants* (n=30) |
|---|---|---|
| First Impressions of Church: What were the participants' first impressions of church? | Positive Impressions | 23 |
| | *Good People* | 15 |
| | *Comfortable* | 2 |
| | *Peace* | 1 |
| | *Enthusiastic* | 3 |
| | *Like Home* | 4 |
| | *Receptive* | 1 |
| | *Moved by Hymns* | 4 |
| | Good Sermons | 1 |
| | Negative Impressions | 7 |
| | *Abnormal* | 3 |
| | *Experiencing Conflict* | 1 |
| | *Suspicious* | 1 |
| | *Resistant* | 1 |
| | *Trying Not to Be Brainwashed* | 1 |

* Some participants reported multiple subthemes.

## Positive Impressions

### Good People

Half of the participants noted that the people of the church were good and kind, so they felt at home and wanted to keep on attending and join the church. Some participants attending Korean churches mentioned that the Korean Christians were kind to them, even though they were foreigners and could not speak Chinese. The participants appreciated the help of the church members.

## Comfortable

A female participant felt comfortable and happy because the church members treated her kindly.

> They are really good. They have no bad motives. They are really good to you. When I first went to church, they did not necessarily treat me very well, but they all treated me well. I felt so comfortable. I felt so comfortable being with them. I felt that I was very happy to go to church. Going to church is enjoyable, comfortable.[59]

## Peace

When one male participant first went to church, he felt "very pleased" and "a kind of peace" in his mind, noting that he had "never experienced such an atmosphere before."[60]

## Enthusiastic

Some participants were very moved to see the enthusiasm of the church members. One participant noted that no one treated her as the Christians did in her home country. Another participant felt that the people of the church were enthusiastic and sincere "because they have Christian faith."[61]

## Like Home

Some participants noted that the church was like home, and the church members like family. One participant mentioned that church was like home when living abroad. What they especially pointed out were the members' helpfulness, loving attitudes and hearts, and kindness.

> The people of the church were very good to me and kind. They are like brothers and sisters and fathers, mothers, grandfathers, and grandmothers. Since I was living abroad, I felt the church was a very kind place and environment.[62]

59. Y, Transcripts of Converts, 273.
60. J1, Transcripts of Converts, 57.
61. C3/F, Transcripts of Converts, 28.
62. Z1, Transcripts of Converts, 284.

When I went to church a couple of times, I found that the people from church were different from other people. They seemed to be like a family. I could see the love in their attitudes and hearts. This attracted me very much indeed, the love between brothers and sisters![63]

## Receptive

One female participant recalled having asked the Christians at her church many "absurd questions" from her atheistic perspective yet felt they had been receptive.

When I first came to church, nobody ridiculed us though we asked many absurd questions, such as, how Jesus was resurrected after his heart stopped and "How do you know the existence of God? Show me the evidence!" [*laughs*] But nobody laughed at us! They understood us very well indeed, because they are all Chinese. The people at the Chinese church could understand other Chinese people very well, because we all have the same background of atheism. So, I was very much comforted by that fact.[64]

## Moved by Hymns

A female participant could feel the divinity when she was singing during the worship service, so she started to believe without reservation. Three participants described their special experience of listening to hymns as "being moved by the Holy Spirit." As a result, they kept on attending the church. For instance, one participant was so happy to hear hymns being sung at her first time at church, even though she did not know God. She went to church every Sunday since then, claiming, "What attracts me most are the hymns."[65]

63. Z3/F, Transcripts of Converts, 303.
64. W4/4, Transcripts of Converts, 233.
65. W2, Transcripts of Converts, 203.

*Good Sermons*

Some of the participants recalled that the content of the sermons was useful because it included moral principles. One participant, who had a positive first impression of Christianity on account of sermons, remembers how the sermons were "kind of theological" and "had no bad content," because they taught "how to love others, to be a good person, to treat others well."[66]

Negative Impressions

Seven participants had a negative impression when they initially attended church. The subthemes of Negative Impression are Abnormal, Conflict, Suspicious, Resistant, and Trying Not to Be Brainwashed.

*Abnormal*

Some participants received strong, negative impressions from Christians during prayer meetings or services. For instance, one participant described that at his first time at church, he thought that Christians were "crazy" and "very strange" for crying when praying and "abnormal" for the way they worshipped.[67] Another participant shared the sentiment of the abnormality of Christians, but in a different way:

> I especially rejected Jesus Christ. I felt that [Christians] are not normal because many people asked me to believe in Jesus, sometimes they were even holding me, saying, "If you believe in Jesus, you could go to heaven, if not, you will go to hell." I felt extremely disgusted and rejected this idea, asking, "What is this? I can live a happy life if I try to do my best."[68]

*Experiencing Conflict*

One participant who was attending a Buddhist university was heavily exposed to Buddhist culture on campus and had taken a mandatory class on Buddhism. He felt conflicted about attending church for the first time.

66. Q, Transcripts of Converts, 158.
67. C1, Transcripts of Converts, 3.
68. W4/F, Transcripts of Converts, 226.

While taking a Bible class taught by church staff, he asked himself "whether this is good or bad."[69]

## Suspicious

One female participant's initial reaction on the subject of God was suspicion. She remembers that when the pastor spoke of God, she "felt very strange" and "suspicious," but when he preached on the ethical principles of living, she "felt that they were right."[70]

## Resistant

One participant was strongly affected by her relatives warning her about the prevalence of cults in Korea, as shown on the news, so she had a "rejecting heart" at first, and "did not want to accept the faith".[71]

## Trying Not to Be Brainwashed

One participant actively tried "not to be brainwashed" by the "crazy" Christians at church, but later confessed that, although she was not interested in faith, she "just started to believe," which was "miraculous" to her.[72]

## Summary

In summary, most participants had positive impressions of church when they first attended, and these first impressions attracted them to continue attending church. These participants felt that the Christians of the church were kind and good people who were helpful and caring. Also, they felt comfortable and at peace, even though it was their first time attending church. The enthusiasm of the Korean church members towards foreigners and fellow Chinese Christians was one of the major factors that moved the participants and attracted them to church. Some of the participants felt that church was like home abroad due to the receptive attitude of love and kindness of the church

69. H, Transcripts of Converts, 48.
70. Y, Transcripts of Converts, 274.
71. X4/F, Transcripts of Converts, 312.
72. P, Transcripts of Converts, 148.

members, regardless of their ethnicity. Many participants were also moved by the hymns—they could feel the presence of the Holy Spirit. In addition, some participants enjoyed the sermons for the ethical teachings, although they did not recognize the spiritual truths behind them.

The analysis of the data shows the importance of the efforts of Christians who serve international students with Christian love, kindness, and enthusiasm. When Christians serve international students who have few friend and resources, they attract these students to their church. Also, the work of the Holy Spirit was evident among the participants attending the church services, especially during the singing of hymns. Only a few participants mentioned sermons when asked about their first impressions or initial feelings at church. Though the participants were at the age of intellectual activeness, most of them shared that their initial positive feelings about the church were related to non-intellectual factors.

The participants' negative impressions of their initial visit to a church can be categorized into four types: criticism based on prejudice, preconceived atheistic ideas, influence of another religion, and caution of cults.

Firstly, one participant was critical of the manner of prayer and worship, describing the Christians she met as "abnormal" and "crazy." Secondly, several participants evaluated their church experiences with their beliefs and values, such as self-reliance and atheism. Thirdly, one participant experienced internal conflict at church because of Buddhist influences at his university. Lastly, one participant was concerned about cults in Korea and could not differentiate Christian churches from such cults.

The next section will present obstacles to conversion that hindered the participants from converting to Christianity in Korea.

## Obstacles to Conversion

This section contains the data analysis pertaining to the question, "What was the obstacle to your conversion?" The researcher identified ten themes: Atheism, Objections from Others, Strong Self, Bad Christians, Buddhism, Perspective on Sin, Views on Values, Cult-like, Image of God as Father, and God's Punishment. The main themes for this section are outlined in Table 8.

Table 8. Themes Related to Obstacles to Conversion

| Category | Themes | Participants*<br>(n=30) |
|---|---|---|
| Obstacles to Conversion: What were the participants' obstacles to conversion? | Atheism | 13 |
| | Objections from Others | 6 |
| | Strong Self | 4 |
| | Bad Christians | 3 |
| | Buddhism | 2 |
| | Perspective on Sin | 1 |
| | Views on Values | 1 |
| | Cult-like | 1 |
| | Image of God as Father | 2 |
| | God's Punishment | 1 |

* Some participants reported multiple themes.

## Atheism

Thirteen participants recognized that the atheistic education and Communism they had learned in China deeply affected their perspectives on God and religion. As one participant commented, "the biggest obstacle blocking my faith in God was the existence of God."[73]

Indeed, atheistic education hindered some participants from believing in the existence of God and the Christian faith. They also regarded atheistic ideology, especially evolutionism and materialism, as "scientific knowledge." For instance, one participant who "did not believe in Creation" when first attending church stated that at the time, "if you tried to persuade me to totally reject evolutionism, it would not have been easy for you because it was a solid thought."[74]

Likewise, one female participant intensely believed in Communism as her faith, denying other religions:

73. C2/F, Transcripts of Converts, 15.
74. Q, Transcripts of Converts, 162.

In 2013, I had a Korean boyfriend. Everyone of his family were Christians. They were continuously praying for me and asking me to go to church, but I did not go to church. I believed in Communism. I believed that everyone should work hard. Why should I believe in religion? I could not believe in the religion of feudalism. And so, I very strongly rejected it.[75]

## Objections from Others

Several participants were burdened about disclosing their new, Christian faith to their parents. One participant felt pressure from his mother, for she had just divorced and wanted him to listen to her. He said, "If she did not want something, then I did not want it, either. I try to do my best to follow her. So, I did not disclose my faith."[76]

Some participants even experienced objections against their Christian faith from their friends. For instance, when one participant decided to be baptized with other students, some of the students who went to the same American missionary's house for Bible study and worship "urged [him] not to be baptized."[77]

## Strong Self

For some of the participants, a strong self or ego prevented them from coming to faith. For one female participant, the most difficult obstacle in deciding to believe in God was the idea of receiving help from others. She believed that "only weak people believe in God," and stated, "My wanting to have religious faith, then, was equal to confessing that I am weak."[78]

Strong self also worked in terms of wanting to hold on to lifestyle choices. For example, one participant thought that becoming a Christian would restrict him and his life. He believed that in order to be a Christian, he "needed to change many things" in his life, but he "did not want to change

75. W5/F, Transcripts of Converts, 243.

76. L3, Transcripts of Converts, 121.

77. W1, Transcripts of Converts, 198.

78. K/F, Transcripts of Converts, 87.

those things."[79] Another participant did not want to give up a sexual relationship but was aware that "this was a kind of obstacle for me."[80]

## Bad Christians

Some participants were dismayed by the attitude of some Christians, so they initially rejected becoming Christians. One participant had taught Chinese to Korean children before in China and had received a negative impression of the parents' attitudes, concluding that, "if Christians are like this, then I can do much better than Christianity."[81] A female participant "was disgusted" that someone who had previously been hurtful invited her to attend church, and this hurt caused her to initially reject God.[82]

## Buddhism

Two participants confessed that their Buddhist background were preexisting obstacles towards conversion. One participant recalled that "it was not easy" to make the decision to accept the Christian faith.[83] Another described feeling "a kind of clash" when undergoing Bible study.[84]

## Perspective on Sin

The Chinese concept of sin, which differs from the Christian concept, became an obstacle for one female participant. According to her, Chinese people and culture understand sin as a transgression of governmental law. As a result, she could not easily accept the "unusual" Christian view of sin: "I did not break the law, so why are you telling me I am a sinner?"[85]

79. J1, Transcripts of Converts, 60.

80. C2/F, Transcripts of Converts, 13.

81. D/F, Transcripts of Converts, 39.

82. W4/F, Transcripts of Converts, 227.

83. H, Transcripts of Converts, 48.

84. L2/F, Transcripts of Converts, 108.

85. D/F, Transcripts of Converts, 40.

## Views on Values

For one female participant, materialism became an obstacle. She grew up observing people measure their potential marriage partner's financial ability, which affected her values. As a result, she "only recognized the worldly philosophy of value" and knew that "this philosophy of value contradicts with the philosophy of the Bible."[86]

## Cult-like

Some participants mentioned that their wariness of cults was an obstacle that kept them from attending church. A female participant recalled that after arriving in Korea, her teachers warned against attending church, for there might be "heretics who will shut you in a small dark room and brainwash you and never let you out."[87]

## Image of God as Father

The image of God as Father also became an obstacle for certain participants, due to their perception and experiences of their biological fathers. One participant viewed God as strict, since he was "afraid" of his own father and thought that God would be like his father. He shared, "For a long time, and still now, that kind of thinking still remains."[88]

One female participant felt that it was difficult for her to understand God as Father, because she did not receive love and support from her father and had to work hard and be independent from a young age.

> From when I was young, I did not rely on other people. So, I was easily wrapped up in myself. It was not easy to make a decision to rely on other people, so it was not easy for me to make a decision to believe in Jesus. . . . I did not get love from my father, but pastors said that I just needed to regard God as my father. But I could not understand that. After I believed in God, I prayed, "God, you just need to accompany me. That's all I need from you. I can do other things by myself. You do not need to do anything. You just accompany me. That's it. I can manage by myself. I am

86. D/F, Transcripts of Converts, 40.
87. P/F, Transcripts of Converts, 147.
88. J1, Transcripts of Converts, 61.

used to managing by myself." So, it was very hard for me to surrender to God and to say that I do not do everything.[89]

## God's Punishment

For one participant, God's punishment on individuals and nations was an obstacle. He said, "Before, I thought that the punishment of God was too heavy."[90]

## Summary

In summary, twenty-three of the thirty participants shared ten different kinds of obstacles in their conversion to Christianity. The most prominent obstacle was closely related to their atheistic education before coming to Korea. Some obstacles were related to their perception of God, sin, and personal values, while others concerned their character and their former religious faith. The next section will present the ways in which participants overcame the above-mentioned obstacles.

## How Participants Overcame Their Obstacles

Based on an analysis of responses to the question, "How did you overcome the obstacle(s) to conversion?" the key emergent themes are: The Word of God, Prayer, Other Christians' Witness, Reasoning, Determination, Baptism, Mystical Experience, and Watching Films. Table 9 outlines the key themes and their subthemes.

89. X/F, Transcripts of Converts, 261.
90. N2, Transcripts of Converts, 141.

Table 9. Themes Related to Overcoming Obstacles to Conversion

| Category | Themes and Subthemes | Participants* (n=30) |
|---|---|---|
| Overcoming the Obstacles: How did the participants over-come the obstacles to conversion? | The Word of God | 7 |
| | *Studying the Bible* | 4 |
| | *Listening to Sermons* | 3 |
| | Prayer | 7 |
| | *Enlightenment through Prayer* | 2 |
| | *Answers to Prayer* | 1 |
| | *Praying during Retreats* | 3 |
| | *Overcoming Suspicion through Prayer* | 1 |
| | Other Christians' Witness | 5 |
| | *Listening to Christian's Witness* | 3 |
| | *Mature Christians* | 1 |
| | *Experiencing Enlightenment* | 1 |
| | Reasoning | 2 |
| | Determination | 2 |
| | Baptism | 1 |
| | Mystical Experience | 1 |
| | Watching Films | 1 |

* Some participants mentioned multiple (sub)themes.

# The Word of God

Some participants solved their obstacles through the Word of God. That is, they were able to understand their problems and find answers by studying the Bible or listening to sermons.

## *Studying the Bible*

Some participants, who rejected and were suspicious of biblical teachings due to their atheistic education in China, came to accept the Christian faith as they studied the Bible. Through Bible study, "suspicion was weakened," evolutionist views were "changed," and these participants were gradually led to accept the Bible.[91]

One such participant shared her representative experience:

> Yes, I learned about Darwinism and evolutionism at school in China, and because of this, sometimes, I was blind. When I was told in Korea that God created the world and humans, I thought that God created the ape and then the ape evolved into human beings. At that time, I had many questions, but now I think the Bible can tell me the answers. . . . I came to know that only God can tell us what is right or wrong. Only Jesus can lead my life to the right way. Now I can say I believe in the Bible.[92]

## *Listening to Sermons*

Although one participant had received a negative first impression of Christianity, she was moved by the Holy Spirit while listening to a sermon during a retreat. She was moved to the point of tears, not because of anything specific that she could remember, but because "it was so touching," and she "felt so full of the Holy Spirit."[93]

Another participant gained a new understanding of Christianity and Marxism through a sermon:

> At the initial stage of my going to church, I thought that the Chinese educational system did not believe in the existence of God, and I was affected by such education and thinking. Later on, through a sermon, I found that many of the greatest scientists were Christians, for example, Newton. Chinese Marxism also applied Christianity to its ideas. I felt like hearing all of these things was not a coincidence but the will of God. So, I believed in God.[94]

---

91. L2/F, Transcripts of Converts, 108; Q, Transcripts of Converts, 161

92. Z2/F, Transcripts of Converts, 293.

93. Z4/F, Transcripts of Converts, 312.

94. Z5, Transcripts of Converts, 326.

## Prayer

Some participants overcame their obstacles to the Christian faith through prayer. Prayer led them to gain enlightenment, receive answers, experience revivalism, and overcome suspicion.

### Enlightenment through Prayer

One participant was able to overcome a personal crisis through prayer and quiet time. During this time of difficulty, "help from others was useless," and she "tried to find an answer from God." The more she came to understand herself, the more she came to understand God and vice versa. She summarily shared a maxim, "the dead end of people is the starting point of God."[95]

Another participant, who wanted to stop attending church because she was hurt and dismayed by other Christians, heard the voice of God saying, "They are also humans, so you should not watch them, but me." Out of a desire "to follow him," she responded, "Then, I will stay at church and look upon You," and she gradually changed as she "wanted to know more of Christ Jesus through worship, sermons, and serving the church with other brothers and sisters."[96]

### Answers to Prayer

One participant experienced God answering her prayers about her Korean speaking exam. She was feeling nervous and was "trembling" just before her exam, so she asked her classmate, a Japanese pastor, to pray for her nervousness. After his prayer, she was able to smile and talk comfortably with the examiner, who noticed and commented on her increased confidence. She recalled, "I was very surprised by my state of mind. Then, after coming out of the room, I said, 'Thank You, Lord! You truly exist.' Since then, I feel that the Lord has been with me."[97]

---

95. L2/F, Transcripts of Converts, 107.
96. W4/F, Transcripts of Converts, 229.
97. W5/F, Transcripts of Converts, 247.

## Praying during Retreats

One church-attending participant was refraining from a serious commitment in faith because he did not want to be restricted by Christianity. After the service of a CHISTA retreat, he was asked to kneel before the altar to pray for forgiveness of sins. At the time, he did not want to pray, because he did not want to tell God of his wrongdoings or change his lifestyle. Eventually, he chose to pray: "I prayed, prayed, prayed, and cried out with tears. At that time, I could feel that God exists."[98]

Another participant, who did not believe in God, had a similar experience at a retreat.

> I didn't know how to pray. I just closed my eyes and felt very much released, very released. I had never shed tears in front of other people in my life. I seldom cried because my character is very strong. When I was praying, I shed a lot of tears, and I kept on shedding tears. I was amazed and started to have some understanding of God.[99]

## Overcoming Suspicion through Prayer

One participant overcame her suspicion of God through prayer. Whenever she felt suspicious, she "prayed and prayed, every time" until her suspicion "was gradually weakened."[100]

## Other Christians' Witness

### Listening to Other Christians' Witness

Some participants were able to overcome their obstacles to the Christian faith through the testimonies of Christians. They had confidence in that person's faith while listening to the witness and saw a good example of a mature Christian. One participant said, "Through people's testimonies and God's guidance, I came to believe in the existence of God. . . . My faith itself is the work of God. Otherwise, it would have been impossible for me

---

98. W2, Transcripts of Converts, 204.

99. Y, Transcripts of Converts, 273.

100. Z2/F, Transcripts of Converts, 294.

to believe in God."[101] Another participant shared, "I started experiencing the mighty power of God as I thought of other people's testimonies, for example, how other people faced death, the power of their prayer. . . . I felt that God really has great power."[102]

## Mature Christians

One male participant considered a Christian friend to be "a good role model" for dating. The mature Christian strictly avoided premarital sex and protected himself from temptation in different situations. The participant, who did not want to commit sexual immorality, saw this Christian's avoidance of sin as a "blessing from God."[103]

## Experiencing Enlightenment

One participant experienced enlightenment when a mature Christian exhorted him not to be bound by the world.

> There was a turning point in my experience of attending church. . . . I liked a sister at that time. I pursued her and could not see anything else but her at church. . . . I felt that she was the best in the world. And then, a leader of my small group knew my situation, and we talked about the problem of faith together. He explained about the bondage of worldly things. When I was listening to what he said, I felt some light enter my heart. Suddenly, my feelings toward the sister disappeared from my heart, and my mind became clear. . . . Before, I had doubted the existence of God. God did not exist. God was made by man. Now, I strongly believe in God. . . . The target of my life is God, and God is shining upon me.[104]

## Reasoning

Some participants solved their obstacles through reasoning. While an atheist, one participant reasoned "that there were many things in this

101. P, Transcripts of Converts, 150.
102. T/F, Transcripts of Converts, 177.
103. J1, Transcripts of Converts, 60.
104. C1, Transcripts of Converts, 3.

world that man cannot understand" and sought God.[105] Another participant, who struggled between the Bible and her atheistic education, persisted in finding the truth and eventually arrived at the conclusion that some scientists "were absurd and insincere" for supporting what they knew "was not the truth."[106]

Reasoning also came from personal backgrounds. One participant of a Buddhist background noticed that "the appearances of the statues of the Buddha in different countries are different," and that Buddha could be "fat, skinny, tall, short, standing, or lying," depending on the "culture and customs of the people of the region." Finally, she "realized that Jesus is the same in any part of the world—the cross."[107] Another participant studying biology had difficulty understanding the punishment of God in the Old Testament, but he overcame this with reasoning based on knowledge of his discipline:

> In the Bible, if some people worshipped an idol, it easily affected other people, so it must be destroyed at the roots. If a cell has a problem in a body, it can affect the whole body. So, it should be rooted out, such as a cancerous cell. The biological understanding inspired me to think this way.[108]

## Determination

One participant worried about telling his family and friends about his new Christian faith: "They would think I was just like a person from another world." However, he became determined to tell them, and just as he had expected, they did not believe him when he announced his conversion.[109]

## Baptism

One participant started to have a great deal of zeal after being baptized. He explained that before, "My faith was not solid. . . . I skipped church without any regret." Baptism became a turning point in his faith, after

105. C1, Transcripts of Converts, 7.

106. Z2/F, Transcripts of Converts, 293.

107. C3/F, Transcripts of Converts, 29.

108. N2, Transcripts of Converts, 140.

109. Y, Transcripts of Converts, 276.

which he "started to read the Bible" and anticipated worship as fellowship with God.[110]

## Mystical Experience

One participant who was a former Buddhist was able to overcome unbelief due to a mystical experience. When approached with the gospel from a short-term mission team, she did not want to accept Jesus Christ as asked. She recalls, however, that at that moment, "a little voice whispered to my heart: 'You will not have any other method or way to save yourself except through me.'"[111] This experience helped her to overcome her struggle and believe in Christ.

## Watching Films

One participant came to know Christ clearly by watching the film, *The Passion of the Christ* and decided to believe in Jesus even though she had some unresolved tension against believing. She said, "After watching it, I felt more driven to make the decision. . . . Before, I only knew that he died for us, but I had no idea of the whole story."[112]

## Summary

In summary, the participants were able to overcome their obstacles to Christian faith through eight different kinds of means that have been categorized as subthemes: The Word of God, Prayer, Other Christians' Witness, Reasoning, Determination, Baptism, Mystical Experience, and Watching Films. The most frequently occurring categories were the Word of God (seven), Prayer (seven), and Other Christians' Witness (five). When participants were moved by the Word of God when reading the Bible or listening to its proclamation, they were able to overcome the obstacles that had kept them from accepting the Christian faith. Praying was the means of experiencing God's power, love, and grace over difficulties which could not be solved alone. Through prayer, participants experienced answering of prayer, discovered the will of

110. Y, Transcripts of Converts, 275.

111. C2/F, Transcripts of Converts, 19.

112. Z4/F, Transcripts of Converts, 314.

God, and encountered revivalism. The next section presents the reason why the participants decide to believe in God.

## Why the Participants Decided to Believe in God

The participants decided to believe in Jesus Christ due to various reasons, categorized into the following subthemes: The Existence of God, Intellectual Deliberation, To Become a New Person, the Love of Christians, the Sacrificial Love of God, Experiencing God's Help, the Word of God, Inner Healing, Forgiveness of Sin, the Holy Spirit, Having Hope, and To Be Like Jesus. The emergent themes for this section are illustrated in Table 10.

Table 10. Themes Related to Participants' Reasons for Believing in God

| Category | Themes | Participants* (n=30) |
|---|---|---|
| Reasons for Believing in God: Why did the participants decide to believe in God? | The Existence of God | 4 |
| | Intellectual Deliberation | 3 |
| | To Become a New Person | 5 |
| | The Love of Christians | 3 |
| | The Sacrificial Love of God | 3 |
| | Experiencing God's Help | 7 |
| | The Word of God | 1 |
| | Inner Healing | 1 |
| | Forgiveness of Sin | 2 |
| | The Holy Spirit | 1 |
| | Having Hope | 1 |
| | To Be Like Jesus | 1 |

* Some participants mentioned multiple themes.

CONVERSION OF CHINESE STUDENTS IN KOREA

## The Existence of God

The existence of God was a "major reason" or "the most important thing" for several participants who grew up with an atheistic education.[113] As the cognitive framework of Christianity is strongly different from the atheistic education system of the participants, some of the participants were able to believe in God when their previously held viewpoints or orientations of atheism changed.[114] Belief in God's existence opened up a clear path towards Christianity, as one participant aptly explained: "Since He exists, and He is God, then I have to believe in him."[115]

Moreover, the participants' response and commitment to their belief in God played an important role, as shown in the following:

> In the beginning, it was very difficult to believe. Later on, we studied the Bible for almost one year in [a pastor's] house. During the studies, I discussed things with him, and I felt the existence of God. . . . He asked us to be baptized. Although I did not know much about Christianity, I said that I wanted to be baptized.[116]

> Yes, God has existed all along, but why didn't I believe? I had been relying on myself. But later on, I stopped relying on myself anymore. I told God, "I'll give everything to you. You bore my cross, so I'll give you my entire burden." As a result, everything worked out much more beautifully than when I had done things all by myself, in terms of what I gained or how I matured. . . . I felt like I had done nothing except simply saying, "I thank you God," "I praise God," or "I love God a lot." I knew God was right by my side.[117]

The intellectual factor (knowing the existence of God) was also deeply related with the experiential factor in the process of conversion. Several participants came to believe in God's existence through their personal experiences. For example, P had been a strong atheist who needed an A+ to receive a scholarship. However, when her professor refused to change her grade from an A, she "prayed hard to God," and when her score was later changed to an A+, she believed in God's existence.[118]

---

113. Z5, Transcripts of Converts, 327; P, Transcripts of Converts, 150.

114. Rambo, *Understanding Religious Conversion*, 61.

115. P, Transcripts of Converts, 150.

116. W1, Transcripts of Converts, 195.

117. W5/F, Transcripts of Converts, 250.

118. P, Transcripts of Converts, 132.

## Intellectual Deliberation

Some participants were able to decide to believe in God as the result of their reasoning. A typical case was with one participant studying biotechnology, who perceived that the "sincerity" and their "love of Jesus" matched the tenet of Christian faith, love. Moreover, his background in biology showed him "that Darwinism and evolutionism is not enough. . . . One simple cell cannot develop into a complex one."[119] Another participant insisted that people should believe in God "because there are so many witnesses."[120]

A female participant decided to believe in Jesus when she discovered the limitedness of herself and other human beings. She articulated this as follows:

> For example, when my feelings got hurt, and when I saw so many negative things in society, and when I thought about someone who was very rich but was lying in a hospital bed, I knew that people are the same: weak. When I thought about this, I decided that I must believe in Jesus with my heart. . . . The greatest reason for me to become a Christian . . . was because I found that I was very limited. The greatest person in the world is also limited, so they cannot save themselves. I am also very limited, so I definitely cannot save myself. I also came to know that people have ugliness in their hearts and minds. People cannot save themselves from their sins.[121]

## To Become a New Person

Some participants decided to believe in Jesus with the hope of becoming a new person, which could also mean living a new life. When one participant first heard the gospel, she considered herself as the "prodigal son," hoped to "start a new life," "be a better person," and that "life would never be the same."[122] A female participant, who had enjoyed reading books about good sense and wanted to be a better person from a young age, initially believed in Christ because she "was hoping he could make me a better person on earth."[123] Likewise, another participant decided to

119. N2, Transcripts of Converts, 138.
120. S, Transcripts of Converts, 173.
121. L2/F, Transcripts of Converts, 209.
122. C2/F, Transcripts of Converts, 17.
123. T/F, Transcripts of Converts, 186.

believe in God because he firmly believed and appreciated that "God can make you a much better person through his guidance . . . [and] can guide your life to make you a whole person."[124]

Some participants decided to become Christians because God had changed their lives. One participant came to believe in God after recognizing that God made her "not need to think too much" about her life anymore, claiming that, "I can be secure and have hope. I do not have to be afraid of death and failure. I felt that such a great God would help me. Before, I was alone, very tired."[125]

Others believed in God to obtain a clear direction in life that would lead to a better life. One such participant stated his main reason for believing: "God could lead all my life, in everything. God could care for and protect me. If I believed in God, I would be blessed."[126] Another participant saw the need for the guidance of "the Spirit of God," saying, "My life needs to have a very clear guide. . . . God can lead my life in the right way and help me learn the truth."[127]

## The Love of Christians

Several participants became Christians through the love of other Christians. One participant decided to become a Christian because unlike with Buddhism, "you can experience love when you are among Christians and have fellowship," and "when you experience the love of God, then you can practice love for other people."[128]

The love of Christians was a strong factor when the participants received help and care at their time of need. Although one participant did not want to believe in Christianity, he felt the great love of Christians at a church when they paid attention to him and gave him "a great deal of help."[129] Another participant became a Christian when he was stressed and lonely as a student studying abroad. He recalls:

124. Z, Transcripts of Converts, 287.

125. Y, Transcripts of Converts, 278.

126. S, Transcripts of Converts, 172.

127. Z2/F, Transcripts of Converts, 296.

128. Q, Transcripts of Converts, 163.

129. L1, Transcripts of Converts, 98.

Then, the missionary and friends from the church were so kind to me, which made me think that someone was caring about me. At that time, I felt that someone loved me, which made me feel very secure. Being alone, I was so lonesome, but since I have known God, I don't feel lonesome anymore but secure.[130]

## The Sacrificial Love of God

Some participants were amazed by the sacrificial love of Jesus in saving the people of the world. As one participant responded, "I believed in Jesus because of my gratitude, with a heart of gratitude . . . for the love that Jesus gave to us."[131] The understanding of sacrificial love was necessarily deepened through Bible study:

> The greatness of love! My analysis with reason and study of the Bible helped me to understand the plan of God's salvation and to believe in God. This kind of love is not like the love of parents. I mean, parents give what the child asks. Also, when you do good things, they praise you and reward you, but the love of Jesus is unconditional. Jesus loves you whether you do good things or not. Jesus first loves you. Love is a prerequisite condition. He is already devoted to you, regardless of who you are. To go up on the cross for those who cursed and hit him is not such a simple thing.[132]

## Experiencing God's Help

For several participants, experiencing God's help was the main reason for believing in God. Help came in many forms, and for one participant, God's help was not only "relief to the spirit and mind," as Chinese people generally consider to be the merit of religion, but also "relief in life."

> I felt that the Christian faith can help me and relieve my mind. If I get into trouble, have problems, I can rely on it. So, I decided to believe. We need to rely on God not only for the spirit and mind, but also for our material needs and the reality of life. Yes, I experienced help in real life. As I told you, when I entered graduate school, I

130. W, Transcripts of Converts, 199.
131. J2/F, Transcripts of Converts, 71.
132. N2, Transcripts of Converts, 142.

experienced help from God. When we commit sins against God, Jesus forgives our sins. Also, when I have problems, he can help me. So, I want to share the gospel with others.[133]

One participant gradually became a Christian as he experienced the love and help of God over time.

I was not like others. People, in general, raise their hands and pray that they will follow Jesus in their life. I was not like that, but gradually, gradually, little by little, I felt that, amazingly, the Lord led my life. I felt that the Lord helped me a lot and loved me a lot. So, I did not say, "I must decide to believe in God."[134]

## The Word of God

One female participant believed in God, because she perceived an invisible truth about the Word of God:

As I read the Bible and listened to sermons and lectures, the Bible was consistent with history, though we could not see it with our own eyes. Also, when I read Proverbs, I recognized that those words cannot be from any man. Surely, they are from God. Though I cannot see the truth, I believe it.[135]

## Inner Healing

One participant believed in God when she experienced the inner healing. Although she had been closed towards God, she still went on a short-term mission trip to Indonesia, where discussions with other Christians revealed to her certain "problems" that she bore in her heart. She shared how watching the mission team's performance for children led her to believe in God:

In Indonesia, we created a play with a theme taken from the Bible. The story strongly stirred me. A boy did an acrobatic performance in which the performer, dressed in a costume, walked and danced on stilts. And he fell down, so he cried. Then, the stilts were stolen. When he was crying, Jesus came to him, saying that he is precious,

133. L1, Transcripts of Converts, 100.
134. J1, Transcripts of Converts, 58.
135. W3/F, Transcripts of Converts, 216.

whoever he is, whether he has something or not. He is so precious to Jesus forever. My parents have never told me that I was precious to them. At that time, suddenly, I felt that from the beginning, I have been precious.[136]

## Forgiveness of Sin

Participants also became Christian because of the forgiveness of sins. One participant stated, "I did many bad things before, but he made me free from what bound me."[137]

## The Holy Spirit

One participant decided to believe in God because of the moving of the Holy Spirit. She recalls: "The Holy Spirit moved in my heart. It was not something of the world that moved me, because I decided by myself from my heart."[138]

## Having Hope

One participant was comforted by other Christians when nobody else did, leading him to become a Christian because he "felt that Jesus could give me hope."[139]

## To Be Like Jesus

One participant wanted to follow Jesus and get closer to him, regarding him as both his role model and goal.

> At that time, I thought that Jesus was the controller of my life. I followed the road that he planned for me. Because I did not know the way of life that he had arranged for me, I kept on trying my best to suppress my desire until I reached the state where "I did not have any desire" [*wu yu wu qiu*, an idea in Taoism and Buddhism],

136. X/F, Transcripts of Converts, 262–63.
137. Z3/F, Transcripts of Converts, 305.
138. Z2/F, Transcripts of Converts, 296.
139. L3, Transcripts of Converts, 123.

so that I might get closer to Jesus. As for me, Jesus is the goal in my heart and my role model because he did what we, all the people of the world, could not do. For example, love your enemy and love strangers. Because of this, he especially impressed me. I really wanted to get closer to him and to be like him.[140]

## Summary

In summary, the participants were able to decide to believe in Jesus Christ for reasons categorized as the following subthemes: The Existence of God, Intellectual Deliberation, To Become a New Person, the Love of Christians, The Sacrificial Love of God, Experiencing God's Help, the Word of God, Inner Healing, Forgiveness of Sin, the Holy Spirit, Having Hope, and To Be Like Jesus.

All the participants came from atheistic educational and social backgrounds, but only four participants were motivated to believe in Jesus due to the fact of the existence of God. Four participants decided to believe in Jesus Christ because they intellectually analyzed and deliberated on Christianity and the limitations of evolutionism and human beings. Five participants wanted to believe in Jesus because they wanted to be a new person by changing their life, being a better person, and having direction in life. Through their encounters with other Christians, they found that only Jesus could satisfy their needs in these areas.

Several participants were able to open their hearts to the Christian faith when they received the love of other Christians. As students studying abroad, without family and sometimes in stressful situations, their hearts were touched when Christians cared for them, and this led them to decide to believe in Jesus. Some participants decided to believe in Jesus when they knew the sacrificial love of Jesus on the cross, a love which they described as unconditional, unimaginable, indescribable, and incomparable in the world. Others decided to believe in Jesus when they experienced the grace of God helping their needs in life. They confessed that through Christianity, they could get what they desired, such as love, comfort, encouragement, and financial help. As God satisfied their needs, they became more open to the gospel and believing in God.

One participant discovered the consistency and excellence of the Bible and then decided to believe in Jesus. Another participant decided to believe

140. H, Transcripts of Converts, 50.

in Jesus when she experienced inner healing while watching a performance of the gospel during a short-term mission trip abroad. One participant decided to be a Christian when he was freed from the bondage of sin. As such, the core content of the gospel, such as the sacrificial love of Jesus on the cross, the forgiveness of sins, and the power of the gospel, can set people free from the bondage of sin and should be the priority of a ministry towards any group of people, even intellectuals.

The direct moving of the Holy Spirit was also the stated reason for one participant. One participant found hope in the Christian faith when he was desperate, so he wanted to keep on attending church and accepted the new faith. Another participant found a role model for his life in Jesus, so he decided to believe in Jesus to be like him. The next section will present influential people in the process of conversion.

## Influential People

Those who influenced the conversion of the participants were the pastors, deacons, and brothers and sisters of their churches, as well as the Korean Christians they met at retreats. A total of fifty-three references concerning these influential people were categorized into four themes: the Servant Attitude of Christians, the Role Model of Christians, the Love of Church Members, and the Love of Pastors. These emergent themes related to influential persons in conversion are displayed in Table 11.

Table 11. Themes Related to Influential People

| Category | Themes | Participants (n=30) |
|---|---|---|
| Influential People: Who was the most influential in the participants' conversion? | The Servant Attitude of Christians | 8 |
| | The Role Model of Christians | 8 |
| | The Love of Church Members | 8 |
| | The Love of Pastors | 6 |

## The Servant Attitude of Christians

Nearly one third of the participants mentioned that they decided to believe in Jesus because they were moved by the Christians serving at retreat programs such as Tres Dias and Connecting Business and Marketplace to Christ (CBMC). One participant decided to become a Christian because he could see that the Christians he met lived out the teachings of the Bible:

> Those people whom I met in the church affected me to a greater extent—the people I met at CHISTA and CBMC. Especially, those working for CBMC served the attendees very kindly. After I attended CBMC, the members of CBMC kept on helping me. I often met with them and discussed my problems with them. The people in the church also affected me a lot. They are much better than non-believers.[141]

## The Role Model of Christians

Eight participants were influenced by mature Christians who showed good Christian witness and acted as good Christian role models in the areas of knowledge of the Bible, faith, love, helping others, and living a true Christian life. These participants were strongly impressed by the picture of Christian living that these Christians exemplified. For instance, one participant, who lived like a "prodigal son" before becoming a Christian, was influenced by the life of her pastor and his wife. Living a morally good life was important to her and was her main reason for becoming a Christian when she first heard the gospel. She recalled, "through their lives, I could see how wonderful and amazing our God was" and "learned the Bible."[142]

Another participant was strongly moved by a brother in his church who shared biblical teachings and love.

> Actually, there was a turning point of my faith. In June 2013, I met a senior in college at that time. He accompanied me, reading the Bible with me and sharing the teachings of the Bible. I had never seen such a person in my life. Before, I just thought that Christians do not smoke, drink, and gamble, but I found that there was someone like him who had so much love. Though I had believed in God in my head, I could not live out the Christian life.

141. Q, Transcripts of Converts, 161.
142. C2/F, Transcripts of Converts, 22.

But, since I met him, I started to change my life as a Christian. Since I met him, I came to believe God more solidly. Such a God, I could believe in. I could believe in God all the more from the deepest part of my heart.[143]

One participant considered a sister in Christ as a "spiritual senior" for the way she modeled the Christian with love and endurance:

She accompanied me doing what I liked, talking and playing together, and in the meantime, she shared the Word of God, explaining how to handle certain matters. She taught me the true Christian life. She had the heart of love. Her heart of love and endurance was not only for me, but also for all the members of my small group and people from my church.[144]

Christians were also influential role models in the way they mentored and gave advice. One participant was able to solve his problem through a brother at church, who gave advice "based on the teachings of the Bible." The participant stated, "When my parents asked me to do something, I would do what they requested, not necessarily completely agreeing with their ideas. But he always persuaded me."[145]

One participant was greatly moved by consistent character of a deacon at church:

The most impressive person is a deacon in my church. I think he is especially warm and humble. Also, he especially accepts other people, even though they are not friendly or are not well liked. He accepts the person who other people cannot accept. . . . If I had just seen him doing good things only once or twice, he would not have been such an impressive person to me. But I continuously found him to be like that.[146]

Participants were also influenced by the passionate faith of Christians. One participant was strongly impressed by a sister who loved the Bible and completely devoted herself to God:

She lives very simply and has not yet married, but she held onto her Bible very tightly. She woke up reading the Bible, and before going to bed, she also read her Bible. I asked her how she could

143. J1, Transcripts of Converts, 58.
144. Y, Transcripts of Converts, 277.
145. W2, Transcripts of Converts, 204.
146. L2/F, Transcripts of Converts, 110.

love God so much. She spoke with the words of God. After listening to her, I felt empowered. I wanted to be a person like her. After that, I started liking her a lot. I always stuck with her, and I wanted to learn to be like her. I realized that there are people like her who are very devoted. She gives 100 percent to God.[147]

One participant, who, before his conversion, had spent his youth with friends not studying but playing and drinking, was deeply affected by his small group leader's witness.

The leader of my small group has shown us his good attitude. Once, I asked him what was different for him after becoming a Christian. He told me that he had lived in America and that he was not an excellent student. After becoming a Christian, he had a goal. I believed what he said was true. I asked him what his goal was. He answered that he wanted to spread the gospel to the world so that everybody could believe in Jesus and get grace from God. Then, I was deeply impressed by his sharing. He was such a sincere person. I completely believed that God really exists. If God is a lie, he could not be sincere like that. His witness enhanced my belief.[148]

## The Love of Church Members

Eight participants specifically mentioned that the love of lay Christians they met in church influenced their decision to become Christian. The help of a Korean Christian moved one participant when she was lonely and having a difficult time during her first winter abroad.

One thing that I especially remember is that during the winter vacation in 2013, a friend and I were alone in the dormitory of the college, which is located in the mountains. There was no restaurant around my campus and no cook at my dormitory. All the students and staff had left the school except for the two of us. After a Korean deaconess found out about our situation, she walked all the way to our dormitory on snowy and icy roads to bring bread, cookies, and other food. She could not drive. I was very much moved [tearing up]. I could see that she was so good and kind.[149]

147. W5/F, Transcripts of Converts, 246.

148. Z1, Transcripts of Converts, 287.

149. Z2/F, Transcripts of Converts, 293.

The kindness and caring love and the lives of the leaders of the church also influenced the participants. For example:

> The deacons of my church are very good and take good care of the members of the church, just as if we were their children. They work hard for the church, too. Later on, I came to understand that they were working for the Lord. I really wanted to study their gentle attitude. During a vacation, I got counseling from a teacher of the church. I could see he was very kind and loving others. He lived out the teaching of the Lord Jesus.[150]

## The Love of Pastors

Pastors, along with their wives, were also influential people through the love they showed to the participants. One participant thought her pastor, a woman, was "just like my mom," because she took care of her lifestyle and studies and also taught music.[151] Another participant could clearly see how his pastor shared the gospel with love:

> My pastor was very good to us. She shared the gospel in a great way. She was patient with us when she shared the gospel with us. She shared the gospel with passion. I could see it from the deepest part of her heart. She had endurance, love, and a good heart. With all of these characteristics, she shared the gospel with us and helped us.[152]

Participants were also influenced by the serving of pastor's wives. When one participant saw that her pastor's wife was "a very sincere Christian" and gave "a great deal of attention" and help, she "decided to be a good Christian and good model of a Christian."[153] Another participant shared a similar story:

> From the first day of my attending the church, she [pastor's wife] kept on contacting me and gave me a Bible, and she helped me a lot. Pastor S kept on teaching me that I must believe in God. God can help you, your everything. But, at that time, the one who helped me through everything was his wife. . . . Um, first of all,

150. J3/F, Transcripts of Converts, 78.
151. X2/F, Transcripts of Converts, 300.
152. L1, Transcripts of Converts, 102.
153. J2/F, Transcripts of Converts, 70.

she taught me Korean, then helped me [to settle down]. Because she was Korean, she helped me easily adjust to the Korean lifestyle and get through difficulties. She introduced me to many Korean friends. Every emotion and everything that I had were from her. So, I felt that she was kind of my God.[154]

## Summary

The participants were greatly influenced by the love, kindness, role model of Christians, their pastors, and their pastors' wives in Korea. The Chinese students commonly mentioned that they did not see people treat others with love as Christians do, especially in terms of serving. This reminds us the importance of how Christians should live out the gospel in love. The next section will present the most attractive characteristics of Christianity to the participants.

## The Most Attractive Characteristics of Christianity

The statements pertaining to the participants' perceptions of the attractive characteristics of Christianity were highlighted, identified, and categorized. From the statements related to the question, "What are the most attractive characteristics of Christianity?," seven themes were extracted: Salvific Characteristics, the Love of Christians, the Truth, Affective Characteristics, Ethical Characteristics, Beneficial Characteristics, and the Superiority of Christians. The emergent themes and their subordinate themes for the most attractive characteristics of Christianity are displayed in Table 12.

154. L3, Transcripts of Converts, 120.

Table 12. Themes Related to the Most Attractive Characteristics of Christianity

| Category | Themes and Subthemes | Participants* ($n$=30) |
|---|---|---|
| Most Attractive Characteristics: What are the most attractive characteristics of Christianity for the participants? | Salvific Characteristics | 12 |
| | Atonement | 3 |
| | Unconditional Love | 3 |
| | Forgiveness of Sins | 3 |
| | Going to Heaven | 1 |
| | Freedom | 2 |
| | The Love of Christians | 8 |
| | The Truth | 5 |
| | Affective characteristics | 5 |
| | Peace | 2 |
| | Joy | 1 |
| | Comfort | 1 |
| | Inner Healing | 1 |
| | Ethical Characteristics | 3 |
| | Walking in the Light | 1 |
| | Honest Perspective on Life | 1 |
| | Sincerity | 1 |
| | Beneficial Characteristics | 2 |
| | Getting Help | 1 |
| | Beneficial to All Persons | 1 |
| | The Superiority of Christians | 1 |

* Some participants mentioned multiple (sub)themes.

## Salvific Characteristics

Twelve of the thirty participants responded that the salvific aspect of Christianity was one of the most attractive characteristics for them. This theme will be further expounded by illustrating the following emergent subthemes: Atonement, Unconditional Love, Forgiveness of Sins, Going to Heaven, and Freedom.

## Atonement

One participant mentioned that Jesus' blood was superior to the teachings of traditional Chinese religions in the cleansing of sins. That is, humans cannot be saved by the works of humans, but only by "the precious blood of Jesus."

> Before, I read the literature of Taoism, Buddhism, and Confucianism. These teach that salvation is [obtained] by relying on oneself, by one's own effort. Once you have committed sin, sin cannot be erased, and you keep on committing sins. Though you do good to help other people, your sin still exists. Because of the precious blood of Jesus, we sinners can be saved and can go to heaven.[155]

Likewise, another participant was also attracted to the atonement of Christ.

> We are all sinners. We are trying to normalize ourselves by doing good acts and being good people and to change ourselves to be better people. We are trying to compensate for our sins through those acts and ideas. But these good acts cannot cut it, in all religions, because you can fall into sin again. Only God can save us from our sins. God has sent his own son to save us, who died on the cross for our sins. . . . Jesus will take away our sins, and we will be saved.[156]

## Unconditional Love

Several participants were drawn to God's unconditional love. Before becoming a Christian, one participant thought that "just like almost everybody, that there is no unconditional love in the world."[157] Another participant found that unconditional love gave her strength:

---

155. W1, Transcripts of Converts, 199.
156. W2, Transcripts of Converts, 210.
157. W2, Transcripts of Converts, 206.

It is the unconditional love of God shown on the cross! There are
many times when I cannot love and forgive people, but, if I have
love from God, I can do it all.[158]

## Forgiveness of Sins

For some participants, God's forgiveness of sins made Christianity appealing, as one participant claimed, "Confess sins always! The Lord wants to
save us."[159] Another participant found the biblical teaching about sin most
appealing, saying, "To believe in Jesus is the way to be forgiven of sins. He
died for us, to save us from our sins."[160]

## Going to Heaven

One participant simply and confidently stated that "The most attractive
aspect of Christianity is the result of our faith, that we can go to heaven."[161]

## Freedom

One participant explained how the truth of the Christian faith was
liberating.

> For the past two thousand years, so many people sacrificed them-
> selves for this truth, so that I can keep on holding this truth. Yes,
> before, I did not know what the truth is, so I just followed other
> people's thoughts and ideas, and the world's, too. When there was
> a difference between others' thoughts and mine, I felt unsafe. I did
> not know whether their thinking was right or wrong. I felt like I
> was controlled by other people. But now I know what the truth is,
> so that I can hold fast to this freedom, hold fast to this truth.[162]

158. D/F, Transcripts of Converts, 44.
159. J2/F, Transcripts of Converts, 72.
160. X1, Transcripts of Converts, 290.
161. C3/F, Transcripts of Converts, 31.
162. Z3/F, Transcripts of Converts, 305.

## The Love of Christians

The second most common theme was the Love of Christians. Common descriptors of this theme included "genuine love," "to love and help each other," and "to experience love at church."

One participant became a Christian because she could strongly feel the love of God and of fellow church members.

> What made me come to church is the love. Love led me to become a Christian. Originally, I did not want to go to church and believe in God, but love drew me to believe in God. Whether it is the love of God or brothers and sisters, they love me. I can feel it very strongly. This love is not like fictitious love and appearance only, like the kind that we can see in the world. It is a genuine love. . . . The love attracts me to the Lord, the church, and my brothers and sisters.[163]

The participants also differentiated between Christians and non-Christians in the way they treated other people:

> [Christians] love and help each other, and also the way they treat each other. These points attracted me. People outside of the church treat other people according to their own purposes. Most of their purpose is to make profit, but I experienced love at church. This love is from their God.[164]

> What attracted me the most is the heart of the Christians. They help many people in need with the love that they have gotten from God. They have a lot of endurance and love.[165]

According to one participant, this Christian love could not be found among non-believers.

> The most attractive aspect is love. You cannot feel or find such a love in any other place. When other Christians told me that they would pray for me, I could feel that I got power upon power. People I do not know pray for each other and help each other at church. I think that love is the most attractive aspect of Christianity.[166]

---

163. N1/F, Transcripts of Converts, 133.

164. N2, Transcripts of Converts, 143.

165. J3/F, Transcripts of Converts, 81.

166. W4/F, Transcripts of Converts, 235.

## The Truth

Five participants responded to and connected with the truth of Christianity when they were asked to elaborate what was the most attractive characteristic of Christianity for them. The truth of Christianity became more appealing when compared with other religions, as with one participant, who saw that the Christian truth was both authoritative and transformative:

> Let me compare Christianity with other religions to answer this question. In my hometown, every house has their own Buddhist idols and worships them by burning incense. My mom burned incense every morning and evening when I was young. I found that my mom prayed only for the business of my father and for our health. Actually, she burned incense whenever she needed something. Though the Buddha teaches people to do good things, people do not follow the teachings but seek only their own good. The attractive aspect of Christianity for me is the truth. Christians do not seek only their own benefits from God. The truth cannot be changed, and also, it teaches us how to apply it in every aspect of our life.[167]

One participant was attracted to how the truth could guide his life. He said, "[the truth] can lead and help me to accomplish what God has entrusted to me with his wisdom and power, something my family and I cannot do."[168] Similarly, another participant believed that even "If a non-Christian reads the Bible, they cannot go astray or do bad things," and the truth teaches "how to be a good person."[169]

## Affective Characteristics

Five out of the thirty participants responded that the most attractive characteristics of Christianity were mainly affective ones. The theme of Affective Characteristics was articulated by the participants under the following subthemes: Peace, Joy, Comfort, and Inner Healing.

---

167. L2/F, Transcripts of Converts, 110.
168. Z2/F, Transcripts of Converts, 297.
169. Z5, Transcripts of Converts, 328.

*Peace*

The atmosphere of the church and its service, and also of Christianity itself, made participants feel peaceful, relaxed, content, and calm, which attracted them to the church and the Christian faith. One participant appreciated the "peace and relaxation" of Christianity, because "by nature, I don't have to beg for anything or to obtain anything."[170] Another participant recalled, "After I came to the church, I felt very calm. I sat down and closed my eyes, very calm.[171]

*Joy*

For one participant, joy was the most attractive characteristic, observing that "people who believe in Christ are very joyful."[172]

*Comfort*

One participant considered comfort as the most attractive characteristic of Christianity:

> I think it is God's comfort, especially related to prayer. For example, God promises that "if you knock on the door, I will open it." Every time I think of God's promise, I know God will listen and answer my prayer. Yes, through prayer I experience God.[173]

*Inner Healing*

A participant who experienced inner healing by sharing her problems with other church members stated the aspect that "God can heal people" was the most attractive characteristic for her. From her experience, she saw church as "a place that is full of love" where "we can open our hearts and share anything with other Christians and God."[174]

170. W5/F, Transcripts of Converts, 251.

171. Z1, Transcripts of Converts, 284.

172. P, Transcripts of Converts, 151.

173. C2/F, Transcripts of Converts, 22.

174. X/F, Transcripts of Converts, 265.

## Ethical Characteristics

Three participants mentioned that ethical characteristics were the most attractive characteristics of Christianity for them. This theme has the following subthemes: Walking in the Light, Honest Perspective on Life, and Sincerity.

### Walking in the Light

One participant commented that "To walk in the way of the light" was most attractive, differentiating living a holy life from walking in the darkness. She recalled:

> When I walked in the darkness, I felt that I was in the valley of dried bones that was mentioned in the Bible. It is dreadfully frightening. I came to understand what holiness is through the teaching of the Bible. The holiness that comes from God makes me delighted and happy in my heart. That can heal me and make me happy. It makes me very comfortable. But, before I understood this, I was not very sensitive to the darkness. So, I kept on being in pain. After I experienced the holiness that came from God, I was completely changed.[175]

### Honest Perspective on Life

One participant was most attracted by "the teaching of having an honest view of life."

> It gave me an honest view of life and honest values in my life. My body is God-given, so I need to care for it. Don't smoke, drink, use drugs, and don't do anything that can harm my body. The people in the world are created by God, so we need to respect all people.[176]

---

175. X/F, Transcripts of Converts, 270.
176. L3, Transcripts of Converts, 122.

## Sincerity

Drawing from her experience at church, one participant narrated how she found the sincerity with which Christians treated each other as the most attractive characteristic.

> First of all, Christians are very kind and sincere, and also, I have never seen anyone who comes to church and has a mean face. They are all happy and pleased. Whether before or after the service, everyone says "Hi!" to each other. It is not on the surface only but from their heart. They are all very glad. They seem to talk to each other with their hearts.[177]

## Beneficial Characteristics

Some participants noted getting help from God attracted them, therefore, Christianity is beneficial to all the people of the world.

## Getting Help

For one participant, getting help from other Christians for her financial difficulties was an important experience.

> They prayed with me. I received offerings from other people. They asked other people to pray for me. They financially supported me. At that time, I did not have any money in my account, but I was able to survive the semester [*laughs*]. So, God cared for me.[178]

## Beneficial to All Persons

One participant recognized the potential, universal benefit of Christianity, claiming that "Christianity is not just for believers, but for all the people of the world who receive the gospel and the teachings of Christ. People can get help from God when they believe in Jesus."[179]

---

177. Y, Transcripts of Converts, 279.
178. D/F, Transcripts of Converts, 38.
179. Z4/F, Transcripts of Converts, 317.

## The Superiority of Christians

When one participant encountered Christianity, he found that Christians were smarter and wealthier than the Chinese non-Christians who scorned Christianity. Until recently, Chinese people have looked down on Christianity as a religion for the poor, old, and sick.

> I thought the people attending church were very good. I thought that there must be some reason why so many famous people in the world are Christians. Yes, they are very clever. Once, some people told me that only old people go to church. They cannot make money, and they have no food to eat, and the church gives them food to eat. Later on, I found that the richer and smarter people are Christians and believe in God more sincerely. So, church and Christianity are very attractive to me.[180]

## Summary

In summary, more than one third of the participants were attracted to Christianity by its salvific characteristics, which includes the foundations of salvation including atonement and unconditional love, as well as the effects of atonement, such as the forgiveness of sins, a sense of freedom, and going to heaven. Participants were well aware of the uniqueness of Christian salvation. Comparing Christian salvation with traditional Chinese religions, several participants concluded that only "the precious blood of Jesus" can forgive and save sinners. They understood human sinful nature and the inability of human beings to save themselves. The participants also described the sacrifice of Jesus on the cross as unconditional love, which cannot be found elsewhere in the world.

Other participants were most attracted by the love of the Christians whom they met. They perceived this love as genuine, not for personal gain, and not to be found among non-believers. Traditional Chinese society is communal. Members share their resources within their networks, *guanxi* ("personal network"), so people do not share their resources with those who are not in the same *guanxi*. Therefore, when witnessing and experiencing Christians helping and praying for those who did not share the same *guanxi*, participants were moved and attracted. When people can see Christians

180. J1, Transcripts of Converts, 62.

loving each other and loving their community, people know they are the disciples of Jesus and become attracted to Christianity.

The Chinese students were also most attracted to the truth of Christianity, to affective characteristics that brought peace, joy, comfort, and inner healing, and to ethical aspects, such as the honesty of Christians. Other students were also most attracted to the personal and universal benefits and to how Christians were sometimes even more superior than they had expected. The next section treats special religious experiences that the participants experienced in the process of conversion.

## Special Religious Experiences

For the question, "What were the special religious experiences of the participants?," relevant statements were extracted, clustered then grouped into the following ten themes: God's Help, the Bible, Praying, Visions and Voices, Preaching, Listening to Witness, God's Guidance, Listening to Hymns, Watching Films, and No Special Experience. Twenty-three of the thirty participants stated that they had had special experiences. These themes, except for the last theme of No Special Experience (seven participants), were found to be conducive to conversion for the participants. The emergent themes for special religious experiences are displayed in Table 13.

Table 13. Themes Related to Special Religious Experiences

| Category | Themes | Participants*<br>(n=30) |
|---|---|---|
| Special Religious Experiences: What were the special religious experiences of the participants? | God's Help | 12 |
| | The Bible | 5 |
| | Praying | 7 |
| | Visions and Voices | 4 |
| | Preaching | 3 |
| | Listening to Witness | 3 |
| | God's Guidance | 2 |
| | Listening to Hymns | 1 |
| | Watching Films | 1 |
| | No Special Experience | 7 |

* Some participants mentioned multiple themes.

## God's Help

Twelve out of the thirty participants mentioned their experience of getting help from God. Most of the participants mentioned receiving special help regarding their academic studies, with grades, school admission, theses, examinations, and scholarships.

One participant acknowledged God for helping her pass the defense of her thesis:

> I was constantly changing my thesis without deciding on the theme, although the hearing was imminent. So, I desperately needed to fix my theme and plan, but I could not do it, which made me so disappointed. In this situation, I said to myself, "My wisdom is so small! God's wisdom is greater than mine." So, I asked the Lord for help in prayer, saying, "My wisdom cannot compare with yours, so I leave it all to you. I first want to write my thesis with your wisdom. I cannot write my thesis with my own wisdom." After finishing the prayer, I suddenly thought of two themes, so I quickly wrote down these two themes for the thesis.

When I presented it to my supervisor, he accepted it, saying, "Very good, very well done!" When he asked me some questions, I answered very quickly, although I had not prepared for it. It is not something I did, and it is not something I could do.[181]

Participants also experienced God's help in their admissions process. Although one participant was notified of failing the Korean language exam for a college's admission interview, the university later sent him a letter of acceptance as an exception to their regulations.[182] Another participant stated that he was able to get into his graduate school because he had prayed with pastors and Christian friends at church.[183]

## The Bible

Special religious experiences included the Word of God, as with one participant who felt the words of the Bible giving her "power, and a beam of light [shining] upon my spirit and heart."[184] When one participant had quiet time or studied the Bible at church, she felt that God was comforting her with the words of the Bible:

> When I was going through the lowest valley of my life, when I was in trouble, I prayed. Actually, I did not have faith and understand God much. But I felt that there was no one except God who could help me. So, I prayed for God's help. And then, I felt that the contentment I felt through quiet time was from God.[185]

Another participant experienced the living power and relevance of the Bible during Bible study.

> We learned the Bible and shared our lives and studies. It is so amazing because I could see that what I experienced on that day was applicable to the passage we studied. The Bible tells me why something happens and what I am supposed to do. It is very amazing that I can get answers from the Bible every time I go to church on Wednesday. I feel like the Bible has life.[186]

181. W4/F, Transcripts of Converts, 232.

182. S, Transcripts of Converts, 177.

183. L1, Transcripts of Converts, 100.

184. Z3/F, Transcripts of Converts, 303.

185. L2/F, Transcripts of Converts, 112.

186. Z5, Transcripts of Converts, 329.

## Praying

Some participants experienced God during prayer, in the form of insight or guidance. During the prayer time of a CHISTA retreat, one participant felt he was "unworthy and was a sinner, but I felt that the love of Jesus is so great that a sinner like me can be chosen and saved."[187]

Another participant identified his problems and controlled his anger through prayer:

> Once, our church had a dinner together, but a friend of mine told me the wrong information so that I could not attend the dinner with the church members. Because of this, I scolded my friend. When I came back to my room that evening, I prayed and asked God whether my action was right or wrong. Then, I could hear a voice from my heart saying that I was wrong, and I should apologize for that. I strongly believe that the Holy Spirit works in us. I believe that the Holy Spirit worked in me. When I got angry, I prayed and got answers from God. Then, I could calm down. I experienced similar things many times. When I prayed, I became calm.[188]

## Visions and Voices

Several participants related that mystical visions and voices enhanced their faith. One participant saw a vision of the cross during a three-day retreat:

> During one prayer, I saw the cross. I felt like God was calling me. My first impression was a great surprise, because the cross is the tool of execution, the symbol of cruelty. But when I saw the cross, it was very beautiful, more beautiful than any other cross I have ever seen. I believe that is the place where our Lord died. I was so moved. I could feel the pain of Christ in that moment. I was so moved that I cried.[189]

Another participant saw a vision of the face of Jesus during a worship service:

> I remember one time during the pastor's preaching, I saw the face of Jesus on the ceiling. It was still in my time of growing closer to the faith. I shared this with my pastor, and he told me that this was

187. C1, Transcripts of Converts, 10.
188. Z5, Transcripts of Converts, 328.
189. L3, Transcripts of Converts, 116.

an encounter between the Lord Jesus and me. [Jesus] was smiling, kind of a gentle smile. I found it so mystical.[190]

Hearing voices also led participants to commitment and the decision to believe. One participant who had been attending church for one year was asked to be baptized. Although she initially did not want to, she chose to be baptized in response to a voice she heard.

> Before, I had strongly thought that I wouldn't quickly decide to be baptized. If I went back to China, I would be living in an area unlike here in terms of Christianity, so my faith would be shaken. When she asked me whether or not I wanted to be baptized, I heard a voice saying, "You need to be baptized, now." At that time, I looked at that sister and said, "I want to be baptized."[191]

Another participant decided to believe in Jesus when a voice revealed he was the only way to salvation.

> At this time, a mission team from Hong Kong came to our campus to visit us and evangelize our students. Actually, it was not easy for me to make this decision, because I was a Buddhist before. While they evangelized the gospel, I was constantly telling myself [that] I didn't want to believe, I would not accept this belief, and I must not change my belief. But one thing was quite amazing. As they finished evangelizing the gospel, they asked me, "Are you willing to accept Jesus as your Lord in your life?" At that time, a little voice whispered in my heart, "You will not have any other method or way to save yourself except me." I felt quite a struggle to make this decision. Finally, I decided to accept this belief, and I became a Christian.[192]

## Preaching

Hearing sermons also led to special experiences. One participant was moved to tears while listening to a sermon, feeling "so much filled by the Holy Spirit."[193] Another participant received encouragement through a

---

190. Z4/F, Transcripts of Converts, 322.

191. Y, Transcripts of Converts, 275.

192. C2/F, Transcripts of Converts, 14.

193. Z4/F, Transcripts of Converts, 313.

sermon at a retreat, gaining "confident faith from the book of Isaiah, 'Do not remember the things of the past.'"[194]

## Listening to Witness

When one participant was listening to the sharing of a deacon from her church, she suddenly felt the Holy Spirit moving her:

> He often invited us to a restaurant. When we were eating together, he told us the story of Jesus Christ. And then, he told me that God has been keeping me all the time. When I heard this, the Holy Spirit moved me. Suddenly, many scenes came across in my mind. When I was young, I left my house and lived abroad, I was hit by a car when I was riding a bicycle, but I did not get hurt at all. Actually, there were many things like that. And then, many other things came across my mind, too. I really thanked the Lord. Since then, I started accepting Jesus Christ.[195]

## God's Guidance

One participant believed that God led her to a specific church where she could learn what she wanted to.

> The special experience is how I came to the present church I attend. Actually, I am Chinese. My Korean is not so good. A friend of mine who plays tennis with me mentioned this church, so I went to the church, and I did not want to leave it. I think God specially arranged this church for me. I had always really wanted to learn a musical instrument. Ever since I have attended this church, I have been learning to play the guitar, clarinet, and piano, which I had not learned before.[196]

## Listening to Hymns

One participant became convicted to confessing her sins while listening to the choir during a service. She remembers, "When I was listening to the

194. D/F, Transcripts of Converts, 36.
195. J2/F, Transcripts of Converts, 67.
196. Z2/F, Transcripts of Converts, 300.

hymns during the service at church, I closed my eyes and confessed a lot of sins that I did not think were sins. I kept on shedding tears and confessing sins. I had never thought like this ever before."[197]

## Watching Films

One participant was greatly moved when watching the film *Jesus* when he was first attending church:

> Initially, when I read the Bible, I did not feel anything special. But when I watched the film *Jesus*, I was especially moved. When I watched the scene where Jesus was nailed to the cross, I could not stand it anymore. I was moved to almost cry out. Tears were continuously flowing down my face.[198]

## No Special Experience

Seven participants said they did not go through any special experience in their conversion. One such participant knew that "definitely God has a different plan for me, so I have been both consistently and gradually waiting upon God's plan to be accomplished in me."[199]

## Summary

In summary, twenty-three of the thirty participants mentioned having special experiences of God's Help, the Bible, Praying, Visions and Voices, Preaching, Listening to Witness, God's Guidance, Listening to Hymns, and Watching Films. These themes were found to be conducive to conversion for the participants. However, seven participants stated that they became Christian gradually without experiencing anything special.

Twelve participants experienced help through prayers when they faced problems in their studies and financial situations. Seven participants experienced the moving of the Holy Spirit during retreats, so that they would understand and believe in the saving grace of Jesus on the cross.

197. Y, Transcripts of Converts, 287.
198. H, Transcripts of Converts, 50.
199. N, Transcripts of Converts, 130.

Their experiences were like revivalism. That is, they confessed their sins, cried, thanked God for the sacrificial love of Jesus on the cross, and began praying out loud. Eleven participants experienced the grace of God through the Word of God in sermons, personal reading, and teachings from other Christians. Two participants saw visions, while two heard voices, all of which enhanced their faith and led them to be baptized and believe in Jesus. One participant confessed her sins while listening to hymns sung by the choir. The next section will present the conspicuous changes of the participants after converting to Christianity.

## Conspicuous Changes after Converting to Christianity

The following section deals with the findings from the data analysis that pertain to the question, "What were the conspicuous changes in the participants after their conversion to Christianity?" Several themes emerged from the data analysis: Improved Relationships, Greater Confidence, Improved Emotional Stability, An Ethical Standard, New Religious Understanding, and New Perspective on Values. The emergent themes and subthemes for this section are illustrated in Table 14.

Table 14. Themes Related to Conspicuous Changes

| Category | Themes and Subthemes | Participants* (n=30) |
|---|---|---|
| Conspicuous Changes: What were the conspicuous changes in the participants after their conversion to Christianity? | Improved Relationships | 26 |
| | *Concern for Others* | 8 |
| | *Forgiving Others* | 6 |
| | *Recovering Relationship with Parents* | 7 |
| | *Becoming Less Selfish* | 2 |
| | *Becoming Social* | 2 |
| | *Becoming Less Competitive* | 1 |
| | Greater Confidence | 8 |
| | *Having Hope* | 3 |

* Some participants mentioned multiple (sub)themes.

| Category | Themes and Subthemes | Participants*<br>(*n*=30) |
|---|---|---|
| | *Respecting Oneself* | 3 |
| | *Becoming Courageous* | 2 |
| | Improved Emotional Stability | 6 |
| | *Becoming Less Angry* | 3 |
| | *Healing* | 1 |
| | No More Anxiety | 2 |
| | An Ethical Standard | 5 |
| | *Having a Standard* | 3 |
| | *Becoming a Better Person* | 2 |
| | New Religious Understanding | 4 |
| | *Correcting Chinese Ideas about Christianity* | 3 |
| | *New Perspective on Other Religions* | 1 |
| | New Perspective on Values | 2 |
| | *New View on Values* | 1 |
| | *Having Eternal Life* | 1 |

* Some participants mentioned multiple (sub)themes.

## Improved Relationships

The transcripts of twenty-six participant interviews yielded many statements relating to improved relationships. The subthemes of Improved Relationships are Concern for Others, Forgiving Others, Recovering Relationship with Parents, Becoming Less Selfish, Becoming Social, and Becoming Less Competitive.

## Concern for Others

Eight participants stated that they became more considerate of and loving towards other people after their conversion. These participants became more sensitive to others, especially if they were not so before conversion. One participant admitted, "I pray for other people more than before."[200] Another participant stated that she now lives for others rather than herself, having learned "to share what I have with people and to care for people around me, showing love to them."[201] A male participant, who already enjoyed helping people, claimed that his intentions changed, saying, "When I offered help [before], I didn't feel comfortable, thinking, 'Why should I help you?' But now when I offer help, I do not consider myself and simply just want to help."[202]

## Forgiving Others

Six participants noted that they could forgive other people after their conversion because of the "sacrificial love of Jesus" and the "love of God." As one participant responded, "Gradually, when I thought of the sacrificial love of Jesus, I could control my anger. I came to treat others with love."[203]

Participants saw a noticeable change in temperament, as those who were vengeful and easily angered were able to forgive and love them.

> When other people hurt me, I do not want revenge. I treat them in a new way. Before, when other people were unpleasant to me, I was very unhappy, and I said to myself, "You must see clearly how I will pay you back for this." But now, it is no problem. If a non-Christian hurts me, I still want to take them to church. It is not easy, but I still love them and bless them. Because of the love of God, I have changed. Whatever I face, I cannot be depressed because God is with me.[204]
>
> Though people hurt me, I stand in the other person's position and try to understand and forgive them, and I also pray for them,

200. P, Transcripts of Converts, 152.
201. Z4/F, Transcripts of Converts, 318.
202. T/F, Transcripts of Converts, 188.
203. Q, Transcripts of Converts, 164.
204. Y, Transcripts of Converts, 281.

because I think they must not be happy. I try to understand and forgive them now. Now, I have changed a great deal.[205]

## Recovering Relationship with Parents

Overall, participants' attitudes and perceptions towards their parents changed, giving them the desire to restore their relationships with them. One participant was able to have strong affection towards her parents after conversion:

> Also, my mother gave birth to me when she was quite young, so she didn't know how to take care of me, and I used to complain about it, like, "How come other mothers can take care of their kids so well, but my mom doesn't even clean our house?" I grumbled in the past. I don't know how, but gradually, [something] affected me so I saw my mom differently after my conversion. Suddenly, a big change! I have much stronger affection towards my parents now.[206]

One participant was able to call and forgive her parents after seeing Jesus forgive others while crucified in the film, *The Passion of the Christ.*

> For example, I hated my parents because of what happened in my childhood, though I know I love them. . . . When I came back to my room after receiving Communion, I was so excited that I thought I should tell them, "I forgive you because of the love of Jesus Christ." So, I contacted them [*laughs*]. I had not contacted them for long time. If not for Jesus, I could not do that [*laughs*] . . . Thank the Lord![207]

Another participant was able to heal the relationship with her mother with much prayer and the interceding of the Holy Spirit.

> Before I converted, my relationship with my mother was very bad. We often argued and fought with each other. But after I converted, the Holy Spirit interceded in the relationship between my mother and me. This process took a long time, and it was not very easy. I needed to pray a lot for God's love to ease the conflict between us.[208]

205. N1, Transcripts of Converts, 136.
206. T/F, Transcripts of Converts, 188.
207. Z3/F, Transcripts of Converts, 307.
208. C2/F, Transcripts of Converts, 19.

## *Becoming Less Selfish*

Some participants admitted to becoming less "selfish" after their conversion, a change that is considered to be much greater than the previous sub-theme, Concern for Others.

> The most conspicuous change is that I am not as selfish as I was when I was young. For example, "This time belongs to me, so you do not disturb me," and "This place belongs to me, so you do not come here." I think that I was selfish in my thoughts. But after becoming a Christian, I am not that selfish. I really want to give my time and energy to people in need.[209]

> You'd better ask my friends [*laughs*]. The most conspicuous change . . . [was the] spiritual leaders who mentor me said that I changed a lot, I can care for other people, I am not so selfish. . . . They told me "Do you know, sister, you have changed a lot? Before, you were very selfish, you did this . . . but now you have really changed a lot."[210]

## *Becoming Social*

Some participants became more sociable and "much more open to others."[211] One such participant shared:

> If there was no church, I would be very lonely. I came to Korea when I was eighteen years old, so if I did not go to church, my personality would not be cheerful. I might be lonely and antisocial. God has arranged all of this for me.[212]

## *Becoming Less Competitive*

One participant had been competitive before his conversion, but afterwards, he stopped comparing himself with other people:

> Before I believed in Jesus, I was so competitive that I thought that I should be better than other people. Now, I can accept the

---

209. N1/F, Transcripts of Converts, 134.

210. Y/F, Transcripts of Converts, 281.

211. P, Transcripts of Converts, 155.

212. Z2/F, Transcripts of Converts, 292.

reality, what I face in my daily life. For example, clothes, food, I do not care much about them and do not compare myself with other people.[213]

## Greater Confidence

The second most frequently occurring theme was the theme, Greater Confidence (eight participants). Common descriptors that participants employed during the interview included: "a child of God," "to have confidence," "to have hope," "to have self-respect," and "to accept myself." This theme has the following subthemes: Having Hope, Respecting Oneself, and Becoming Courageous.

### Having Hope

After conversion, several participants gained hope in life because of their Christian beliefs. One participant who had no hope before conversion and "did not know what to do in the future . . . came to have hope," because "the Lord will guide and arrange my future."[214]

Another participant claimed that others around her saw her "become more optimistic, really optimistic," and said things like, 'This person entrusts all of her things to God! She has hope!'"[215]

To each of these participants, hope meant overcoming uncertainty and difficulties, but to one participant who had previously attempted to end his life due to family problems found a reason to live in having hope:

> My life suddenly was full of hope, because when I was in China . . . my parents divorced, they were always fighting, even at my school. I really couldn't stand it anymore. I tried to commit suicide without success. After I entered Christianity, I found that there is hope in the world. I tried to forgive my parents and many other people. Jesus forgave these people, so why can't I forgive my parents? Because of these ideas, I thought I could have hope for my life.[216]

213. N2, Transcripts of Converts, 144.
214. W2, Transcripts of Converts, 209.
215. W4/F, Transcripts of Converts, 236.
216. L3, Transcripts of Converts, 123.

*Respecting Oneself*

As the participants recognized their new status as Christians, as children of God, they found their new value in God and were able to respect themselves. One participant boldly claimed, "I'm a child of God and there's nothing better than this."[217]

Participants also shared how their Christian faith gave them new-found worth that was not tied to other people:

> Now, I came to know that I have nothing to be proud of. But when I think of the Lord, I could feel the Lord saying to me, "You are very special. You are different in my eyes. You are very special!" Ah! I felt that I am worthy, the Lord made me worthy. I am a child of God. I could have a self-respect in God that I did not have in the world before.[218]

One participant could do what she really wanted to do within the will of God since she could accept herself after conversion:

> Now, I do not follow the value system of the world. Before, I followed it—if all the people said something was good, then I just did it. After believing in God, I wanted to understand what seed God has sown in my heart and what I want to do. That is, what is it that God wants to say to the deepest part of my heart? I want to face the real part of myself, because I was completely wrapped up in myself. For instance, even though I liked something, if other people said that it was not good, then I did not take it. But now, if I like something, I just take it. I try to live the life that I really want to live. My personality has become cheerful. I can truly face myself. I can accept myself, though I'm not perfect.[219]

*Becoming Courageous*

Participants also gained more courage than before, as one participant who "could not go out at night [to] dark places because of fear" was able to overcome all of her fears because she believed "in God and his

---

217. W5/F, Transcripts of Converts, 252.
218. W4/F, Transcripts of Converts, 229.
219. X/F, Transcripts of Converts, 267.

protection."[220] When one participant became a Christian, she "changed to have more courage." She stated:

> In the past, I was shy. I did not like to speak in front of other people. I did not dare speak. But now, I feel that the Lord has given me great courage. I can speak what I want to express with courage.[221]

## Improved Emotional Stability

The third most frequently occurring theme was Improved Emotional Stability (six participants). This theme has the following subthemes: Becoming Less Angry, Healing, and No More Anxiety.

### Becoming Less Angry

Another noticeable change after conversion was in how participants became less angry, especially because of their management of anger. One participant stated that after believing in Jesus, "I could calm down my anger, so now I do not get angry very much."[222] Another participant also became calmer in dealing with her anger, relying on Scripture:

> Before, I got angry easily [laughs]. Now, I do not get angry easily. Before, when I got angry, I took revenge. But after becoming a Christian, I became very calm. I know who I need to deal with, the origin of my anger, and how to overcome it. Also, now I know that I should treat my anger not by getting angrier, but with the Word of God. I can be satisfied when I do that.[223]

Yet another participant even stated, "I cannot remember the last time I got angry."[224]

---

220. N1/F, Transcripts of Converts, 134.
221. J3/F, Transcripts of Converts, 82.
222. H, Transcripts of Converts, 52.
223. L2/F, Transcripts of Converts, 112.
224. C3/F, Transcripts of Converts, 33.

## Healing

One participant was hurt whenever she heard other people mentioning her parents' divorce. Through prayer, she was healed of her past wounds.

> When other people told me that I was a child of divorced parents, I felt like they were attacking me. And I cried when I heard that. I thought the same, so I shared this with a pastor's wife. She told me that I needed to have inner healing and pray for that. Whenever I prayed, I was freed and recognized the fact that I was a child of divorced parents, so that I needed to be loved, in order to heal the hurt of the past. Now, I am healed, and I feel much better. I really thank God.[225]

## No More Anxiety

As participants prayed and grew in faith, they felt less anxiety and "could experience more peace."[226] One participant responded:

> I feel that this is the right place, and I grew a lot spiritually and in my character formation. And my old thinking changed, too. I don't have the anxieties that I had back in China. In the past, I had anxiety over things I was not familiar with. I think such a drastic change happened about eight months after my arrival.[227]

## An Ethical Standard

The fourth theme that was discovered was about having An Ethical Standard. The subthemes are Having a Standard and Becoming a Better Person.

## Having a Standard

After becoming a Christian, participants gained a moral standard which they sought to uphold. One participant stated, "When I was with my family and friends, I sometimes thought that I could not do what they

---

225. J2/F, Transcripts of Converts, 74.
226. T/F, Transcripts of Converts, 188.
227. W5/F, Transcripts of Converts, 245.

did because I am a Christian.[228] Another participant confessed, "Before becoming a Christian, I did not ever think what I did was not right. I felt that it was quite normal."[229] One participant also gained a standard of honesty in her life:

> I think it is again a matter of a standard. People make many kinds of imitations, they lack honesty, and even in the small things, I am trying not to lie but to be honest. People do not want to listen to God but to have their own way. However, if they have wisdom, they will go back to God, putting down everything, and trusting God's plan.[230]

## *Becoming a Better Person*

Some participants felt they had become better people due to their faith. One participant explained, "I pray every day that the Lord lead my life, just like now. . . . I became a good person because I wanted to be a good person from my deepest heart."[231] These participants considered themselves to be "better" because of the visible changes in their "bad habits . . . bad actions, those that God disliked and was not pleased with."[232]

> My expectations for myself have become higher than ever before. I do not smoke and drink anymore. I do not swear and use bad language, and I do not see what I should not see. I feel that I have changed since I became a Christian.[233]

> I have quit smoking now. Before, I tried to quit smoking but failed every time. After becoming a Christian, I could not taste anything when I smoked, so I quit smoking. I smoked, drank, and played computer games. After I became a Christian, I felt no more emptiness and stopped smoking and playing computer games. I felt that I became much better than before, believing in the Lord, and also more pleasant.[234]

228. N2, Transcripts of Converts, 143.
229. N1/F, Transcripts of Converts, 135.
230. W3/F, Transcripts of Converts, 222.
231. Z2/F, Transcripts of Converts, 298.
232. S, Transcripts of Converts, 174.
233. W1, Transcripts of Converts, 200.
234. Z1, Transcripts of Converts, 289.

## New Religious Understanding

The fifth theme is New Religious Understanding. Four participants provided data related to the theme. The subthemes were Correcting Chinese Ideas about Christianity and Having a New Perspective on Other Religions.

### Correcting Chinese Ideas about Christianity

As the participants became Christians, they changed their ideas about Christianity. One participant who had previously "thought that church was a place that only old people went to" found this notion to be false.[235] Another participant was able to influence his parents, who opposed his Christian faith and called the religion brainwashing.

> Some Chinese people say that Christianity is brainwashing, but Christianity is a very good religion that can guide people. My parents think that Christianity is a very good religion. They do not think that it is theirs to follow. Although they say, "You changed into a very good person," they do not want to accept Christianity as their religion.[236]

### New Perspective on Other Religions

One participant gained a new perspective on idol worshipping after believing in God:

> Before, because my grandmother was a Buddhist, and I had a close relationship with her, whenever I saw idols, I wanted to worship them in my mind. I heard that idols ask people to serve them with food and wine, but God does not need that kind of worship with food and drink. This is very strongly inscribed in my heart. So, I do not take idols seriously.[237]

---

235. Y, Transcripts of Converts, 271.
236. C1, Transcripts of Converts, 9.
237. H, Transcripts of Converts, 52.

## New Perspective on Values

The sixth theme, New Perspective on Values, has two subthemes: A New View on Values and Having Eternal Life.

### A New View on Values

One participant developed a new view on values, giving an example that "Because I believe in heaven, I can think and make decisions differently."[238]

### Having Eternal Life

One participant shifted to having a spiritual, eternal view of life, based on the truth of Christianity.

> Before, I thought that if you have enough money, fame, and virtue, then it is good enough. But, later on, I found that you can be satisfied when you have eternal life. Many people say that you must take care of yourself first, and then later you take care of others. I do not agree. I think you must take care of other people even though other people want to harm you. God will protect us. I feel the most important thing is the understanding of the truth, the real truth.[239]

## Summary

In summary, the participants noticeably changed in many ways after they converted to Christianity. First, they improved their relationships with other people. For instance, the participants were more concerned for others, forgiving, less selfish, more social, and less competitive. As the participants experienced the sacrificial love of Jesus Christ who died on the cross to forgive sinners, they, too, could love and forgive other people. As a result, their relationships with their family, friends, and other people improved.

Second, when the participants converted, they gained confidence. They came to have hope in their new faith. Through their new identity as children of God, they were able to accept and respect themselves unlike

238. K/F, Transcripts of Converts, 95.
239. J1, Transcripts of Converts, 64.

before. They also became more courageous as they believed God was with them and took care of them.

Third, the converted participants acquired greater emotional stability. They became less angry or anxious, no longer wanting to be angry and believing that God could take care of them in all things. A participant also experienced inner healing of hurt from parents and others.

Fourth, the participants acquired a new ethical standard of living after converting to Christianity. According to their new standard, they quit bad habits, stopped lying, and lived honestly. They could feel that they had become better persons. The participants had higher expectations of themselves and evaluated the world with the truth of Christianity.

Fifth, some participants gained a new religious understanding after their conversion. Although Chinese people typically regard Christianity as a brainwashing religion or a religion only for the old, these participants found these views to be untrue and shared their newfound faith with other people. The participants were also able to discard previous ideas of idol worship.

Sixth, after converting to Christianity, the participants gained a new perspective on values. Because the participants had belief in the eternal life, they could devalue the things of the world and have heaven as a reference point for making decisions. The newfound truth and faith in eternal life made the participants transform their perspective on values. The next section will present commitment of the participants to Christianity after conversion.

## Commitment to Christianity

The following section deals with findings from the data analysis related to the participants' commitment to Christianity. To understand the perceptions of the participants, the researcher used declarative sentences and questions. For instance, "Jesus died for us, sacrificed himself. What is your response to that sacrificial love of Jesus? Thinking about it now, what would you say?" Several themes emerged from the data analysis: Doing Evangelism, Living a God-Centered Life, Obeying God, Dedicating Oneself to God, Serving the Church Full-Time, and Loving Others. Table 15 shows these themes.

Table 15. Themes Related to Participants' Commitment to Christianity

| Category | Themes | Participants*<br>(n=30) |
|---|---|---|
| Commitment: How committed are the participants to their new faith? | Doing Evangelism | 13 |
| | Living a God-Centered Life | 10 |
| | Obeying God | 6 |
| | Dedicating Oneself to God | 6 |
| | Serving the Church Full-Time | 3 |
| | Loving Others | 1 |

* Some participants mentioned multiple themes.

## Doing Evangelism

Thirteen participants responded to the question about commitment by talking about evangelizing. One participant's statement captures the essence of this theme: "I want to be a witness for Jesus to many people."[240]

In particular, participants emphasized their desire to share the gospel because "The Bible says we need to share the gospel with the people of the world."[241] This sense of duty was not separate from love, as one participant added, "I love Jesus Christ. I want to share what I think is good with other people. Let's say, there is a restaurant that serves very delicious food, then I will tell people to come eat there with me."[242]

Participants also wanted to dedicate the way they lived as a form of evangelism. One participant wanted to serve as a role model for attracting people to Christ, and another felt the need to live according to the Word of God to share the gospel.

> I want to be an ambassador for Christ. I want to make good use of my talent and time. I want to be a real Christian so that people

---

240. S, Transcripts of Converts, 175.

241. N2, Transcripts of Converts, 145.

242. P, Transcripts of Converts, 153.

could see me as like other Christians in my church. Then, other people would want to be Christian because of me.[243]

Regarding how I reward the Lord, I need to control my desire, need to keep the Word of God and commandments, to live a life worthy of Jesus' sacrifice, and share the gospel with the people, more people in order to let them know the gospel and the Lord's love. I need to control myself, then share the gospel with people. These are all the things I can do for the Lord.[244]

Participants also prioritized the gospel over their careers, seeking a career that would allow them to evangelize. One participant wanted to become a professor to help students through the gospel because she thought she would know their needs:

He is worthy to be known to many other people through me. . . . I have the hope to serve the Lord on campus as a professor. When I become a professor, I will pray for the students, and I will have fellowship with the students, because students have much pain. They wander, and they do not know anything due to their young age. I can understand their feelings. They run around without a goal. So, I really want to help them. I want to serve the Lord all my life until I go to heaven.[245]

Another participant "thought about being a short-term missionary after having a stable job. . . . Yes, putting myself down is a big challenge."[246] One participant even wanted "to be a movie director in order to make a great movie about the gospel and hire all famous movie stars."[247]

## Living a God-Centered Life

One third of the participants responded that they wanted to live a God-centered life. For the participants, life had to revolve around God: "I take Jesus as my goal, my role model, and I am trying to do my best to be like him."[248] One participant declared, "I need to glorify God in my life" and

243. J2/F, Transcripts of Converts, 72.
244. L3, Transcripts of Converts, 119.
245. W4/F, Transcripts of Converts, 238.
246. W3/F, Transcripts of Converts, 222.
247. J1, Transcripts of Converts, 64.
248. H, Transcripts of Converts, 53.

wanted to do his best in all things to show that he was a Christian. She summarily stated, "I think commitment means that you should live a life that is centered on God. Let the Lord lead me."[249]

Another participant gave a more detailed look into the God-centered life:

> Regarding commitment, whoever I meet, or whatever I do, I should recognize that the Lord is the center of everything. I need to think of the Word of the Lord every day, and I also need to have a close relationship with the Lord. Whatever the Lord moves me to do, I need to obey the Lord's will. I need to work for the Lord every day.[250]

## Obeying God

Six participants wanted to obey God and the Word of God, to the extent of lifelong, serious commitment. One participant stated, "I used to make decisions on my own. Since I became a Christian, Jesus has controlled my life. Commitment is obedience."[251] Another said, "If the Lord asks me to do something, whatever the cost, I would like to do it."[252]

In some responses, to "follow" was synonymous with obeying. "Because he is really my God, really. He led my life, and I experienced some things. So, I wanted to follow him, to go with him."[253] One participant wanted to "obey what God says" and "follow his image in order to be like him, to be complete, and to grow up to the level of Jesus."[254] For another participant, life's purpose was to follow, which meant obeying God's commands, praying, and reading the Bible:

> I will keep on following Jesus. First, I should know clearly who Jesus is. I need to know him through the Bible. Then, I should do what he commands, do what he asks us to do. Though Satan and the world can tempt you, you still follow Jesus closely by way of

---

249. X/F, Transcripts of Converts, 268.

250. J3/F, Transcripts of Converts, 82.

251. J1, Transcripts of Converts, 64.

252. N1/F, Transcripts of Converts, 137.

253. W4/F, Transcripts of Converts, 231.

254. Z2/F, Transcripts of Converts, 299.

praying and reading the Bible. Do not leave God when you are tempted.[255]

## Dedicating Oneself to God

Some participants were willing to dedicate themselves to God, as with one participant, who had previously considered work as "more important than any other thing," but was now "happy to dedicate myself to God."[256]

Dedication also held a sense of giving everything that one could give to God, out of wholesome commitment. One participant captured this well, saying, "Commitment is to enter into the world of God with all your heart, mind, and life and dedicate yourself to God and work for him."[257] The following responses describe such dedication:

> I want to dedicate all that I have to Jesus Christ. The more my faith has grown, the more I think of commitment. At the beginning of this year, I set a goal to dedicate all of my life to the Lord. And then, gratitude is the theme of my faith. Whenever I think of faith, I think of gratitude. I will regard all that God gives me, my ability and everything else, as sacrifices and offer them to God.[258]

> In the past, I thought if I put in the effort, I would get something back, but it's different now. I'm doing something for the Lord. Now I will tell my Lord what I want to do or try, so please listen to my prayer and prepare the way for me. I will wholeheartedly offer it to you. I no longer ask for anything now.[259]

## Serving the Church Full-Time

Three participants wanted to serve the Lord as full-time workers. Out of a grateful heart, one participant wanted "to study in seminary and become a pastor."[260] Another participant felt a burden to eventually become a full-time worker:

255. W, Transcripts of Converts, 201.
256. X/F, Transcripts of Converts, 266.
257. L2/F, Transcripts of Converts, 110.
258. J2/F, Transcripts of Converts, 75.
259. W5/F, Transcripts of Converts, 252.
260. Z5, Transcripts of Converts, 331.

I want to serve the Lord as a full-time worker. I think if I serve the Lord more and longer, I'll be able to experience more grace and power beyond what I ask for and expect. Now I have things to do, and sometimes I am still weak in my faith, but I must serve the Lord as a full-time worker later and keep a very deep relationship with God.[261]

One participant felt a strong conviction to become a missionary:

Actually, I attended many short-term missions, and I found that the place where Christians live should is the mission field and that Christians should become missionaries. I decided to commit myself to be a missionary every time when I attended retreats, such as a conference called Mission China. Up to now, the Lord keeps such a will in my heart, and it has not disappeared. When I came to believe in God, I felt thankful to the missionary for leading me to God. I hope that more people come to know God through me.[262]

## Loving Others

Even though one participant felt aversive towards new or non-believers, she became committed to loving them because God loved them.

I should love others with all my heart, because there are many sisters who never met Jesus. They first came to church when their friends asked them to, and they were assigned to my small group. I learned that they have many kinds of problems, and initially, I did not like to talk with them. I felt that they were not saved. Their lives were not good, and they did not seem to have a good spirit. I really couldn't stand them anymore. Later on, I thought to myself, "If God loves us, then why can't I love them?" I couldn't do it by myself, so I prayed that I could love them by relying upon God. Then, they could come to know the meaning of church and gradually be changed. I really like that.[263]

---

261. C1, Transcripts of Converts, 10.
262. D/F, Transcripts of Converts, 42.
263. Y/F, Transcripts of Converts, 280.

## Summary

In summary, when participants were asked about their commitment, they commonly answered that they wanted to follow God and do what God asks Christians to do in various ways.

In terms of themes, commitment meant evangelizing and sharing the gospel with their words, actions, and even careers, because of the sacrificial love of Jesus and God had commanded so. Second, participants also wanted to live a God-centered life, by listening to the Word of God and loving God. Next, participants wanted to obey God and the Word of God, which was akin to following God. Fourth, some participants wanted to dedicate themselves to God wholeheartedly, showing a great level of commitment. Fifth, the participants wanted to serve Christ as full-time workers, as either pastors or missionaries. Finally, one participant wanted to love other people, even though she did not want to and could not, because God loved them and so that they might change. The next section presents comparative analysis of the major themes for preparing selective coding.

## Comparative Analysis of the Major Themes

Making comparisons is an essential task in developing a theory. According to Strauss and Corbin, constant comparisons are a fundamental analytic tool that helps the analyst identify the similarities and differences of concepts by comparing incidents or concepts.[264]

This section presents a comparative analysis of the major themes treated in the above sections. A total of six pairs of items were compared in order to identify the major factors affecting conversion and their relationship in the process of conversion:

1. Obstacles to Conversion and Means of Overcoming the Obstacles

2. State of Life before Conversion and after Conversion

3. State of Life before Conversion and Personal Motives for Going to Church

4. Positive and Negative Feelings When Initially Attending Church

5. The Most Attractive Characteristics of Christianity and Reasons Participants Believed in Christianity

264. Corbin and Strauss, *Qualitative Research 3e*, 73.

6. Special Religious Experiences and the Reasons Why Participants Believed in Christianity.

## Obstacles to Conversion and Means of Overcoming the Obstacles

The participants were brought up in an atheistic educational system that emphasized the non-existence of God and self-reliance rather than reliance on God. As a result, most of the participants confessed atheism, a distorted image of God and Christian concepts, or a strong self as an obstacle to conversion. Nevertheless, the participants overcame those obstacles, mostly through the Word of God, prayer, or the witness of other Christians. A few other participants overcame through a mystical experience, watching films, reasoning, or their own determination. Figure 6 summarizes the comparison between obstacles to conversion and how the participants overcame them.

| Obstacles to Conversion | Means of Overcoming the Obstacles |
|---|---|
| Atheism (13)<br>Objections from Others (6)<br>Strong Self (4)<br>Bad Christians (3)<br>Buddhism (2)<br>Perspective on Sin (1)<br>Views on Values (1)<br>Cult-like (1)<br>Image of God as Father (1)<br>God's Punishment (1) | The Word of God<br>  Studying the Bible (4)<br>  Listening to Sermons (3)<br>Prayer<br>  Enlightenment through Prayer (2)<br>  Answers to Prayer (1)<br>  Praying during Retreats (3)<br>  Overcoming Suspicion through Prayer (1)<br>Other Christians' Witness<br>  Listening to Christians' Witness (3)<br>  Mature Christians (1)<br>  Experiencing Enlightenment (1)<br>Reasoning (2)<br>Determination (2)<br>Through Baptism (1)<br>Mystical Experience (1)<br>Watching Films (1) |

| Atheism<br>Strong Self<br>Misunderstanding God | Overcoming | Word of God<br>Prayers<br>Christians' Witness<br>Mystical Experience/<br>Baptism |
|---|---|---|

Figure 6. Comparing Obstacles to Conversion and Means
of Overcoming the Obstacles

## State of Life before Conversion and after Conversion

The participants experienced transformative changes after they converted to Christianity, as analyzed above. Before their conversion, most of the participants had lived a competitive and success-oriented life, and they felt insecure, depressed, and exhausted due to the pressures of their studies. Some had lived without a goal, standard, or meaning, so they felt empty and meaningless. Living and studying abroad, some participants experienced financial destitution, maladjustment, poor linguistic competence, and loneliness.

The participants noticeably changed in many ways after they converted to Christianity. As they experienced the sacrificial love of Jesus, they became less selfish and competitive and were able to forgive and love other people. Also, they found their new values and status in God, so they gained confidence, new hope, and self-respect. Their new Christian faith brought the participants emotional stability, allowing them to overcome anger, anxiousness, and bitterness rooted deeply in their hearts. They also had a new standard and perspective on life, so they became honest and better persons. Figure 7 summarizes the comparison of the participants' state of life before and after their conversion.

| Before the Conversion | After the Conversion |
|---|---|
| **Insecure/No Goal**<br>No Confidence (6)<br>Living Blindly (5)<br>Lonely (5)<br>Wanting Love (3)<br>Depressed (2)<br>No Goal (4)<br>Meaninglessness (2)<br>Empty (4)<br>No Hope (3) | **Becoming Stable/Having Hope**<br>Becoming Courageous (2)<br>Respecting Oneself (3)<br>Having Hope (3)<br>Becoming Less Angry (3)<br>Healing (1)<br>No More Anxiety (2) |
| **Self-Centered/Crisis**<br>No Standard (10)<br>Success-oriented (6)<br>Self-complacent (7)<br>Competitive (4)<br>Enjoying Life (4)<br>Complex Crisis (2)<br>Bad Grades (2)<br>Financial Problems (1) | **Becoming a Better Person**<br>Having a Standard (3)<br>Concern for Others (8)<br>Forgiving Others (6)<br>Recovering Relationship with Parents (7)<br>Becoming Less Selfish (2)<br>Becoming Social (2)<br>Becoming Less Competitive (1)<br>Becoming a Better Person (2)<br>New View on Values (1)<br>Having Eternal Life (1) |

Figure 7. Comparing State of Life before and after Conversion

## Relationship between the State of Life before Conversion and Personal Motives for Going to Church

The participants' state of life before converting to Christianity is closely related to their initial motives for going to church. The data analysis of both topics reflects similar themes and a close relationship. The participants who lived a lonely life without friends and family and felt no love wanted to go to church to make friends and attend church activities. Some students went to church because they faced personal problems. Personal crises were one of their major motives for going to church. They voluntarily went to church to find answers for their problems. Also, participants who had not experienced Christianity in China went to church out of curiosity. Figure 8 shows the relationship between the participants' state of life before conversion and their personal motives for going to church.

| State of Life Before Conversion | Personal Motives for Going to Church |
|---|---|
| Lonely (5)<br>Wanting Love (3) | Loneliness (5)<br>Activity (4) |
| Depressed (2)<br>Meaninglessness (2)<br>Empty (4) | Problem (4) |
| Ordinary Life (3)<br>No Hope (3)<br>No Goal (4) | Curiosity (6) |

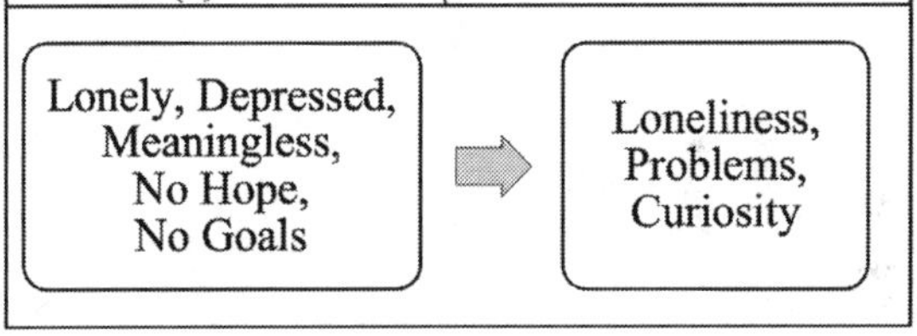

| Lonely, Depressed, Meaningless, No Hope, No Goals | ⇨ | Loneliness, Problems, Curiosity |
|---|---|---|

Figure 8. The Relationship between the State of Life before Conversion and Personal Motives for Going to Church

## Positive and Negative Impressions When Initially Attending Church

When initially attending church, participants described two different kinds of impressions, which were either positive (twenty-three) or negative (seven). The positive responses were mainly due to the attitude of the Christians towards them, hymns, and sermons, which made them feel peaceful, comfortable, and as if they were at home. Some of the negative responses were due to their preconceived ideas about Christianity. Some responses were related with impressions and thoughts on the appearance of worship services and prayer, which were regarded as abnormal. Others were related with religious differences that led to internal conflict when they attended the church activities. Figure 9 summarizes the comparison of the positive and negative impressions participants had when they first attended church.

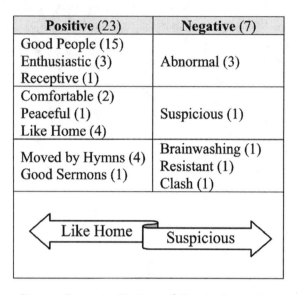

| Positive (23) | Negative (7) |
|---|---|
| Good People (15) Enthusiastic (3) Receptive (1) | Abnormal (3) |
| Comfortable (2) Peaceful (1) Like Home (4) | Suspicious (1) |
| Moved by Hymns (4) Good Sermons (1) | Brainwashing (1) Resistant (1) Clash (1) |

Figure 9. Comparing Positive and Negative Impressions
When First Attending Church

## The Most Attractive Characteristics of Christianity and Reasons for Believing in God

The comparison between the Most Attractive Characteristics of Christianity and Why the Participants Decided to Believe in God was made under seven themes: Salvific Characteristics, the Love of Christians, the Truth, Affective Characteristics, Ethical Characteristics, Beneficial Characteristics, and Superiority of Christians. Of these, the theme of Superiority of Christians has no comparison due to no mention of a corresponding reason for believing. Table 16 compares the most attractive characteristics of Christianity for the participants and the reasons the participants believed in Christianity.

Table 16. Comparing the Most Attractive Characteristics
of Christianity and Reasons for Believing in God

| | The Most Attractive Characteristics* (n=30) | Reasons for Believing in God* (n=30) |
|---|---|---|
| Salvific | Unconditional Love (3) Forgiveness of Sins (3) Atonement (3) Going to Heaven (1) Freedom (2) | The Sacrificial Love of God (3) Forgiveness of Sin (2) The Holy Spirit (1) Having Hope (1) |
| Christian Love | The Love of Christians (8) | The Love of Christians (1) |
| Intellectual | The Truth (5) | Intellectual Deliberation (3) The Word of God (1) The Existence of God (4) |
| Affective | Peace (2) Joy (1) Comfort (1) Inner Healing (1) | Inner Healing (1) |
| Ethical | Walking in the Light (1) Honest Perspective on Life (1) Sincerity (1) | To Be Like Jesus (1) To Become a New Person (5) |
| Beneficial | Getting Help (1) Beneficial to All Persons (1) | Experiencing God's Help (7) |
| Superior | Superiority of Christians (1) | No Mention |

* Some participants mentioned multiple (sub)themes.

First, the salvific aspects of God's grace was the most attractive characteristic to the participants. That is, twelve participants mentioned that salvific grace (Unconditional Love, Forgiveness of Sins, and Atonement) and its results (Going to Heaven and Freedom) were the most attractive characteristics of Christianity for them. In comparison, the salvific grace of God was the second most important reason for believing in God. Seven participants stated that they decided to believe in Jesus because of salvific grace (The Sacrificial Love of God, Forgiveness of Sin, The Holy Spirit, and Having Hope). This shows the significance of presenting the salvific grace of God, in terms of the abovementioned themes, as the core of the gospel and foundation of the Christian faith. It is noteworthy that although twenty-three participants noted themes other than salvific grace as their reasons for believing, this does not necessarily mean that these participants did not experience salvific grace as part of their conversion. In other words, although every participant mentioned experiencing salvific grace, each gave varying reasons when asked the reason for believing in Christianity.

Second, eight participants were attracted by the love of Christians, while one participant stated this theme as the reason for believing. The kindness and love of Christians towards students studying abroad was effective in attracting the participants.

Third, five participants mentioned the truth as the most attractive characteristic of Christianity, while eight participants noted that their reason for believing in Jesus was related to intellectual factors, such as The Word of God, The Existence of God, and Intellectual Deliberation. Since all participants were brought up with an atheistic education, the existence of God according to the teaching of the Bible was a determining factor that could lead them to Christianity. Their contact with Christianity could lead them to contemplate its truthfulness and make the decision to accept their newly found truth. Moreover, one participant decided to believe in Jesus because of the Word of God. Therefore, the basic and fundamental truths of the Bible, including the salvific grace of God and the existence of God, were important content for the Chinese students.

Fourth, five participants were attracted by affective characteristics (Peace, Joy, Comfort, and Inner Healing). However, only one participant stated she decided to believe in Jesus because of inner healing.

Fifth, three participants were attracted by the ethical factors of Christianity, which were included the themes of Walking in the Light, Honest Perspective on Life, and Sincerity, while six participants decided to believe in Jesus because of the themes To Be Like Jesus and To Become a New Person. These six participants were not satisfied with themselves and decided to believe in Jesus, because they found answers for improving their lives in Jesus and his teachings.

Sixth, only two participants mentioned beneficial aspects (Getting Help and Beneficial to All Persons), but seven participants stated that they decided to become a Christian because of Experiencing God's Help. As students studying abroad without their usual support back home, they received help in various ways, such as getting admitted to universities and receiving scholarships, writing a thesis, meeting their material needs, and overcoming a crisis.

Special Religious Experiences and Reasons for Believing in God

Some participants indicated that a special religious experience was the reason they decided to believe in God. For instance, twelve participants experienced God's Help, and seven mentioned it as their reason for believing in Jesus. Eight participants noted they had special experiences when they read the Bible and listened to preaching, while one participant decided to believe in Jesus because of the Word of God. Though some participants did not identify their reason for believing as the Bible or the Word of God, others mentioned the Bible indirectly, as through the themes, the Existence of God, the Sacrificial Love of God, and Forgiveness of Sins. Although four participants had mystical experiences, such as seeing visions and hearing the voice of God, they did not state it as their reason for believing. The theme of Praying also had a mystical aspect, because seven participants experienced revivalism while praying at a retreat. For instance, they suddenly started to shed tears while praying and repented their sins for the first time in their life, experiencing the forgiveness of their sins. Yet, they did not identify this as their reason for believing, although these experiences affected their understanding of Christianity greatly. Table 17 compares participants' special religious experiences and the reasons why they believed in Christianity. The following section deals with selective coding.

Table 17. Comparing Special Religious Experiences
and Reasons for Believing in God

| Special Religious Experiences* (n=30) | Reasons for Believing* (n=30) |
| --- | --- |
| God's Help (12) | Experiencing God's Help (7) |
| The Bible (5) | The Word of God (1) |
| Preaching (3) | The Existence of God (4) |
| God's Guidance (2) | The Holy Spirit (1) |
| Visions and Voices (4) | Intellectual Deliberation (3) |
| Praying (7) | The Sacrificial Love of God (3) |
| Listening to Witness (3) | Forgiveness of Sin (2) |
| Listening to Hymns (1) | Having Hope (1) |
| Watching Films (1) | The Love of Christians (3) |
| No Special Experience (7) | Inner Healing (1) |
| | To Be Like Jesus (1) |
| | To Become a New Person (5) |

* Some participants mentioned multiple themes.

# Selective Coding

In the process of building a theory in grounded theory, selective coding (or theoretical coding) is the final stage in which the analyst integrates and refines the theory.[265] To develop a theory on conversion, the most important content that needs to be explored are the factors and their relationships to each other in the process of conversion.

As mentioned in chapter 3, the highest-level categories were delineated by the interview questions, thus marking the various factors and phases of the conversion process. The questions and the highest-level categories generally fell under three phases of conversion: (1) background and life before conversion, (2) initial contact (encounter) with the gospel, action/interaction, and making the decision to believe, and (3) consequences of conversion. In order to compare and theoretically integrate the themes

265. Strauss and Corbin, *Qualitative Research*, 143.

within the highest-level categories, however, the phase-oriented boundaries of these categories were removed.

First, for theoretical integration, relevant major categories were chosen, then compared to each other. After, these major categories were visualized to show their flow in the process of conversion. Next, this flow became the basis for a storyline, which captured the theoretical relationships between major factors of conversion. Finally, I took the themes of the categories most influential to conversion and classified them according to six dimensions of conversion. This classification served to remove the phase-oriented boundaries of the existing categories and visualize which dimension contained the largest number of themes. As a result, I could identify the most significant dimension of conversion, from which the core category was derived.

## Theoretical Integration of the Analysis of Conversion

Analyzing data related to factors, process, and theoretical integration is a major part of theory building in grounded theory. Strauss and Corbin state that "concepts must be linked and filled in with detail to construct theory out of data."[266] During the selective coding, I compared categories and their themes to identify those considered to have the most common and crucial factors for conversion. As a result, ten major categories were identified, as shown in Table 18. Then, these ten categories were integrated into a fishbone diagram, as shown in Figure 10, in order to show the overall flow of these categories with respect to the process of conversion. The next section discusses the storyline derived from this integration.

Table 18. Factors Affecting Conversion According to
Themes Grounded in the Data

| Major Categories | Themes |
| --- | --- |
| Before Conversion | Ordinary Life, Self-Centered Life, Insecure Life, Crisis, Religious |
| Motivation | Curiosity, Loneliness, Activity, Problems |
| First Impressions | Positive Impressions, Negative Impressions |

266. Strauss and Corbin, *Qualitative Research*, 103.

| Major Categories | Themes |
| --- | --- |
| Obstacles | Atheism, People's Objections, Strong Self, Bad Christians, Buddhism, Perspective on Sin, Views on Values, Cult-like, Image of God as Father, God's Punishment |
| Means of Overcoming | The Word of God, Prayer, Christians' Witness, Reasoning, Determination, Baptism, Mystical Experience, Watching Films |
| Reasons for Deciding to Believe | The Existence of God, Intellectual, To Become a New Person, Love of Christians, Sacrificial Love of God, Experiencing God's Help, Word of God, Inner Healing, Forgiveness of Sin, Holy Spirit, Having Hope, To Be Like Jesus |
| Influential People | Serving Christians, Christian Role Models, Love of Church Members, Love of Pastors |
| Most Attractive Characteristics | Salvific, Love of Christians, The Truth, Affective, Ethical, and Beneficial Characteristics, Superiority of Christians |
| Special Religious Experiences | God's Help, The Bible, Praying, Visions and Voices, Preaching, Listening to Witness, God's Guidance, Listening to Hymns, Watching Films, No Special Experience |
| Consequences | Improved Relationships, Greater Confidence, Emotional Stability, Ethical Standard, New Religious Understanding, New Perspective on Values |

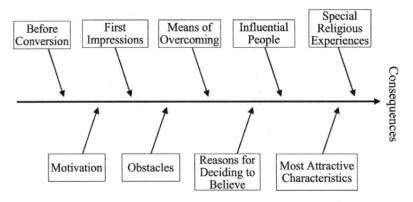

Figure 10. Factors Affecting Conversion and Their Flow According to Categories Grounded in the Data

## Storyline of the Conversion of Chinese Students

I conceptualized the storyline according to the ten major categories. The categories analyzed are related not only to the context (situation) of the participants and factors affecting conversion, but also to the process of conversion, which includes the relationships among the factors. The storyline of the conversion factors and process is as follows.

The participants were educated as atheists from a young age. Most of them lived a self-centered life with atheistic perspectives and without a standard, so they felt insecure and in crisis. Loneliness and personal problems were their main motives for going to church. The people who invited them to go to church were Korean and Chinese Christian friends, church members, pastors, and missionaries. When they went to church, most felt welcomed by the enthusiastic Christians, so they felt comfortable and had a positive impression of church and Christians. Nevertheless, some of them had negative impressions due to their preconceptions about Christianity, but these were not a serious hindrance to attending church.

The participants had various kinds of obstacles for accepting Christian faith and its teachings. Atheism was the most conspicuous obstacle because of their atheistic education, which rejected the existence of God and distorted the teachings of Christianity. Some obstacles were due to their personal characteristics, such as having a strong sense of self, or their family background, such as the image of their father. These obstacles were overcome as they experienced the grace of God through the Word of God, prayer, and other Christians' witnesses. They were enlightened when they listened to preaching and testimonies. Some were also able to overcome their obstacles when their prayers were answered or when they experienced revivalism while praying at a retreat.

When the participants first went to church, many characteristics of Christianity attracted them to keep attending church. According to the data analysis, there were seven characteristics, which are explained as follows. First, many of the participants were attracted by the sacrificial love of God and its consequences: atonement, forgiveness, unconditional love, eternal life, and freedom. Second, the participants found that Christians were different from non-Christians in how they treated other people, that is, Christians love other people. Third, the truth attracted the participants. They were able to find truth in the Bible and thought that the Bible was written by God, not by wise people. They believed in the existence of God through the teachings of the Bible, which was a great breakthrough, since they had had an atheistic education.

Fourth, affective factors attracted the participants. For instance, they not only felt peace and joy, but also felt comfortable at church. Fifth, ethical characteristics were another important attractant. Some of the participants confessed that they were confused and did not recognize what was right when they saw the wrongdoings of others. Through Christianity, they found a standard for living, so they were able to walk in the light and live with sincerity and kindness. Sixth, some of the participants noted that the help they received from God attracted them to Christianity. Since they were living and studying abroad, they experienced various difficulties, such as adjusting to a new country, studying in a new language, living without friends and family, facing financial issues, etc. However, as they attended church and prayed for their problems, they received help from God and solved their problems. They believed that God helped them in their difficulties. Seventh, the participants were attracted to Christianity because they saw the superiority of Christians. They acknowledged the strengths of Christians, both in their achievements and behavior.

The participants noted that they decided to believe in Jesus for twelve reasons, which include some of the above-mentioned characteristics, such as experiencing God's help, the Word of God, the existence of God, the sacrificial love of God, the forgiveness of sins, the love of Christians, and inner healing. The other reasons were intellectual deliberation, having hope, the Holy Spirit, to become a new person, and to be like Jesus. Some of the participants reflected on what they learned at church and decided to believe in Jesus. One participant, who was once desperate due to his family situation, found hope in Christianity because he received the love of God and the love of the Christians who helped him. Another participant wanted to become a new person after hearing a church member's testimony about changing into a new person.

As the participants converted to Christianity, they changed into new people, emotionally stable and saw themselves as better people. They gained self-confidence, courage, and hope. They become less anxious and angry. Their behavior also greatly changed after their conversion. They were able to have new standards and perspectives and lived accordingly. They became less selfish and competitive and were able to forgive and be concerned about other people. Therefore, their relationships with others improved greatly.

## Classifying the Factors Affecting Conversion According to Six Dimensions

This section describes the process of determining the factors of conversion that were most influential in the conversion of the participants. After the storyline was created, the ten major categories were narrowed, then classified according to six dimensions of conversion. The purpose of this classification was to remove the boundaries of the highest-level categories and compare the subsumed themes, so that a core category could be derived.

First, the ten major categories were further narrowed by deciding which were the most indicative of a positive response to the gospel and contained the most significant factors of conversion. In this manner, the major categories (Before Conversion, Motivation, First Impressions, Obstacles, Means of Overcoming, Reasons for Deciding to Believe, Influential People, Most Attractive Characteristics, Special Religious Experiences, and Consequences) were narrowed to five categories (First Impressions, Overcoming Obstacles, Reasons for Believing, Most Attractive Characteristics, and Special Religious Experiences). Second, the themes in these five categories were classified under six dimensions of conversion: cognitive, affective, evaluative, experiential, communal, and ideational. This classification visualized the dimension containing the largest number of themes, which served as an indicator of influence.

The dimensions of conversion proposed by Paul Hiebert and Eiko Takamizawa were used as a tool for comparing the themes or factors affecting conversion. Corbin and Strauss state that a "theoretical framework can be used to offer alternative explanations for finding."[267] Paul Hiebert's mental component dimension and Eiko Takamizawa's phenomenological dimension were utilized in this regard.[268] Hiebert explains the culture, the gospel, and the worldview based on three dimensions: the cognitive, affective, and evaluative dimensions. He explains these dimensions from the perspective of the gospel as follows: (1) the cognitive level is related to knowledge and truth, "with an understanding and acceptance of biblical and theological information and with a knowledge of God"; (2) the affective level relates to feeling "awe and mystery in God's presence, guilt, or shame for our sins, gladness for our salvation, and comfort in the fellowship of God's people"; and (3) the evaluative level concerns values and

267. Corbin and Strauss, *Qualitative Research 3e,* 40.
268. Corbin and Strauss, *Qualitative Research 3e,* 40.

allegiances.[269] Takamizawa suggests that "religious commitment involves three dimensions of the phenomenological level: ideational, communal, and experiential/spiritual."[270] According to Takamizawa, "ideational dimension refers to the content of the belief, communal to human relationship within the group, experiential/spiritual to the members' subjective experiences that connect to the Deity."[271]

My analysis of the factors affecting the participants' conversion found that all of the factors could be classified under Takamizawa's three dimensions of the phenomenological level and Hiebert's three dimensions of the human mental component related to the gospel. This finding may mean that the participants were exposed to various kinds of gospel presentations, so that they had the opportunity to encounter the Christian faith in a way that fit their personal characteristics. Table 19 shows the dimensions and the factors affecting conversion according to the themes analyzed above. This table was used as an explanatory framework to generate a theory by comparing conversion factors found in this study. The next section presents observations based on Table 19 and how the core category of this study was derived.

---

269. Hiebert, *Anthropological Insights*, 30–35.

270. Takamizawa, "Religious Commitment Theory," 165.

271. Takamizawa, "Religious Commitment Theory," 165.

Table 19. Dimensions and Factors Affecting Conversion
According to the Themes Grounded in Data

| Dimensions (total responses) | Conversion Factors* ($n$=30) (Themes are from First Impressions, Overcoming Obstacles, Reasons for Believing, Most Attractive Characteristics, and Special Religious Experiences) |
|---|---|
| Cognitive (6) | *Impressions (1)*: Good Sermons (1) |
| | *Overcoming (2)*: Reasoning (2) |
| | *Reasons (3)*: Intellectual Deliberation (3) |
| Affective (19) | *Impressions (10)*: Comfortable (2), Peace (1), Enthusiastic (3), Moved by Hymns (4) |
| | *Reasons (2)*: Inner Healing (1), Having Hope (1) |
| | *Attractive (7)*: Freedom (2), Peace (2), Joy (1), Comfort (1), Inner Healing (1) |
| Evaluative (15) | *Reasons (6)*: To Become a New Person (5), To Be Like Jesus (1) |
| | *Attractive (9)*: The Truth (5), Walking in the Light (1), Honest Perspective on Life (1), Sincerity (1), Superiority of Christians (1) |

The table is grouped under: Mental Component (40)

* Some participants reported multiple (sub)themes.

| Dimensions (total responses) | Conversion Factors* ($n=30$) (Themes are from First Impressions, Overcoming Obstacles, Reasons for Believing, Most Attractive Characteristics, and Special Religious Experiences) |
|---|---|
| **Phenomenological (119)** Experiential (76) | *Overcoming (20)*: Studying the Bible (4), Listening to Sermons (3), Enlightenment through Prayer (2), Answers to Prayer (1), Praying during Retreats (3), Overcoming Suspicion through Prayer (1), Listening to Christian's Witness (3), Baptism (1), Mystical Experience (1), Watching Films (1) |
| | *Reasons (14)*: The Existence of God (4), Experiencing God's Help (7), The Word of God (1), Forgiveness of Sin (2) |
| | *Attractive (4)*: Forgiveness of Sins (3), Getting Help (1) |
| | *Special (38)*: God's Help (12), The Bible (5), Praying (7), Visions and Voices (4), Preaching (3), Listening to Witness (3), God's Guidance (2), Listening to Hymns (1), Watching Films (1) |
| Communal (31) | *Impressions (20)*: Good People (15), Like Home (4), Receptive (1) |
| | *Reasons (3)*: The Love of Christians (3) |
| | *Attractive (8)*: The Love of Christians (8) |
| Ideational (12) | *Reasons (3)*: The Sacrificial Love of God (3) |
| | *Attractive (9)*: Atonement (3), Unconditional Love (3), Going to Heaven (1), Freedom (2) |

* Some participants reported multiple (sub)themes.

## Deriving the Core Category

The conversion factors in Table 19 are the themes found in the five major categories: First Impressions, Overcoming Obstacles, Reasons for Believing, Most Attractive Characteristics, and Special Religious Experiences. In Table 19, significant observations are as follows.

First, of the total of 159 individual responses classified, 40 responses are in the mental component dimensions, and 119 responses are in the phenomenological dimensions. Second, the dimension with the most responses is the experiential dimension (76), which has more than twice as many responses as the communal dimension (31), the second largest dimension.

Third, within the mental component dimension, the affective dimension has the greatest number of responses (nineteen), while the cognitive dimension has the fewest responses (six) out of all six dimensions. This shows that affective factors played a greater role in the participants' conversion than cognitive factors did. Fourth, although thirteen participants mentioned atheism as an obstacle to believing in Christianity (see chapter 4, subheading, "Obstacles to Conversion"), the cognitive dimension has only three responses from Reasons for Believing in God. This shows that participants who had intellectual obstacles to conversion were more influenced by non-cognitive factors when it came to believing in the existence of God. From this, we can infer that *cognitive factors, such as knowledge and doctrine, were not as influential as other kinds of factors.* That is, participants who considered atheism as an obstacle to conversion came to believe in the existence of God most likely through the experiential and communal dimensions.

Fifth, the experiential dimension contains the highest proportion of responses from several categories, as follows. All twenty responses from Overcoming Obstacles are in the experiential dimension. There are more responses from Reasons for Believing in God in the experiential dimension (fourteen) than in any other. From Special Religious Experiences, all thirty-eight responses (excluding No Special Responses) are under the experiential dimension. *Based on all of the above observations, the experiential dimension holds the most influential factors that affected the participants' conversion to Christianity.*

Moreover, situating the experiential dimension within the context of the research data led me to infer that the experience of God's grace and love was the most influential factor of conversion. From this dimension, the core category emerged. Almost all of the participants experienced problems and viewed their lives as problematic prior to conversion, before or after coming to Korea to study. Then, the participants met Christians, attended services and retreats, heard the gospel, and underwent many other situations detailed earlier in this chapter. These experiential factors are the most influential in leading the participants to believe in God, as well as the most indicative of experiencing God's grace and love. *Therefore, I conclude that Experiencing God is the core category derived from the data analysis of this research.*

In the broader context of the conversion process and the participants' Conspicuous Changes and Commitment to Christianity, *Experiencing God is considered as the turning point in which their problems were overcome, and their lives no longer seemed to be problematic.* Before conversion, nearly all of the participants faced problems or viewed their lives as problematic. For example, they felt insecure, exhausted, and even depressed due to academic pressure. Some lived without their own standard of living, following others without meaning or purpose. In Korea, some participants experienced crisis due to relationships, financial difficulties, maladjustment, poor language skills, and more. When the participants experienced God, they were led to believe in God, which became a turning point for them to overcome a wide range of problems.

Integrating the core category of Experiencing God and the idea of overcoming problems, Figure 11 displays a diagram of the basic schema of the conversion process of Chinese students in Korea. The next section discusses the types of conversion that the participants experienced.

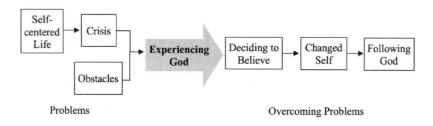

Figure 11. Basic Schema of the Conversion Process

## Types of Conversion

The way of designating the types, or motifs, of conversion can vary according to the perspective of the conversion factors. One may categorize types according to either the manner of encountering God or theoretical perspectives. Lofland and Skonovd make "conversion motifs" by integrating both. They suggest six motifs of conversions, which include "salient thematic elements and key experiences combined with objective situations."[272] The six motifs are: intellectual, mystical, experimental, affectional, revivalist, and coercive.

272. Lofland and Skonovd, "Conversion Motifs," 354–75.

However, these motifs are not appropriate to explain the conversions of the participants in this study, because none of them were converted through coercive factors or experimental factors. Rather than developing types or motifs of conversion based on a theoretical framework, what the convert states as the reason for deciding to believe is a more accurate way to represent the types of conversion. This is due to the complexity of the process of conversion. Many factors, not just one, affect conversion. For instance, those participants who had mystical experiences did not identify their mystical experience as their reason for deciding to believe in Jesus. As such, designating their conversion type as mystical would not represent the converts' own view of their conversion. *What the convert perceives as the most influential factor can best represent the type of conversion, rather than what others perceive through a theoretical framework.*

For this reason, I decided to ground the types of conversion in the participants' given reasons for deciding to believe in God, as detailed in chapter 4, subheading, "Why the Participants Decided to Believe in God." As a result, I present twelve types of conversion based on the themes emerged from the analysis of the participants' responses to the question, "Why did you decide to believe in Jesus?":

1. Believing in the Existence of God

2. Intellectual Deliberation

3. To Become a New Person

4. The Love of Christians

5. The Sacrificial Love of God

6. Experiencing God's Help

7. Amazed by the Consistency of the Word of God

8. Inner Healing

9. Forgiveness of Sin

10. The Work of the Holy Spirit

11. Having Hope

12. To Be Like Jesus.

The next section presents a theory of conversion generated from the data analysis shared thus far.

## A Conversion Theory

The study of conversion has to be comprehensive because it must not only explore the affecting factors, but also simultaneously analyze the process, especially since conversion is a process, not an instantaneous event. So, this study analyzed the factors together with the process. Furthermore, the types of conversion were based on what the participants defined as their reason for believing in Jesus, not on a theoretical perspective or an event that happened at a specific moment in time.

In this study, the core and salient concept overarching the significant concepts of this study is Experiencing God. Integrating the core category with the major categories, I present the following theory: *Chinese students studying in Korea were inclined to convert to Christianity upon experiencing God. Experiencing God was the turning point in which their problems were overcome, and they no longer viewed their lives as problematic. Moreover, by experiencing God, they could also overcome their obstacles to conversion, such as atheism, which hindered them from converting to Christianity.*

Figure 12 shows a paradigm of conversion, including the factors, process, and types of conversion of Chinese students in Korea.

| Conversion Process | | | | | | |
|---|---|---|---|---|---|---|
| Problems | | Overcoming Problems | | | | |
| Situation | Lifestyle | Experiencing God | Types of Conversion | Consequences | Commitment | |
| Insecure, Low Self-esteem, Crisis, Emptiness, Tired, No Hope, No Goal, etc. . . | Living Blindly, Excessive, Strong Self, Following the World, Success-oriented, etc. . . | Worship, Bible Study, Devotionals, Prayers, Revivalism, etc. . . | Intellectual Deliberation, To Become a New Person, Word of God, Inner Healing, etc. . . | Confidence, Hope, Joy, Freedom, Better Person, Less Angry, Having a Standard, etc. . . | Evangelism, God-Centered Life, Obeying God, Dedication to God, etc. . . | |

Figure 12. A Paradigm of Conversion

## Summary of Selective Coding

To conclude, the summary of selective coding is as follows. First, ten major categories containing the most common and crucial factors for conversion were chosen and integrated in a fishbone model. Next, a storyline was created using these categories, in order to show the broader, processual workings of conversion. Afterwards, these major categories were narrowed to five categories most indicative of a positive response to the gospel and most directly relevant to the conversion process. The themes of these five categories were classified under six dimensions of conversion. Subsequently, observations and analysis led to the conclusion that the experiential dimension was the most significant. Then, the core category, Experiencing God, was derived from this dimension. Next, twelve types of conversion unique to this study were identified, based on the participants' own responses to why they decided to believe in God. Finally, a conversion theory was generated as a result of the theoretical integration and analysis above.

Significant findings are summarized as follows. First, the most influential conversion factor for the participants was experiential, while cognitive factors were the least influential overall. Second, the process of conversion contains the basic schema of overcoming problems. That is, through experiencing God, most participants could overcome problems in their lives, including obstacles to converting to Christianity. This schema also includes the participants' consequences, such as improved relationships and greater concern for others, and commitment to Christianity, in the sense of following God, as a result of conversion. The following chapter presents the conclusion of this study.

# 5

# Conclusion

THE PURPOSE OF THIS study was to explore the Chinese students' conversion to Evangelical Christianity while they were studying in South Korea, especially to develop a theory related to the factors, process, and types of conversion using qualitative methodology. This concluding chapter consists of a summary of the research procedure, a summary of key findings, a conversion theory generated from the analysis, findings in relation to previous studies on Chinese intellectuals' conversions, implications for practice, and recommendations for future research.

## Summary of the Procedure

The procedure of this study for data gathering and analyzing can be summarized as follows. In regard to the characteristics and purpose of this study on conversion, I utilized grounded theory methodology, which is most appropriate for exploring factors and process of events or phenomena.

First, I conducted interviews with thirty Chinese students who converted while studying in Korea. The interviews were followed by theoretical sampling to identify concepts and themes that could be used to develop a theory limited to the research data.

Second, I transcribed and translated the interviews into English. In addition, I made observations at some of the Chinese churches that the participants attended, including worship services, Bible studies, retreats, and outdoor activities. To increase the validity of the study, I also interviewed seven pastors who worked with Chinese students.

Third, I analyzed the data according to the methodology of grounded theory by utilizing NVivo 11. Open coding and axial coding were used to identify concepts and categories. The highest-level categories created during the axial coding reflected the process of conversion in its different stages. The constant comparison method was used throughout the process of analysis, from the open coding to the selective coding.

Fourth, I did comparative analysis of major categories and summarized the comparisons as tables. Fifth, I conducted the selective coding, which theoretically integrated major categories and comprised of an analysis, according to several dimensions of conversion. This resulted in the emergence of the core category. During selective coding, integrated categories were also presented as diagrams to show the factors and process of conversion, and the types of conversion were discussed.

Finally, I developed a conversion theory from the theoretically integrated findings and also proposed a paradigm of conversion.

## Summary of Key Findings

The following is a summary of key findings grounded in the data of this research.

- Finding 1: Regarding the background of the participants, nineteen of the thirty participants lived an insecure life prior to their conversion to Christianity. Nineteen participants also lived a self-centered life.

- Finding 2: Approximately three-fourths of the participants (twenty-three) went to church because their friends invited them.

- Finding 3: Regarding the motives for first going to church, six participants went to church out of curiosity, five because of loneliness, four because of activities, while others did not state a specific motive.

- Finding 4: Twenty-three participants had a positive first impression of the church they first attended, and because the Christians were good people, enthusiastic, and receptive, these participants felt comfortable, peaceful, and at home.

- Finding 5: The most influential factors in the conversion of the thirty participants who had received atheistic education in China were in the experiential dimension of conversion.

- Finding 6: When the participants experienced God, atheism was no longer a hindrance, although thirteen participants reported that atheism had been an obstacle for them to convert to Christianity.

- Finding 7: Within the mental component dimension, which consists of evaluative, affective, and cognitive dimensions, the affective was most influential.

- Finding 8: The process of conversion for many of the participants includes the basic schema of overcoming problems. That is, experiencing God was a turning point for participants to overcome problems in their lives, overcome obstacles to conversion, and no longer see their lives as problematic.

- Finding 9: After the participants became converted, their relationships improved, and they became less selfish and more concerned for other people.

- Finding 10: Twenty-nine participants wanted to commit themselves to Christianity and God in various ways, in response to the saving grace of Jesus.

## A Conversion Theory

This study presents a theory on the conversion of the Chinese students in Korea, situated within the context of this research and grounded in the data analysis:

Chinese students studying in Korea were inclined to convert to Christianity when they experienced God. Experiencing God was the turning point for overcoming problems, allowing them to overcome obstacles to conversion, overcome present difficulties, and no longer view their lives as problematic.

## Findings in Relation to Previous Studies of the Conversion of Chinese Intellectuals

Conversion studies of Chinese intellectuals in North America offer useful information on the characteristics of the conversion factors and process in a cross-cultural context. Nevertheless, the subjects and circumstances of research on Chinese intellectuals' conversion in North America are considerably different from those of this study for at least three reasons. First, the Chinese intellectuals who converted in North America were mostly immigrants, whereas nearly all of the subjects of this study are students who were not seeking long-term residency in South Korea. Second, although there are many Chinese churches and Chinese communities in many North American cities, there are only a handful of Chinese immigrant churches and communities in South Korea. Third, most of the Chinese intellectuals in North America who were studied in existing research had experienced major political unrest in China.

Although there are large differences between the subjects of the Northern American studies and the Chinese students I studied in Korea, there are some commonalities: (1) they grew up in a Communist country with atheist teachings, (2) their host countries value democracy and religious freedom, and (3) Christianity is a major religion in their host countries. In terms of these commonalities, comparing the conversions of Chinese intellectuals in North America with the findings of this study may lead to several significant insights.

Fenggang Yang studied Chinese immigrants' conversion factors at the macro-level, embracing social and cultural contexts in the United States.[1] Yang has pointed out not only the limitations of the individualistic approach taken by the dominant theories of religious conversion, but also the inadequacy of the assimilation explanations of immigrant conversion when treating religious conversion cases among the Chinese in the United States. Brian Hall identifies social and cultural contextual factors affecting Chinese students' conversion in American universities, such as the collapse of traditional Chinese culture, Western modernization, and the prestige of Christianity.[2] The commonalities among Chinese converts created by the dramatic changes during a particular time of social and cultural turmoil in their country overshadow the individual personalities and interpersonal bonds that are often stressed in conversion studies. Therefore, Yang argues that "social and cultural changes in China in the process of coerced modernization are the most important factor for Chinese conversion to Christianity," viewing the institutional factors as of "secondary importance."[3]

Xuefeng Zhang explored how religious organizations have influenced Chinese immigrants' conversion to evangelical Protestantism in the United States. His research is mainly based on ethnographic fieldwork in a Chinese Christian church and a para-church organization (China Outreach Ministries), all located in the United States. Zhang argues that institutional

1. Yang, "Chinese Conversion," 237–57.
2. Hall, "Social and Cultural Context," 131–47.
3. Yang, "Chinese Conversion," 237.

factors greatly influence Chinese immigrants' conversion.[4] Describing the endeavors and the effectiveness of Christian institutions in evangelizing Chinese immigrants, Zhang does not seem to agree with Yang's argument that institutional factors are of secondary importance.

Unlike the Chinese intellectuals in Yang's study, the participants in this study did not experience social and cultural upheavals due to their younger age. Instead, they reaped the benefits of economic growth and the Open Door Policy of the Chinese government. Therefore, Yang's argument cannot explain the conversion of these students in Korea. Interpersonal relationships and institutional factors are among the major factors affecting the conversion of Chinese students in Korea. Most of the students first went to church with a Christian friend, and the churches and mission institutions played a central role in their conversion.

Yuting Wang studied the religious conversion to Christianity of Chinese students based on in-depth interviews.[5] His comparative study examines the different patterns of religious conversion to Christianity in two Chinese student communities. Wang argues that context is the primary factor, more important than socio-cultural changes, in the process of conversion among current Chinese students on college campuses. My study also found that the context of the converts is significant. As they live and study abroad, they face various difficulties that lead them to seek help from God. Many of the converts confessed that they experienced help from God when they had difficulties.

Kwai Hang Ng studied Chinese conversion to Christianity through the perspective of assimilation theories.[6] He argues that converting to Christianity for Chinese immigrants is a process of learning the American way through a creative deployment of their own cultural categories, symbols, and practices. This explanation also emphasizes the importance of socio-cultural factors among Chinese converts in America. However, the converts in my study did not have the intention of immigrating to Korea and also did not feel the need to assimilate to Korean society. Rather, they were attracted to convert due to spiritual truth, the love of God, and the loving kindness of Christians.

Tsu-Kung Chuang studied the factors influencing the conversion to Christianity of Chinese intellectuals in North America mainly using

4. Zhang, "Chinese Conversion," 149.
5. Wang, "Conversion to Christianity."
6. Ng, "Seeking Christian Tutelage," 195–214.

quantitative methodology, employing questionnaire surveys among Chinese intellectuals and mainland Chinese ministry workers, combined with interviews with mainland Chinese converts.[7] He found that these intellectuals were looking for a faith that was valid in the context of their scientific pursuits, in their hopes for China, and in their private lives. Based on his findings, Chuang suggests that the gospel message should be presented in a more rational and intellectual way so that the message may be accepted cognitively.[8] Samuel Ling, based on his experience of serving Chinese intellectuals in the United States, notes: "We are discovering that it often takes a long time for a PRC to think and rethink the claims of Christ. Thus we are rediscovering the importance of the *intellectual* aspect of faith, i.e., the role of understanding."[9]

Although it is important to consider the significance of cognitive factors in the conversion of Chinese intellectuals, we must also recognize other important factors. This study found that cognitive factors such as knowledge and doctrine were not necessarily the most influential for atheistic Chinese converts. Instead, the Chinese students were more inclined to convert to Christianity when they experienced God. Furthermore, this finding suggests the need to reevaluate the cognitive belief theory, which stresses ideational components of the process and argues that people readily commit themselves to a particular religion because of what they believe.[10] Though the Chinese students received atheistic education in China and atheism was the most salient obstacle for converting, most of them converted to Christianity because of their personal experience of God's grace and love.

Drawing on psychological, sociological, cultural, and theological studies, Lai Fan Wong studied the conversion of Chinese intellectuals who immigrated to the United States.[11] In his research, he found that several factors were correlated to conversion, such as the immigrants' interactions with strongly welcoming Christians and the experience of psychological stress or crisis. This study also found that most Chinese students were surprised by the loving kindness of the Christians they met. The students experienced help from God, which gave them release from their stresses and freed them from various problems and crises. People living in foreign countries must

7. Chuang, "Conversion of Chinese Intellectuals."

8. Chuang, "Conversion of Chinese Intellectuals," 119.

9. Ling, "Critical Points," 190.

10. Kilbourne and Richardson, "Conflict and Conversion," 1–21.

11. Wong, "From Atheists to Evangelicals."

reshape their lives in circumstances that are insecure due to uprooting, lack of resources, and linguistic and cultural maladaptation. As such, the cross-cultural approach is the most desirable way to reach out to international students facing various difficulties.

Lewis Rambo, Steven Bauman, and Jiazhi Fengjiang, in "Toward a Psychology of Converting in the People's Republic of China," explore the psychological nature of Chinese college students' conversion to Christianity in China. In her ethnographic case study of Chinese university undergraduate and graduate students, Fengjiang found that rather than intellectual factors, social interactions were crucial in the conversion cases, even for those whose initial motive was an intellectual quest. According to Fengjiang, the communal element of Christianity, such as community service and friendships, helped students to cope with life events emotionally and intellectually.[12] This is congruent with the finding of this study: in response to questions concerning first impressions of church, overcoming obstacles to conversion, reasons for deciding to believe in God, and the most attractive characteristics of Christianity, only six responses were in the cognitive dimension, while thirty-one responses were in the communal dimension. Fengjiang states that a critical motivation for the Chinese students to convert to Christianity was "an unexpected life event or a stressful period that was difficult to cope with."[13]

## Implications for Practice

The purpose of this study was to explore factors affecting conversion, together with the process and types of conversion, in order to develop a conversion theory. This study identified significant factors and constructed a theory explaining the conversion of Chinese students. This section presents three practical implications which may benefit ministries serving Chinese international students: the overcoming problem approach, the coming home approach, and the role model approach.

---

12. Rambo et al., "Psychology of Converting," 901.

13. Rambo et al., "Psychology of Converting," 901.

## The Overcoming Problem Approach

To be an effective gospel worker, making the gospel relevant to the life situations of potential converts is crucial. This study found that the majority of the Chinese students in Korea felt insecure and were exhausted due to competition and academic pressures. As a result of the One Child Policy, the parents of these only children can be highly demanding. The participants felt powerless and did not know what to do for their future. Many of them viewed their lives as unhappy and problematic. They themselves were success-oriented, self-complacent, self-centered, and mostly atheists.

Therefore, ministries for Chinese students should be based on a holistic mission strategy, rather than only presenting the gospel without considering the needs and situation of potential converts.[14] Proclaiming the gospel is mandatory and essential, but ministries should not stop there. I found that the Chinese students were attracted not only to the salvific aspect of Christianity, but also to receiving help and loving kindness. Indeed, thirteen of the Chinese students confessed that they decided to believe in Jesus because of receiving help and love from God and Christians. In the conversion process, communal factors, which were the second most influential, contained what Christians did to serve and help the participants. Christians should try to holistically meet the Chinese students' needs, both spiritual and practical.

People may have culture-specific obstacles regarding the Christian faith. A deep understanding of these obstacles is just as important as knowing how to overcome them. Nearly half of the Chinese students confessed that atheism was a persistent obstacle, due to their atheistic upbringing in China. This study found that Chinese students converted to Christianity not through cognitive factors, but mainly through experiential factors. When the participants experienced God, their atheistic beliefs were no longer a hindrance. Therefore, ministries should provide Chinese students with diverse opportunities to experience God, so that they might overcome the obstacles hindering them from converting to Christianity.

## The Coming Home Approach

Chinese people have strong family bonds. Many famous Chinese poems are about missing family and home. The Chinese students said that their

14. Chuang, "Conversion of Chinese Intellectuals," 163.

churches in Korea felt like home, because they could see the unconditional love and kindness that they could only receive at home. Chinese Christians generally refer to their church as their "spiritual home." I recall how, in one mission field, Chinese Christians who were working abroad would arrive at our church and say that they had arrived home. Likewise, the participants confessed that they felt comfortable, joyful, and peaceful when attending church, and they were also moved by the love that Christians showed them. One Chinese student said that he decided to become a Christian because of the genuine love of the Christians at his church. To make church a place like home is an ideal strategy for effectively approaching Chinese students living abroad.

Additionally, almost every participant referred to small group meetings, such as Bible study meetings, when they talked about their church. The Chinese students who are attending a church with an effective small-group system claimed that their small group members are like their own brothers and sisters. Thus, small groups can also provide Chinese international students with a "sense of belonging and intimate relationships."[15]

## The Role Model Approach

Chinese students want to find role models in their lives. Many participants stated that they did not have their own standard of living. Some of them were attracted to Christianity by the ethical standards of Christianity and by the sincerity and honesty of the Christians they encountered. They wanted to convert to Christianity because they wanted to become a new person, to be like Jesus, and to be a better person. Christians should not only emphasize the values and ethics of Christianity, but also live according to these values and be good role models for Chinese students. We should follow Jesus ourselves before asking others to follow him.

## Recommendation for Future Research

I would like to make a recommendation for furthering research on conversion. I developed this study using grounded theory methodology. Phenomenology might also be a meaningful way to study conversion for those who want to describe or interpret the essence of the conversion

15. Chuang, "Conversion of Chinese Intellectuals," 165.

experience, According to van Manen, phenomenology is the most appropriate methodology for investigating the meaning of the lived experience.[16] Because conversion is an experience of a life-changing transformation, phenomenological research on conversion would provide readers with a deep understanding of God's saving works and the distinctive ways of turning to God, which can enrich our dogmatic understanding of conversion in which conversion is one specific point in the order of salvation. To this end, van Manen's hermeneutic phenomenology is appropriate for studying conversion, with its emphasis on reflecting on experience and abstaining from getting caught up in theoretical, polemical, suppositional, and emotional approaches.

To do research on conversion using the method of phenomenology, I suggest the following guiding research question, based on Manen's questions for studying conversion.[17] What meaning do converts confer to their conversion experience? This research question may be explored with the following sub-questions: What is the conversion experience like? What is the meaning of conversion to them? How does the meaning of the conversion experience arise? How do they live through an experience like that? What is the uniqueness of conversion? How does the phenomenon of conversion originate? How can we grasp the phenomenon of conversion in its inception and existence?

Finally, the methodology of this conversion study could be applied to other groups.

16. Manen, *Phenomenology of Practice*, 43.
17. Manen, *Phenomenology of Practice*, 32–36.

# Appendix A
# Translation of Consent Form

Consent Form

Title of Research: Conversion of Chinese students in Korea to Evangelical Christianity: factors, processes, and types

1. I have read the instructions and informed consent form related to the study of the researcher.

2. I have read about the benefits and risks, and I am satisfied with the answers received concerning what I wanted to know.

3. I voluntarily agree to participate this research.

4. I agree to this research collecting data according to regulation of the Institutional Review Board (IRB).

5. I agree to the researcher doing research and keeping the results. I also agree to the IRB, Torch Trinity Graduate University, and any institution commissioned by the Department of Health and Welfare checking this study, which includes my information.

6. I understand that I can withdraw from this research at any time during the research, and I understand that I will not receive any harm if I participate in this research.

7. My signature means that I have received the consent form, which I will keep until the completion of the research.

Participant Name:

Signature:

Date:

# Appendix B

# Translation of Demographic Questionnaire

Demographic Questionnaire

Name:

1. When did you arrive in Korea?

2. When did you begin studying in Korea? What is your program?

3. What is your major?

4. If applicable, when did you graduate? What are you doing now?

5. Which church are you currently attending?

6. When did you first hear the gospel?

7. When did you start attending church?

8. What ethnicity is your pastor?

9. When did you decide to believe in God?

10. When were you baptized?

11. What is your religious background prior to conversion?

# Appendix C

## Location of Voice Recording Materials

Location of Voice Recording Materials

| Convert | ID for Voice Recording | Page Range in Transcripts |
|---------|------------------------|---------------------------|
| C1 | 16300–001 | 1–11 |
| C2/F | 15709–005 | 12–24 |
| C3/F | 160422–003 | 25–33 |
| D/F | 160126–001 | 34–45 |
| H | 160422–002 | 46–53 |
| J1 | 160311–004 | 54–64 |
| J2/F | 160420–001 | 65–76 |
| J3/F | 160311–004 | 77–83 |
| K/F | 151230–002 | 84–95 |
| L1 | 160406–001 | 96–102 |
| L2/F | 160311–003 | 103–112 |
| L3 | 150713–001 | 113–125 |
| N1/F | 160422–004 | 126–136 |
| N2 | 160408–001 | 137–145 |
| P/F | 150717–003 | 146–155 |
| Q | 160219–001 | 156–166 |
| S | 150709–013 | 167–178 |
| T/F | 150709–015 | 179–193 |
| W1 | 160318–002 | 194–201 |

| Convert | ID for Voice Recording | Page Range in Transcripts |
|---------|------------------------|---------------------------|
| W2 | 160304–003 | 202–210 |
| W3/F | 150717–001 | 211–223 |
| W4/F | 160426–002 | 224–238 |
| W5 | 150717–002 | 239–258 |
| X/F | 160421–002 | 259–269 |
| Y/F | 160318–001 | 270–281 |
| Z1 | 160423–006 | 282–289 |
| Z2/F | 160322–001 | 290–300 |
| Z3/F | 160408–002 | 301–307 |
| Z4/F | 160311–002 | 308–322 |
| Z5 | 160423–007 | 323–330 |

*Note*: 160422–003, for example, means that the interview was conducted on April 22, 2016.

# Bibliography

Bainbridge, William Sims. "The Sociology of Conversion." In *Handbook of Religious Conversion*, edited by H. Newton Malony and Samuel Southard, 178–91. Birmingham: Religious Education, 1992.

Bays, Daniel H. *A New History of Christianity in China*. West Sussex: Blackwell, 2012.

Begley, C. M. "Using *Triangulation* in Nursing Research." *Journal of Advanced Nursing* 24.1 (1996) 122–28.

Berkhof, Louis. *Systematic Theology*. Grand Rapids: Eerdmans, 1979.

Berling, Judith A. *A Pilgrim in Chinese Culture: Negotiating Religious Diversity*. Maryknoll, NY: Orbis, 1997.

Bieler, Stacey. "Contemporary Chinese Intellectuals, II: Undercurrents Leading to Tiananmen Square, 1980–1989." In *Chinese Intellectuals and the Gospel*, edited by Samuel Ling and Stacey Bieler, 33–56. San Gabriel, CA: P&R, 1999.

Bowden, John. *Christianity: The Complete Guide*. New York: Continuum, 2005.

Buckser, Andrew, and Stephen D. Glazier. *The Anthropology of Religious Conversion*. Lanham, MD: Rowman & Littlefield, 2003.

Casino, Tereso. "Are Diaspora Missions Valid? Disciple-Making among Filipino Kabayans." In *Scattered*, edited by Luis Pantoja et al., 123–45. Manila: LifeChange, 2004.

Castles, Stephen, and Mark J. Miller. *The Age of Migration: International Population Movements in the Modern World*. 4th ed. New York: Guilford, 2009.

CCCOWE. "List of Chinese Churches." Accessed November 25, 2015. http://www.cccowe.org/church/html/browse.html#U.

Chao, Jonathan. "The Gospel and Culture in Chinese History." In *Chinese Intellectuals and the Gospel*, edited by Samuel Ling and Stacey Bieler, 9–24. San Gabriel, CA: P&R, 1999.

Charmaz, Kathy. *Constructing Grounded Theory: A Practical Guide through Qualitative Analysis*. Thousand Oaks, CA: Sage, 2006.

Ching, Julia. *Chinese Religions*. Maryknoll, NY: Orbis, 1993.

Cho, Gwi-sam. "The Missiological Answer of the Korean Church on the Pain of the Foreign Diaspora in Korea." Paper presented at the International Consultation on Global Diaspora: Trends and Strategies, Namyangju, Korea, August 4–6, 2008.

Choi, In Gee. "A Case Report of Chinese Students Ministry in Pusan National University." Paper presented at the Forum for the Mission of Foreign Students, Seoul, Korea, December 6, 2013.

Chuang, Tsu-Kung. "The Factors Influencing the Conversion of Mainland Chinese Intellectuals toward Christianity in North America." PhD diss., Trinity Evangelical Divinity School, 1995.

————. *Ripening Harvest: Mission Strategy for Mainland Chinese Intellectuals in North America*. Paradise, PA: Ambassadors for Christ, 1995.

Corbin, Juliet, and Anselm Strauss. *Basics of Qualitative Research 3e: Techniques and Procedures for Developing Grounded Theory*. Thousand Oaks, CA: Sage, 2008.

Creswell, John W. *Qualitative Inquiry & Research Design: Choosing among Five Approaches*. Thousand Oaks, CA: Sage, 2013.

————. *Research Design*. Thousand Oaks, CA: Sage, 1994.

Denzin, Norman K. "The Art and Politics of Interpretation." In *The SAGE Handbook of Qualitative Research*, edited by Norman K. Denzin and Yvonna Lincoln, 500–515. Thousand Oaks, CA: Sage, 1998.

Fan, Lizhu, and Na Chen. "Conversion and the Resurgence of Indigenous Religion in China." In *The Oxford Handbook of Religious Conversion*, edited by Lewis R. Rambo and Charles E. Farhadian, 556–77. New York: Oxford University Press, 2014.

Feng, Liu Xiao. "From Enlightenment to Exile." In *Chinese Intellectuals and the Gospel*, edited by Samuel Ling and Stacey Bieler, 57–62. San Gabriel, CA: P&R, 1999.

Freedman, Maurice. "On the Sociological Study of Chinese Religion." In *Religion and Ritual in Chinese Society*, edited by Arthur P. Wolf, 351–69. Stanford: Stanford University Press, 1974.

Gaiser, Frederick J. "A Biblical Theology of Conversion." In *Handbook of Religious Conversion*, edited by H. Newton Malony and Samuel Southward, 94–107. Birmingham: Religious Education, 1992.

Gaventa, Beverly R. "Conversion in the Bible." In *Handbook of Religious Conversion*, edited by H. Newton Malony and Samuel Southward, 41–54. Birmingham: Religious Education, 1992.

George, Sam. "Diaspora: A Hidden Link to 'From Everywhere to Everywhere.'" *Missiology* 39.1 (2011) 45–56.

Gernet, Jacques. *China and the Christian Impact: A Conflict of Cultures*. Translated by Janet Lloyd. New York: Cambridge University Press, 1985.

Ging, Kai Xuan. "An Unexpected Harvest." In *Mainland Chinese in America: An Emerging Kinship*, edited by Ambassadors for Christ, 31–38. Paradise, PA: Ambassadors for Christ, 1991.

"Government Attracting 200,000 Foreign Students until 2020." *Yonhab News*, October 29, 2012. https://www.yna.co.kr/view/AKR20121029115800004.

Hall, Brian. "Social and Cultural Context in Conversion to Christianity among Chinese American College Students." *Sociology of Religion* 67.2 (2006) 131–47.

Han, Kwon Shik. "Conversion of Iranian and Indonesian Muslims in South Korea to Evangelical Christianity." PhD diss., Torch Trinity Graduate University, 2012.

Hanciles, Jehu J. "Migration and Mission: Some Implications for the Twenty-first Century Church." *International Bulletin of Missionary Research* 27.4 (2003) 146–53.

Helm, Paul. *The Beginnings: Word & Spirit in Conversion*. Burks, UK: Hazell, Watson & Viney, 1986.

Hiebert, Paul G. *Anthropological Insights for Missionaries*. Grand Rapids: Baker Academic, 1985.

————. *Anthropological Reflection on Missiological Issues*. Grand Rapids: Baker, 1994.

Houston, Tom, et al. "The New People Next Door: Occasional Paper No. 55." Paper presented at the Forum of the Lausanne Committee for World Evangelization, Pattaya, Thailand, September 29—October 5, 2004.

Hua, Y. "An Analysis of Reasons and Approaches of Chinese Student Conversion to Christianity." *Journal of China Youth Today* 11 (2010) 75–80.

———. "An Investigation of Christian Beliefs among University Students in Shanghai." *Youth Study* 11 (2008) 27–34.

Huberman, A. Michael, and Matthew B. Miles. *Qualitative Data Analysis*. Thousand Oaks, CA: Sage, 1994.

Hunter, Alan, and Kwong Chan Kim. *Protestantism in Contemporary China*. New York: Cambridge University Press, 1996.

Kang, Hae Jin. "Missions to the Foreign Students as a Module of Missionary Training Curriculum." *Christianity Today Korea*, October 17, 2014. https://www.christiantoday.co.kr/news/275665.

Kilbourne, Brock, and James T. Richardson. "Paradigm Conflict, Types of Conversion, and Conversion Theories." *Sociology of Analysis* 50 (1988) 1–21.

Kim, Kyung Taek. "Foreign Students Returning as Leaders of Their Home Country." *Kuk-Min Daily*, July 16, 2013. http://news.kmib.co.kr/article/view.asp?arcid=0007375488.

Kim, Yoo Jun. "Yonsei University and Foreign Student Ministry." Paper presented at the Forum for Foreign Student Mission 2013, Seoul, Korea, December 6, 2013.

Korean Ministry of Education. "Foreign Students in 2015." https://www.moe.go.kr/boardCnts/viewRenew.do?boardID=350&lev=0&statusYN=C&s=moe&m=0309&opType=N&boardSeq=60923.

———. "Statistics of Foreign Students in 2019." https://www.moe.go.kr/boardCnts/view.do?boardID=350&lev=0&statusYN=W&s=moe&m=0309&opType=N&boardSeq=79011.

———. "Summary of the Basic Statistics of Education for 2015." https://www.moe.go.kr/boardCnts/viewRenew.do?boardID=350&lev=0&statusYN=C&s=moe&m=0309&opType=N&boardSeq=60923.

KOSTA. "Vision." Accessed September 2, 2015. Kostaworld.org/homepage_30th/board/introduce.

KOWSMA. "KOWSMA Bulletin." Presented at Forum for the Mission of Foreign Students, Seoul, Korea, December 6, 2013.

Lamb, Christopher, and M. Darrol Bryant. *Religious Conversion: Contemporary Practices and Controversies*. New York: Cassell, 1999.

Lambert, Tony. *China's Christian Millions*. London: Monarch, 1999.

———. *The Resurrection of the Chinese Church*. Wheaton: Shaw, 1994.

Lane, T. Dennis. "Conversion in an Evangelical Context: A Study in the Micro-Sociology of Religion." PhD diss., Northwestern University, 1980.

Lee, Sang In. "Who Are *panta ta ethne* (Matt. 28:29)?" *Scripture and Interpretation* 1.1 (2006) 50–67.

Lee, Sang Shick. "The Present State of the Future of Cooperating Mission for the Chinese Students in Korea." *China to God*, August 1, 2015. http://www.chinatogod.com/main/z2s_c_v.php?no=3192&div=2.

Lee, Sun Yong. "Why So Many Churches in Korea?" *The Korea Herald*, January 15, 2014. http://www.koreaherald.com/view.php?ud=20140115000985.

Leedy, Paul D., and Jeanne Ellis Ormrod. *Practical Research: Planning and Design*. Upper Saddle River, NJ: Prentice Hall, 2001.

Ling, Samuel. "Critical Points in the Conversion Process." In *Chinese Intellectuals and the Gospel*, edited by Samuel Ling and Stacey Bieler, 189–96. San Gabriel, CA: P&R, 1999.

————. "A Second Chance." In *Chinese Intellectuals and the Gospel*, edited by Samuel Ling and Stacey Bieler, 1–8. San Gabriel, CA: P&R, 1999.

Lofland, John. "Becoming a World-Saver: A Theory of Conversion to a Deviant Perspective." *American Behavioral Scientist* 20 (1977) 805–18.

Lofland, John, and Norman Skonovd. "Conversion Motifs." *Journal for the Scientific Study of Religion* 20 (1981) 373–85.

Manen, Max van. *The Phenomenology of Practice: Meaning-Giving Methods in Phenomenological Research and Writing.* Walnut Creek, CA: Left Coast, 2014.

Marshall, Catherine, and Gretchen B. Rossman. *Designing Qualitative Research.* Thousand Oaks, CA: Sage, 2010.

McGuire, Meredith B. *Religion: The Social Context.* Belmont, CA: Wadsworth, 1992.

Merleau-Ponty, Maurice. *Phenomenology of Perception.* New York: Humanities, 1962.

Merriam, S. B. *Qualitative Research and Case Study Applications in Education.* San Francisco: Jossey-Bass, 1998.

Moberg, David O. *The Church as a Social Institution: The Sociology of American Religion.* Englewood Cliffs, NJ: Prentice Hall, 1962.

Morris, George E. *The Mystery and Meaning of Christian Conversion.* Nashville: World Methodist Evangelism, 2004.

Ng, Kwai Hang. "Seeking the Christian Tutelage: Agency and Culture in Chinese Immigrants' Conversion to Christianity." *Sociology of Religion* 63.2 (2002) 195–214.

Ott, Craig. "Diaspora and Relocation as Divine Impetus for Witness in the Early Church." In *Diaspora Missiology: Theory, Methodology, and Practice,* edited by Enoch Wan, 87–110. Portland: Institute of Diaspora Studies of USA, 2011.

Park, Chan Shik, and Noah Jung. *Diaspora Mission and Migrant Mission in the World.* Seoul: Institute of Christian Industry and Society, 2013.

Park, Mu Ik. *The Religions of Korea 1984–2014.* Seoul: Korean Gallup Research, 2015.

Rambo, Lewis R. "Anthropology and the Study of Conversion." In *The Anthropology of Religious Conversion,* edited by Andrew Buckser and Stephen D. Glazier, 211–22. Lanham, MD: Rowman & Littlefield, 2003.

————. "The Psychology of Conversion." In *Handbook of Religious Conversion,* edited by H. Newton Malony and Samuel Southard, 159–77. Birmingham: Religious Education, 1992.

————. *Understanding Religious Conversion.* New Haven: Yale University Press, 1993.

Rambo, Lewis R., et al. "Toward a Psychology of Converting in the People's Republic of China." *Pastoral Psychology* 61.5 (2012) 895–921.

Robinson, Thomas A., and Hillary P. Rodrigues. *World Religions: A Guide to the Essentials.* Grand Rapids: Baker Academic, 2014.

Ruokanen, Miikka. *Christianity and Chinese Culture.* Edited by Miikka Ruokanen and Paulos Huang. Grand Rapids: Eerdmans, 2010.

Santos, Narry F. "Exploring the Major Dispersion Terms and Realities in the Bible." In *Diaspora Missiology: Theory, Methodology, and Practice,* edited by Enoch Wan, 19–37. Portland: Institute of Diaspora Studies of USA, 2011.

Seol, Dong Hun. *Research on the Actual Conditions of Migrant Workers and the Demands for Services to Support Them.* Seoul: Korea International Labor Foundation, 2003.

Seoul Metropolitan Government. "Seoul Metropolitan Government Will Take Care of the Inconveniences of 18,000 Chinese Students Living in Seoul." http://www.seoul.go.kr/archives/21441.

Shi, Kun. "Knowing Chinese Students and Scholars: The Background and Strategy to Evangelize Mainland Chinese Intellectuals." In *Mainland Chinese in America: An Emerging Kinship*, edited by Ambassadors for Christ, 81–89. Paradise, PA: Ambassadors for Christ, 1991.

Sisci, Francesco. *China: In the Name of Law: A New Global Order*. Florence: goWare, 2016.

Smith, Jonathan A., et al. *Interpretative Phenomenological Analysis: Theory, Method and Research*. Thousand Oaks, CA: Sage, 2009.

Snow, David A., et al. "Frame Alignment Process, Micromobilization, and Movement Participation." *American Sociological Review* 51 (1986) 464–81.

Stark, Rodney, and Charles Y. Glock. *Religion and Society in Tension*. Chicago: McNally, 1965.

Straus, Roger A. "Changing Oneself: Seekers and the Creative Transformation of Life Experience." In *Doing Social Life*, edited by John Lofland, 252–72. New York: Wiley & Sons, 1976.

Strauss, Anselm, and Juliet Corbin. *Basics of Qualitative Research: Techniques and Procedures for Developing Grounded Theory*. Thousand Oaks, CA: Sage, 1998.

Sutherland, Edwin H. *On Analyzing Crime*. Chicago: University of Chicago Press, 1973.

Takamizawa, Eiko. "Religious Commitment Theory: A Model for Japanese Christians." *Torch Trinity Journal* 2.1 (2003) 164–97.

Taw, Timothy. *John Sung My Teacher*. Singapore: Christian Life, 1985.

Taylor, Bryan. "Conversion and Cognition: An Area for Empirical Study in the Microsociology of Religious Knowledge." *Social Compass* 23.1 (1976) 5–22.

Temple, C. William. "Perspective Transformation among Mainland Chinese Intellectuals Reporting Christian Conversion while in the United States." PhD diss., Trinity Evangelical Divinity School, 1999.

Tippett, Alan R. "Conversion as a Dynamic Process in Christian Mission." *Missiology* 5.2 (1977) 203–21.

———. "The Cultural Anthropology of Conversion." In *Handbook of Religious Conversion*, edited by H. Newton Malony and Samuel Southard, 192–208. Birmingham: Religious Education, 1992.

Tira, Sadiri Joy. "Landscape of the Global Diaspora at the Dawn of the 21st Century." Paper presented at the Global Diaspora Missiology Consultation, Edmonton, Canada, November 15–18, 2006.

Ullman, Chana. *The Transformed Self: The Psychology of Religious Conversion*. New York: Plenum, 1989.

Wan, Enoch. "The Phenomenon of Diaspora." In *Diaspora Missiology: Theory, Methodology, and Practice*, edited by Enoch Wan, 103–21. Portland: Institute of Diaspora Studies of USA, 2011.

Wan, Enoch, and Sadiri Joy Tira. "Diaspora Missiology." In *Missions Practice in the 21st Century*, edited by Enoch Wan and Sadiri Joy Tira, 27–54. Pasadena, CA: William Carey International University Press, 2009.

Wang, Yuting. "Religious Conversion to Christianity among Students from the Republic of China: A Comparative Study." Paper presented at the annual meeting of the Association for the Sociology of Religion, San Francisco, August 14, 2004.

Wang, Yuting, and Fenggang Yang. "More than Evangelical and Ethnic: The Ecological Factor in Chinese Conversion to Christianity in the United States." *Sociology of Religion* 67.2 (2006) 179–92.

Wells, David F. *Turning to God: Reclaiming Christian Conversion as Unique, Necessary, and Supernatural*. Grand Rapids: Baker, 2012.

Wickeri, Philip L. *Reconstructing Christianity in China: K. H. Ting and the Chinese Church*. Maryknoll, NY: Orbis, 2007.

Wielander, Gerda. *Christian Values in Communist China*. New York: Routledge, 2013.

Wong, Lai Fan. "From Atheists to Evangelicals: The Christian Conversion Experiences of Mainland Chinese Intellectuals in the United States of America." ThD diss., Boston University School of Theology, 2006.

Xi, Lien. *The Conversion Missionaries: Liberalism in American Protestant Mission in China, 1907–1932*. University Park, PA: Pennsylvania State University Press, 1997.

Xiaofeng, Liu. "From Enlightenment to Exile." In *Chinese Intellectuals and the Gospel*, edited by Samuel Ling and Stacey Bieler, 57–62. San Gabriel, CA: P&R, 1999.

Yang, C. K. *Religion in Chinese Society: A Study of Contemporary Social Functions of Religion and Some of Their Historical Factors*. Berkeley, CA: University of California Press, 1970.

Yang, Fenggang. "Chinese Conversion to Evangelical Christianity: The Importance of Social and Cultural Contexts." *Sociology of Religion* 59.3 (1998) 237–57.

Yang, Guen Seok. "Globalization and Christian Responses (in Korea)." *Theology Today* 62 (2005) 38–48.

Yiang, An-Dong. "Removing Obstacles: From Atheism to Knowing God." In *Mainland Chinese in America: An Emerging Kinship*, edited by Ambassadors for Christ, 17–24. Paradise, PA: Ambassadors for Christ, 1991.

Yim, Ki Hun. "Yonsei University Has 3,653 Foreign Students." *The Korea Economy*, September 17, 2014. https://www.hankyung.com/society/article/2014091634091.

Ying, Fuk-tsang. "Mainland China." In *Christianities in Asia*, edited by Peter C. Phan, 149–70. West Sussex: Blackwell, 2011.

Zehnder, David J. *A Theology of Religious Change: What the Social Science of Conversion Means for the Gospel*. Eugene, OR: Pickwick, 2011.

Zhang, Jun Min. "A Study of the Ministry for Chinese Students in Korea: Centered on the Ministries for the Chinese Students in the Seoul Area." ThM diss., Juan International University, 2014.

Zhang, Xuefeng. "How Religious Organizations Influence Chinese Conversion to Evangelical Protestantism in the United States." *Sociology of Religion* 67.2 (2006) 149–59.

Zhou, Jinghao. *Chinese vs. Western Perspectives: Understanding Contemporary China*. New York: Lexington, 2013.